The Insular Cases *and the Emergence of*
American Empire

LANDMARK LAW CASES

AMERICAN SOCIETY

Peter Charles Hoffer
N. E. H. Hull
Series Editors

BARTHOLOMEW H. SPARROW

The Insular Cases
and the Emergence
of American Empire

UNIVERSITY PRESS OF KANSAS

Published by the University Press of Kansas (Lawrence, Kansas 66045), which was
organized by the Kansas Board of Regents and is operated and funded by Emporia
State University, Fort Hays State University, Kansas State University, Pittsburg State
University, the University of Kansas, and Wichita State University

Library of Congress Cataloging-in-Publication Data

Sparrow, Bartholomew H., 1959–
The insular cases and the emergence of American empire /
Bartholomew H. Sparrow.

p. cm. — (Landmark law cases & American society)
Includes bibliographical references and index.
ISBN 978-0-7006-1481-3 (cloth : alk. paper)
ISBN 978-0-7006-1482-0 (pbk. : alk. paper)
1. United States—Insular possessions—History.   2. United
States—Territories and possessions—History.   3. Constitutional
history—United States.   I. Title.   II. Series.
KF4635.S63   2006
342.73'0413 — dc22   2006013438

British Library Cataloguing-in-Publication Data is available.

Printed in the United States of America

10 9 8 7 6 5 4 3 2

The paper used in this publication meets the minimum requirements of the
American National Standard for Permanence of Paper for Printed Library Materials
z39.48-1984.

To Polly Lanning Sparrow

CONTENTS

EDITORS' PREFACE

The United States of America was founded in part on the proposition that empire was inherently corrupt and tyrannical. Although greedy for land, our leaders had always held out the prospect of full and equal participation in the life of the nation to those whose lands we coveted. Hence we marched across the continent annexing, purchasing, conquering, and then incorporating territory as new states in the Union. Sometimes our reach exceeded our grasp, as we cast avaricious eyes on Cuba, Mexico, Central America, Canada, and distant islands in the Pacific, but a combination of local resistance, distance, good sense, and even less admirable motives like racism stayed our hand.

Then came the Spanish-American War, with its prospect of genuine empire in the Caribbean and the Pacific. The diplomatic, military, and cultural issues this prospect raised at home and abroad have had their chroniclers. Now comes Bartholomew Sparrow to examine the legal and constitutional issues in a wide-ranging, clear-sighted, and compelling essay on the so-called *Insular Cases*. For in their wisdom, and for other reasons, the justices of our highest court created a new category of territory, "unincorporated" for the purposes of statehood. These new territories had some but not all the rights and privileges of other Americans. In effect, some were more equal than others.

As Sparrow explains, the cases ran from 1901 well into the next decades, covering matters as seemingly diverse as tariffs, double jeopardy, and the very meaning of citizenship. They challenged a series of high courts, and the justices were not always up to the task.

Sparrow not only presents a thorough and enlightened account of these cases but also contextualizes them. For they arose in an era of racial animosity and discrimination, confrontation between labor and capital, and America's emergence as a world power. In his deft hands, the cases remind us how we handled our first episode of globalization.

Finally, Sparrow weighs the meaning of the cases, tracking them through legal and political science scholarship. From that scholarship, he derives a new and exciting way to evaluate shifts in constitutional interpretation.

ACKNOWLEDGMENTS

Professor Sanford Levinson encouraged me to take on this project. Without his recommendation and confidence, there would be no book. His essay "Installing the *Insular Cases* in the Canon of Constitutional Law" was a source of inspiration and anticipates several of the arguments I make in the chapters that follow. Professor Levinson also provided me with valuable criticism on an earlier draft of the manuscript and saved me from a number of errors.

Professor Louis A. Pérez, who also reviewed the manuscript for the University Press of Kansas, found still other errors and made several helpful recommendations on how to improve the manuscript.

Michael Briggs of the University Press of Kansas has been supportive, decisive, and quick in his correspondence; he has been a pleasure to work with. Peter Hoffer, coeditor of the Landmark Cases in American Society series, challenged me to be clear and accessible and suggested how I might best organize the material in my chapters. I am also grateful to Fred Woodward, publisher at the University Press of Kansas, and to others at the Press who made the book possible.

Friends and colleagues gave generously of their attention, energy, and time to read the manuscript. They supported the project, corrected mistakes, and encouraged further research. I am particularly grateful to Paul Kens, who shared his expertise in late nineteenth-century and early twentieth-century constitutional law and offered indispensable advice on how to improve the manuscript, and to Christina Duffy Burnett, who shared her insights and own research; both Paul and Christina went well beyond their professional duties. And Mark Graber's comments on a conference paper led me to consult new sources and proceed in new directions.

I further benefited from the comments of and close readings by Mark Lawrence, George Forgie, Lanny Thompson, and Julian Go; Roger Louis and Tony Hopkins provided additional guidance. Shannon Bow O'Brien, George Gavrilas, Milton Jamail, Patrick Mac-Donald, and Peter Trubowitz, all in the Department of Government at the University of Texas, also kindly read and commented on the manuscript, as did Paul Ciavarri, a friend and former graduate student of mine. Last, I owe a special debt to Sophie Sparrow — professor of law and sister — for her attention to detail and helpful suggestions. As for the advice I ignored and other omissions and shortcomings, I take full responsibility.

John Higley, chair of the Department of Government at the University of Texas, and Richard Lariviere, dean of the College of Liberal Arts, supported me with a Dean's Fellowship that provided a semester's leave in the fall of 2004 and allowed me to complete a draft of the manuscript.

Seth Miller and Chris Vaughn provided me with fast, resourceful, accurate research assistance. I could not have asked for better help. Jonathan Chausovsky and Neal Allen, with the Public Policy Institute, also provided research assistance at earlier stages of the project, and I thank them both.

And I owe special thanks to Greg Kahn.

Polly Lanning Sparrow contributed as a reader and as a spouse. She has given me the time, opportunity, and full personal life that allowed me to write the book.

Introduction

Any project of extending the sphere of the United States, by annexation or otherwise, is met by the constitutional lion in the path.

CAPTAIN ALFRED THAYER MAHAN,
The Interest of America in Sea Power, Present and Future, 1898

This is a study of empire, a term that only recently has returned to fashion. Almost all political scientists, constitutional scholars, journalists, and other Americans think of the United States as a federal republic — that is, made up of its member states and ruled by its elected representatives — but the reality is something else: the United States exerts sovereignty over territorial inhabitants who do not have full voting representation in the U.S. House, the Senate, or the Electoral College. Neither, and earlier, did the inhabitants of these territories have a voice in the decisions that their islands be annexed by the United States, with the exception of the residents of the Northern Marianas. These territorial inhabitants and their territorial governments, as a result, occupy a political limbo — despite the fact that their inhabitants are officially designated as "U.S. citizens." They are both a part of the United States and apart from the United States. The indeterminate status of the inhabitants and local governments of the United States' island territories was established by the U.S. Supreme Court's decisions in the *Insular Cases.*

Although the history of the United States' island territories follows from that of the previous continental territories — as I shall show shortly — the U.S. Constitution itself has almost nothing on the territorial expansion of the United States. Only in Sections 2 and 3 of Article IV does the Constitution (briefly) mention Congress's power to admit new states and exercise authority over the territory and property of the United States. Even then, the Constitution says nothing about the extent of the territory or property of the United States, or of the number of new states that might be added to the Union. Yet the fact of the extraordinary geographic expansion of the United States is critical to understanding the rise of the nation as a world power and global empire. A vast and sparsely populated North American continent, with its rich agricultural and mineral resources and its largely temperate and favorable climate, attracted and absorbed millions of immigrants. *Land* provided the foundation for the tremendous growth in the population and wealth of the United States and facilitated its emergence as a great power and then superpower.

It took political action to acquire that land. By the terms of the 1783 Treaty of Paris after the American Revolution, Britain ceded the trans-Appalachian West — the eastern half of the Mississippi River valley — to the young United States. Twenty years later, President Thomas Jefferson made the extraordinary purchase of the "Louisiana" territory from France, thereby doubling the size of the United States with the stroke of a pen. President James Madison added West Florida in 1811 and Florida proper in 1819; President Polk secured the Mexican Cession in 1848, and Secretary of State William Seward persuaded President Andrew Johnson and the U.S. Congress to buy Alaska in 1867. In these and other instances, the land acquired by the U.S. government was organized into territories and then into states that were to become part of the Union.

Congress administered these newly acquired areas. It divided areas into districts and/or territories and later annexed the territories (or parts of territories) as separate states. In fact, almost all the nonoriginal states of the Union owe their existence to this process of expansion and political absorption. Thirty-one of the fifty states were formerly U.S. territories and regarded as states "in embryo," given that U.S. expansion during the eighteenth and nineteenth centuries had always been followed by the organization of territorial governments and then the annexation of territories as states of the Union — states that were to be admitted on an *equal footing* with the existing states. Every time the United States extended the domain of its sovereignty, the protections of the U.S. Constitution followed. The Constitution "followed the flag," in the words of William Jennings Bryan in the presidential election campaign of 1900.

The Constitution followed the flag in two ways. *Geographically*, as the United States expanded north to Michigan, Minnesota, the Dakotas, and Montana, south to New Orleans and Louisiana, Alabama, Mississippi, and Florida, and west beyond the Mississippi River out to California and Oregon, Congress extended constitutional liberties and added new states to the Union. Only six nonoriginal states did not have territorial governments. Vermont was independent, although always assumed to be part of the United States, until its admission in 1791; Texas was an independent republic from 1837 to 1845, prior to being annexed by the United States; and California was a military district from 1848 to 1850, before its admission into the Union. Kentucky, meanwhile, had been part of Virginia until 1792; Maine had been part of Massachusetts until 1820; and West Virginia had been part of Virginia until 1863.

Temporally, the Constitution followed the flag, since Congress did not immediately admit new states once the United States acquired new areas. Instead, Congress had to decide when to create territorial governments and when to allow the territories to become member states of the Union. Not surprisingly, then, the length of time between when an area came under U.S. sovereignty and when Congress admitted it as a state or part of a state varied considerably. Congress admitted California after only 2 years and formed the state of Louisiana in just 9 years' time. But it took Hawai'i 61 years to become a state (1959) from the time when it was acquired (1898); 64 years passed between when New Mexico and Arizona came under U.S. sovereignty (1848) and when they were both admitted as states (1912); Alaska (1867) took 92 years to become a state (1959); and Oklahoma (1803) took 104 years (1907). And until the territories became states, Congress dictated territorial policy.

Notwithstanding this variation, all the territories of continental North America were eventually admitted as states or as parts of other states, with Tennessee (1796) being the first territory to become a state, and Hawai'i the most recent (1959). (I follow the official state spelling for "Hawai'i" unless I am quoting directly or referring to the title of a particular law or governmental institution.) So even as the United States kept growing in geographic size, it was — remarkably — able to keep its representative form of government. The United States could be an "empire of liberty," as Thomas Jefferson called it. Or, as the political scientist William Riker wrote in 1964, federalism was "an effective alternate to empire."

Yet the process of geographic expansion followed by the organization of territorial governments and then the admission of new states into the Union came to a sudden halt after the Spanish-American War of 1898, when the United States acquired Cuba, Puerto Rico, the Philippines, and Guam according to the terms of the peace treaty with Spain. Ending this taken-for-granted process of territorial absorption were the U.S. Supreme Court's decisions in the *Insular Cases*, a series of cases that directly addressed the political and constitutional status of the United States' island territories. Only months after President William McKinley won reelection in 1900, the Supreme Court suddenly had to decide whether Puerto Rico, the Philippines, and Hawai'i (annexed in 1898) were part of the United States with respect to the U.S. tariff law.

The nine cases to be decided by the Court were known as the *Insular Cases*. They were also known as the *Insular Tariff Cases* (since eight of them were tariff related), the *Porto Rican Cases* (since seven of them involved Puerto Rico), and the *Insular Test Cases* (since these were the first cases to test whether the new island territories were foreign or domestic for the purposes of the tariff and other constitutional questions). Constitutional scholars, historians of Puerto Rico, the Philippines, and the U.S. territories, biographers of Supreme Court justices, and others subsequently included later Supreme Court decisions among the *Insular Cases* — decisions that ruled on additional constitutional questions concerning the territories — such as the right to a trial by jury, the prohibition against double jeopardy, and governmental immunity from suit. (See "A Note on the *Insular Cases*" and the chronology at the end of the book for an explanation of the criteria used in selecting the thirty-five *Insular Cases*.)

The Supreme Court's decisions in the *Insular Cases* of 1901 generated great controversy, consistent with Alfred Thayer Mahan's warning quoted in the epigraph to this introduction that "extending the sphere of the United States" would be "met by the constitutional lion in the path." Although continental expansion had previously provoked constitutional questions, never before had the United States added areas this populated and this remote from American shores.

The nation's leading constitutional scholars and political writers argued in the leading academic journals and political magazines over the political status of the island territories and their inhabitants, and over which provisions of the U.S. Constitution should apply to the inhabitants of these new island territories. The debate was over how to define the "United States," in effect, and how to interpret the Constitution with respect to U.S. territories. Observers at the time reported that the *Insular Cases* aroused more political passion than had any action by the Supreme Court since its decision in *Dred Scott v. Sandford* (1857). And for good reason. The Supreme Court's rulings on how the territories and their inhabitants fit into the existing political and constitutional systems of the United States had tremendous implications for the racial composition of the American people, for the United States' strategic position in the world and the internationalization of the American economy, for the balance of power between Congress and the presidency, and for republican government in the United States.

The Supreme Court's decisions of 1901 and later years created a novel, even revolutionary, constitutional doctrine: the Incorporation Doctrine. The United States' island territories in the Caribbean Sea and the Pacific Ocean were "unincorporated" territories that were to receive only unspecified "fundamental" constitutional protections, whereas the "incorporated" territories of continental North America were a part of the Union and enjoyed the full protections of the U.S. Constitution. The new tropical territories were thereby a part of the United States, but not entirely so. And their inhabitants had some constitutional protections, just not all of them.

The origin of the Supreme Court's distinction between the United States' incorporated and unincorporated territories was Justice White's concurring opinion in *Downes v. Bidwell*, decided on May 27, 1901. But it took until 1905, when White drafted his lead opinion in *Rassmussen v. United States*, for a majority on the Court to support the Incorporation Doctrine as the rationale for the Court's decision. And not until after White's death, and the preceding deaths of Chief Justice Fuller and Justices Harlan, Brewer, and Peckham, did the Incorporation Doctrine achieve its complete triumph in the last of the *Insular Cases*, *Balzac v. Porto Rico* (1922), where Chief Justice Taft relied exclusively on the doctrine when drafting the Court's unanimous decision.

White's doctrine thus won out over an alternative view of the United States' relationship with its territories, namely, Justice Brown's "extension theory." This theory held that Congress had to expressly *extend* the Constitution to any territories for the Constitution to apply, since the territories themselves — old or new — were *not* necessarily a part of the United States. Rather, the United States consisted solely of its member states, in other words, until such time that Congress acted to expand the Union.

The Incorporation Doctrine also triumphed over the strict constructionism of Chief Justice Fuller and Justices Harlan, Peckham, and Brewer — the four justices who dissented in *Downes v. Bidwell.* In their dissents, Fuller and Harlan argued that the U.S. Constitution *did* apply in full to the areas annexed by the terms of the 1899 peace treaty with Spain. They argued that the Constitution applied *ex proprio vigore* — that is, by its own force.

With the Supreme Court's creation of the new political status of "unincorporated" territories, though, the *Insular Cases* broke with the history of the late eighteenth- and nineteenth-century United States. Congress's power to regulate the territories and possessions of the United States under the Constitution's territory clause — that "Congress shall have Power to dispose of and make all needful Rules and Regulations respecting the Territory or other Property belonging to the United States" (Article IV, Section 3, Clause 2) — had always been tempered by the assumption that such power was to be exercised only temporarily. (Indicative of this premise, Article IV, Section 3, Clause 1, which immediately precedes the territory clause, empowers Congress to add new states to the Union.) With the decisions in the *Insular Cases,* though, Congress's territorial authority was no longer to be just temporary. New territories might never become states if Congress did not want them to be.

The immediate impact of the Supreme Court's decisions in 1901 was to ratify the expansionism of President William McKinley, Vice President (and later President) Theodore Roosevelt, Philippine governor (and later president and U.S. Supreme Court chief justice) William Howard Taft, Secretary of War (and later Secretary of State) Elihu Root, Senator Henry Cabot Lodge, and other prominent Republicans. And over the next two decades, in the full set of *Insular Cases,* the Supreme Court worked out exactly which constitutional provisions applied to the new island territories and which did not.

Although the *Insular Cases* provoked great controversy when the Supreme Court first issued its decisions, they lie forgotten today — deep in the shadows of other decisions of the Fuller Court, such as the *Sugar Trust Case* (*United States v. E. C. Knight,* 1895), *In Re Debs*

(1895), *Plessy v. Ferguson* (1896), and *Lochner v. New York* (1905). The reason for this neglect, I suspect, is the Constitution's near silence on the subject of territorial expansion. And this silence breeds neglect, since students of American politics and government look to the Constitution as the blueprint of the U.S. political system and as guideline for their subjects of study. Thus does much of political science, constitutional law, and political history focus on the formal and informal powers of the three great institutions of government: the Congress; the presidency and executive branch; and the Supreme Court and federal court system. Perhaps at least as much scholarship looks at political process: voting and election campaigns; legislative procedures, rules, and norms; and the activities of political parties and political organizations. Other studies examine the formation and impact of public opinion, the making and implementation of public and foreign policy, and the conduct of public relations and operation of the media.

But much less scholarship examines U.S. expansion and the emergence of an American empire. This is where the *Insular Cases* make for much more than historical interest.

First, the rulings still stand. Puerto Rico, Guam, American Samoa, the U.S. Virgin Islands, and the Northern Marianas (a 400-mile-long chain of fourteen islands in the far western Pacific) all remain "unincorporated territories" of the United States (the United States acquired five of the six islands constituting Eastern Samoa in 1899; it acquired the U.S. Virgin Islands in 1917, and the Northern Marianas became a territory in 1976), while *Downes v. Bidwell* and the other *Insular Cases* continue to be cited by U.S. courts, including the Supreme Court. Furthermore, the decisions in the *Insular Cases* and in *Downes v. Bidwell*, in particular, established the political and constitutional subordination of the United States' island territories. And the U.S. government continues to have sovereignty over U.S. citizens and areas that do not have and have not had equal representation, since territorial inhabitants, even if U.S. citizens, are unable to vote for federal officeholders — although they can do so if they move their residence to one of the fifty states. For the inhabitants of these island territories, the United States does not have a government of the governed. This lack of representation became entrenched with the decisions in the *Insular Cases*, even if its legacy can be traced back to the founding and to the origins of the U.S. territorial system.

Second, the fact of the territories undermines the principle of "limited government," as Judge José Cabranes, Judge Juan Torrella, José Trías Monge, and Efrén Rivera Ramos — all of whom are of Puerto Rican background — point out. Territorial government is *not* limited in the sense of being subject to checks and balances, since Congress, the presidency and executive branch, and federal courts may assert their powers over the territories at any time. Contrary to the provisions of the Ninth Amendment that the rights enumerated in the Constitution "shall not be construed to deny or disparage others retained by the people," and to those of the Tenth Amendment, that "the powers not delegated to the United States by the Constitution, nor prohibited by it to the States, are reserved to the States respectively, or to the people," the rights of the U.S. territorial citizens — presumably among "the people" of the United States — are nonetheless *not* fully reserved to them or their territorial governments.

Third, the *Insular Cases'* endorsement of expansion marks the emergence of an American empire, to define "empire" as the acquisition and control of a territory and its inhabitants without consent. U.S. territorial inhabitants have been, and are, subject to the continued legal domination of the United States (notwithstanding the several nonbinding referenda on the political status of Puerto Rico). And with the Supreme Court's endorsement of Congress's plenary authority over the U.S. island territories, the United States came to imitate the older European powers that had long exerted sovereignty over remote colonies and dependent nations — including, nominally, those in North America.

At the same time, the decisions in the *Insular Cases* gave rise to a *second* kind of empire, one where the United States has exerted its influence informally instead of through territorial ownership. In the early twentieth century the United States actually had more territory under its sovereignty than it ever had before or has had since. Yet the United States let Cuba go, and later the Philippines. The justification for the power of the United States to actually *divest* itself of its territories — an unprecedented development that contrasts with the prohibition of states' ability to secede — can be found in the briefs and opinions of the *Insular Cases*, as well as in the arguments of political and constitutional experts of the day. The United States did not have to have an empire based on territory: it could exert informal control instead.

———

Curiously, though, few Americans know of the *Insular Cases*. Presidents and politicians in Washington, D.C., and in the states do not mention the cases. Journalists do not comment on them. Students do not learn about them in high school or college. And few legal scholars, political scientists, or historians write about them. Indicative of the neglected status of the *Insular Cases*, as Professor Sanford Levinson points out, is that Robert McCloskey does not mention them in his widely assigned and classic text on the judiciary, *The American Supreme Court.* Neither do almost any of the dozens of casebooks that survey U.S. constitutional law.

This neglect comes at a high cost. For a study of the *Insular Cases* informs us about less-studied aspects of constitutional law, American political history, and U.S. foreign policy: the near silence of the Constitution on the geographic expansion of the United States; the development and reality of the U.S. territorial system, one that both preceded and succeeded the Supreme Court's decisions in the *Insular Cases;* the admission of new states into the Union; and the meaning and criteria of citizenship. The Supreme Court's resolution of how to handle these issues of the early twentieth century has shaped American foreign policy and the U.S. political system to this day.

Many have written expertly on related subjects, such as the important rise of the United States as a world power and the Spanish-American War. Others have revealed the racism and ethnocentrism prevalent throughout the history of the United States. Still others have traced the rise of Progressivism, growth of public administration, and rise of the bureaucratic state in the early twentieth century. And economic historians have explored the development and emergent dominance of big business in the late decades of the nineteenth century and early decades of the twentieth century. But a study of the Supreme Court's decisions in the *Insular Cases* shows how these realms intersected on the question of how the United States was to handle its new, extended possessions and why the fact of these possessions still matters.

The purpose of this study, then, is to move the *Insular Cases* back into prominence, to encourage their return to the legal "canon" of Supreme Court cases as Levinson proposes — that is, to add them to the list of recognized Supreme Court cases essential for and familiar to students of constitutional law and U.S. political history.

The following chapters expand on these points. Chapter 1 explains how the *Insular Cases* marked a tipping point in the history of U.S. geographic expansion from the establishment of the Northwest Territory to the annexation of Hawai'i in 1898. Throughout this period of expansion the U.S. government followed the precedent of the 1787 Northwest Ordinance: Congress organized acquired areas into territories and then admitted them as states. This precedent was at once benign, insofar as it extended civil liberties to territorial citizens, and oppressive, insofar as it reserved for Congress plenary power over the territories and, especially, over the public lands, or "soil," lying within the territories and new states.

Chapter 2 discusses how the United States' new island territories represented a challenge to the assumed process of territorial development. It also reviews the three basic arguments being made at the time — before the Court's decisions — on how to define the "United States" and on the nature of the relationship between the forty-five states and the new offshore territories. One was a view of the United States as just the states; a second view was one of the United States as encompassing both the territories and the states; and a third view was of the United States that could include some incorporated territories, and exclude other unincorporated territories.

Chapter 3 discusses the racial, strategic, and economic explanations of the United States' new island acquisitions. Legal and political academics, government officials and politicians, and the American public at large overwhelmingly believed that the new island territories were inhabited by inferior persons — that is, by persons unsuited to becoming U.S. citizens absent a long apprenticeship under American rule, and possibly not even then. Nonetheless, the McKinley and Roosevelt administrations, many political and legal experts, journalists, and much of the public believed that the United States, as a rising world power, was entitled to its colonies; in fact, it *had* to have them were it to compete internationally with the great powers of Europe and Asia. Although the decisions held serious consequences with respect to questions of race and grand strategy, the direct issue that the Supreme Court had to confront in *Downes v. Bidwell* and most of the other *Insular Cases* of 1901 was the constitutionality of the U.S. tariff law as it applied to trade between the territories and the states. And the tariff issue had its own vigorous politics and considerable stakes.

Chapter 4 examines *Downes v. Bidwell,* the most important of the *Insular Cases. Downes* was the most eagerly awaited decision of May 27, 1901, as well as the single most controversial decision of the *Insular Cases.* Chapter 4 presents the arguments made on both sides of the case and explains the several opinions written in the Court's decision. The chapter also introduces the members of the Supreme Court who wrote opinions in *Downes v. Bidwell* (and who decided the other *Insular Cases* of 1901): Justice Brown, who wrote the lead opinion and who served on the bench from 1890 to 1906; Justice White (1893–1920), who wrote a concurring opinion; Justice Gray (1881–1902), who wrote another (short) concurring opinion; Chief Justice Fuller (1888–1920), who wrote the dissenting opinion; and Justice Harlan (1877–1911), who wrote a second dissent. The chapter concludes by reviewing the newspaper reactions and academic responses to the Court's decision in *Downes.*

Chapter 5 discusses the nine other *Insular Cases* of 1901. It reviews the issues and opinions of the six other decisions of May 27— that is, aside from *Downes* — and discusses two cases that the Court delayed deciding until December 1901. The chapter then considers *Neely v. Henkel. Neely v. Henkel,* decided on January 14, 1901, was one of the most important of the *Insular Cases* for the reason of both its precedent and the contradiction it poses to the others as I shall explain. Chapter 5 also introduces the four other members of the Supreme Court: Justice McKenna, who served on the Court from 1898 to 1925; Justice Shiras (1892–1903); Justice Brewer (1889–1910); and Justice Peckham (1896–1909). Finally, chapter 5 looks at the public response to these other decisions of 1901.

Given the Court's narrow endorsement of U.S. government policies and the controversy over *Downes* and the other decisions — eight of the ten decisions were decided by five-to-four votes and contained heated dissenting opinions — chapter 6 looks at President Roosevelt's efforts to fill the vacancies left by the resignations of Justice Gray in the summer of 1902 and Justice Shiras in late 1902. The chapter then discusses the Court's decisions in the later *Insular Cases* with respect to the constitutional issues left unresolved in the *Insular Cases* of 1901. Chapter 6 discusses, too, the evolution of Court personnel in the period between 1902 and 1922 (see the chronology at the end of the book) and introduces the new justices appointed to the bench.

Chapter 7 explains the Court's rulings in criminal cases, including those adjudicating territorial citizens' rights to a jury trial and to indictment by grand jury, the prohibition against double jeopardy, and other rights of the accused. The chapter begins with a discussion of the Supreme Court's decisions in *Hawaii v. Mankichi* (1903), then turns to *Dorr v. United States* (1905) — a case that represents a turning point in the Court's decision making in the *Insular Cases* — and ends with *Balzac v. Porto Rico* (1922), the last of the *Insular Cases*. (I use "Puerto Rico," which some reporters and writers also used at the time, unless I am quoting directly or referring to a particular name or title that uses "Porto Rico"; "Porto Rico" was the official U.S. spelling until 1923.)

Chapter 8 addresses one of the imperial legacies of the *Insular Cases:* the subordinate and ambiguous positions occupied by the territories in the U.S. constitutional system, where the existence of the territories challenges the principles embodied in the Declaration of Independence, the Articles of Confederation, and the Constitution itself, given that Puerto Rico, Guam, American Samoa, the U.S. Virgin Islands, and the Commonwealth of the Northern Marianas Islands are the political inferiors of the states proper and subject to the plenary power of the legislative, executive, and judicial branches. Chapter 8 addresses, too, the evolution of the status of territorial inhabitants following the decisions in the *Insular Cases,* as well as the diversity of governing regimes across the U.S. island territories.

Chapter 9 explores the second imperial legacy of the *Insular Cases:* the fact that the decisions also allowed the United States to control an informal empire. That is to say that the United States did not have to expand geographically; it could rule informally, instead, through other governments, with the help of U.S. forces and international institutions. Crucial in the establishment of this nonterritorial, informal empire was the ability of the United States to divest itself of territories. Here, too, the *Insular Cases* provided the doctrine that allowed the United States to divest Cuba, the Philippines, and potentially other U.S. territories. The chapter concludes, and the book ends, with a discussion of how we can understand the relationship between the U.S. Constitution and the decisions in the *Insular Cases* — how the United States can still exercise authority over people outside the states, and thus without full membership in the American political community.

The Broken Skein

American Territorial Expansion and 1898

Isolation—the mother of barbarism—is becoming impossible. The elbows of nations
touch. The mysteries of Africa are being laid open, the pulse of her commerce is
beginning to beat. South America is being quickened, and the dry bones of Asia are
moving . . . The world is to be Christianized and civilized. . . . [W]hat is to
prevent the United States from becoming the workshop of the world, and
our people "the hands of mankind?" . . . America holds the future.
JOSIAH STRONG, *Our Country*, 1891

The fact that the United States exercises and has exercised sovereignty over areas outside the separate states is nothing new; the United States has always exerted authority over areas outside the states. This was true at the founding, it was true throughout the nineteenth and twentieth centuries, and it is true today. Until 1898, however, members of Congress, presidents and their cabinet officers, and the American public had always taken for granted that the government's authority over these nonstate areas was to be temporary. But with the territories acquired after the Spanish-American War and the Supreme Court's decisions in the *Insular Cases*, the United States disrupted this taken-for-granted process. Suddenly, the United States had unprecedented offshore possessions under its control — several densely populated islands (or, more accurately, island groups), some lying thousands of miles away. At the same time, most politicians, political experts, and members of the public thought that the inhabitants of these islands — Cubans, Puerto Ricans, and Filipinos, in particular — were unfit to become Americans, and that their islands would probably never become states of the Union.

The assumption of Congress's temporary control of U.S. territories dates back to the Northwest Ordinance of 1787. This ordinance, which established the government of the Northwest Territory, specified that new areas were to be organized into territories and then, whether in whole or in part, admitted as states: Congress was to administer the territories *"for the purpose of temporary government,"* until such time that Congress could admit the several new states "on an *equal footing* with the original States," as soon as "consistent with the general interest" (emphasis added). By so doing, the Northwest Ordinance set the precedent for the administration of the later territories of continental North America. "That the Territories are to be regarded as inchoate States as future members of the Union," the historian Max Farrand wrote in 1900, "has been and is the fundamental basis of our Territorial system."

The United States obtained the Northwest Territory as a result of Britain's cession of the trans-Appalachian West in the Treaty of Paris of 1783. Several states had to forgo their claims that had originated in their colonial charters with respect to land rights extending up to the Mississippi River in order that the Articles of Confederation be ratified, and the area surrendered by several of the states came under the sovereignty of the U.S. government. This area was the "public domain" — land that belonged in its entirety to the U.S. government, and not to any of the states. (The District of Columbia also belongs to the U.S. government and not to any of the states, where the Constitution's enclave clause of Article I, Section 8, Clause 17 explicitly provides for a "federal district" to be the seat of the national government, as well as for the U.S. government's purchase of areas within the several states for forts, arsenals, dockyards, and other essential buildings.)

The state of Maryland gets the credit for creating the public domain. Delegates from Maryland insisted that they would not ratify the Articles of Confederation unless the states with land claims on the trans-Appalachian West — Virginia, New York, North Carolina, Pennsylvania, Connecticut, Massachusetts, and Georgia — forfeited their claims to the U.S. government. Maryland resolved "that a country unsettled at the commencement of this war, claimed by the British crown, and ceded to it by the Treaty of Paris, if wrested from that common enemy by the blood and treasure of the thirteen States, should be considered as common property, subject to be parceled out by Congress, into free, convenient and independent governments, in such manner and at such times as the wisdom of that Assembly shall hereafter direct." Virginia, New York, and the other claimant states reluctantly ceded their lands over to the U.S. government, beginning with Virginia in 1783 and ending with Georgia — which did not release its claims until 1802.

The Northwest Territory (the "Old Northwest") made up most of this new western land. It stretched north from the Ohio River to the Great Lakes and Canada, and west to the shores of the Mississippi. The remainder of the trans-Appalachian West consisted of the Southwest Territory (Tennessee) and Georgia's land claims (now the states of Mississippi and Alabama). Kentucky went directly from being part of Virginia to becoming its own state.

Once the United States acquired the trans-Appalachian West, American political leaders readied to "prepare a plan for the temporary government of the western territory." Thomas Jefferson, the chairman of the committee charged with preparing a plan for the western territory, prepared a first draft of the Northwest Ordinance in 1784, and James Monroe, the future secretary of state and U.S. president, wrote the final draft. Congress passed the Northwest Ordinance in July 1787, while still under the Articles of Confederation. And Jefferson, Monroe, and the U.S. Congress expressly designed the Northwest Ordinance for the short-term administration of the Northwest Territory.

With the Northwest Ordinance already familiar to the delegates meeting at the Constitutional Convention in Philadelphia in the summer of 1787, the subject of the American West and the territorial expansion of the United States received limited discussion at the Constitutional Convention, and almost no mention in the Constitution itself — the obvious importance of the Northwest Territory and trans-Appalachian West notwithstanding. The delegates in Philadelphia simply assumed that the Union would grow in size, with Vermont, Kentucky, Tennessee, Maine (sometimes written as "Mayne"), and a small, undetermined number of states from the Northwest Territory sooner or later to be added — three to five, according to the Northwest Ordinance — to the original thirteen. The delegates could have hardly been expected to foresee the eventual size of the Union or predict the future number of states to become members of the United States. "There was no probability that the number of future states would exceed that of the Existing States," Roger Sherman of Connecticut remarked. "If the event should ever happen it was too remote to be taken into consideration at this time. Besides We are providing for our posterity, for our Children & grand Children, who would be as likely to be citizens of new Western States as of the old States."

Other delegates were more cautious. Hugh Williamson of North Carolina thought that the "new states from Westward . . . would be small States, they would be poor States, they would be unable to pay in proportion to their numbers; their distance from market rendering the produce of their labour less valuable; they would consequently be tempted to combine for the purpose of laying burdens on commerce & consumption." Williamson was clearly less enthusiastic. Elbridge Gerry of Massachusetts warned that the western states would, once they acquired power, abuse it. "They will oppress commerce, and drain our wealth into the Western Country." Gerry recommended that the number of new states not be allowed to exceed that of "the Atlantic States." George Mason of Virginia and Gouverneur Morris of Pennsylvania warned, too, of the possible influence that the additional states might have. They feared that expansion "would fall with greatest weight on the old States."

The prevailing opinion among the delegates in Philadelphia and even among these cautious delegates, however, was that the young United States would be incapable of restricting westward emigration — as was already proving to be the case in the Northwest Territory, which by 1796 had more than 60,000 inhabitants. "If it were possible by just means to prevent emigrations to the Western Country, it might be good policy," George Mason remarked. But since people act according to their own interests, "the best policy is to treat them with that equality which will make them friends, not enemies." Delegate Hugh Williamson agreed: "Attempts at compulsion was not the policy of the United States." James Madison, too, insisted on the admission of western states on equal terms with the other states. The prudent policy would be to make the inhabitants of these new areas their friends and allies, rather than tempt them into secession or rebellion by keeping them indefinitely as dependencies — the logic, of course, that had induced the colonial rebellion in British North America in the first place.

The delegates at the convention therefore established rules so the inhabitants of the new areas could easily become members of new states and thus become part of American political society. The histories of

Franklin (1774–1776) and Transylvania (1780–1784) — attempts at the establishment of independent political communities in what are now western Tennessee and western Kentucky, respectively — were sobering reminders for the founders and manifest cases in point. The founders accordingly made it easy for new states to join the United States, so that the persons of new regions could become members of a (new) state.

The text of the Northwest Ordinance reflected this practical ideal of political equality for territorial inhabitants: Articles I through IV were to "be considered as *articles of compact*, between the original States and the *people and States* in the said territory" (emphasis added). The persons of the new regions could thus form temporary governments, petition for statehood, and then be admitted on equal terms with the existing states. One of Congress's first acts when it convened in 1789 after the ratification of the Constitution was to re-pass the Northwest Ordinance, consistent with the founders' wishes to preempt any resentment by inhabitants of the public domain and to defuse any sentiment for secession or rebellion. Soon thereafter, the Supreme Court affirmed that the Northwest Ordinance was valid under the Constitution of 1789.

Yet George Mason and Gouverneur Morris turned out to be right: the geographic expansion of the United States *was* to have a revolutionary impact on the old states of the Union. With the Louisiana Purchase of 1803, the United States added the vast area extending from the Mississippi delta to the Canadian border and from the Mississippi River to the Rockies, and thereby doubled in size. Then there was the addition of Florida soon thereafter, in 1819. It was in the course of the Supreme Court's resolution of a conflict involving the territory of Florida, in *American Insurance Company v. Canter* (1828), that Chief Justice John Marshall endorsed the power of the United States to acquire territory. Congress's power "of making war, and of making treaties," Marshall wrote, bestowed on the government "the power of acquiring territory, either by conquest or treaty."

Following the United States' 1846 annexation of Oregon (what is now Oregon, Washington, Idaho, and portions of Montana and Wyoming), the nation added another half-million square miles with the Treaty of Guadalupe Hidalgo of 1848 after the Mexican War. Then the U.S. government made the Gadsden Purchase in 1853, buying from Mexico a wide strip of land in southwestern New Mexico and southern Arizona for the purpose of building a railway line. The cumulative effect of the Louisiana Purchase, Florida Cession, British Cession, Mexican Cession, and Gadsden Purchase was that the Northwest Ordinance cast a much larger shadow than anyone might have imagined.

One of the Northwest Ordinance's lasting effects was its precedent as *process:* the new areas coming under the dominion of the United States followed the same sequential pattern of territorial development laid out in the Northwest Ordinance. So as the United States extended outward from the East Coast, so, too, did Congress set up district governments (only up to 1845, however, in what are now the lower forty-eight states), organize territorial governments, and then continue to admit new states into the Union: by 1800, the United States had 17 states; by 1825, it had 24 states; by 1850, it had 30 states; by 1875, it had 37 states; and by 1900, it had 45 states. The territories were "in a state of infancy advancing toward manhood," as Chief Justice Marshall put it in *Loughborough v. Blake* (1818), and "looking forward to complete equality so soon as that state of manhood shall be attained."

The Northwest Ordinance also *protected civil liberties.* The first three articles of the Northwest Ordinance guaranteed territorial citizens — that is, adult white male Americans — freedom of religion, the right of contract, free speech, trial by jury, due process, habeas corpus, and other protections consistent with the Constitution and Bill of Rights. Congress also specified in the organic acts passed for the establishment of territorial governments that territorial officials had to swear to uphold the Constitution of the United States.

Third, the Northwest Ordinance's Article IV provided that the citizens of the territories were the *economic equals* of those in the states. The "inhabitants and settlers" of the Northwest Territory were to pay part of the federal debts, present or future. Also, they were to contribute their "proportional part" of government expenses, consistent with Congress's assessments on the original states or other new states, and the navigable waters and "carrying places" between the Mississippi and Saint Lawrence rivers were to be "common highways" and "forever free" for both "the inhabitants of said territory and the citizens of the United States."

A fourth reason that the Northwest Ordinance had such an impact was its *assumed neglect of indigenous persons*. That is to say that it took it for granted that the new areas acquired by the United States were effectively empty of inhabitants (American Indians excepted). This assumption never came into serious question over the course of the United States' expansion across a sparsely populated continental North America. It was true of Ohio and Oregon, just as it held for Missouri and Minnesota, Arizona, and Idaho. Neither the Northwest Ordinance nor the Constitution's territory clause mentions territorial inhabitants or discusses the absorption (or, for that matter, the exclusion) of other persons. In fact, none of the congressional legislation for the establishment of territorial governments and for the admission of new states mentions inhabitants or aboriginal populations. Politicians and the public presumed that the inhabitants of the territories and future states were white émigrés from the existing states or northwestern Europe.

The presumption was that the inhabitants of the territories — and, therefore, of future states — would be "just like us." And it was in large part because of the denser population of Mexicans south of the Rio Grande that the United States took only the northern half of Mexico in the settlement of the Mexican War; few Americans wanted millions of Mexicans to join them as people of the United States. Meanwhile, the numbers of Spanish-origin and Mexican persons inhabiting California and the other areas of the Mexican Cession of 1848 were too few in number and too dispersed to constitute a challenge or barrier to the western migration and settlement of white Americans.

American Indians, for their part, did not count. In the minds of the founders and most Americans of the eighteenth and nineteenth centuries, the Indians were outsiders — different peoples, different nations. Indicatively, the Articles of Confederation omit any mention of Indians; the Constitution mentions them only twice — once with respect to apportionment ("Indians not taxed" did not count toward the number of representatives a state could have in Congress) and once with respect to commerce (Congress could regulate the Indian trade). Although the Northwest Ordinance *did* mention the Indians, its language was far removed from the practices of the frontier or in the chambers, corridors, and cloakrooms of Congress: "The utmost good faith shall always be observed toward the Indians; their lands and property shall never be taken from them without their consent; and in their property, rights, and liberty they never shall be invaded or disturbed unless in just and lawful wars authorized by Congress; but laws founded in justice and humanity shall, from time to time, be made, for preventing wrongs being done to them and for preserving peace and friendship with them" (Art. III, sec. 14).

The new lands were not entirely empty of other peoples, however. Americans first confronted non-Anglo inhabitants — apart from Indians — in and around New Orleans and the other riverside settlements of late eighteenth-century "Louisiana." These were the trappers, traders, rivermen, farmers, fishermen, free blacks, and other persons of the new territory of Louisiana. A good many Americans, Federalists especially, resisted the absorption of these new peoples into the United States given that these persons often spoke no English, came from different cultures (e.g., French, Spanish, Dominican), and had other legal traditions (i.e., the rationalist Napoleonic Code). Most were Catholics, too — anathema to Protestant America.

New Orleans, one Federalist wrote, is "a place inhabited by a Mixture of Americans, English, Spanish, and French and crouded [*sic*] every year . . . with two or three thousand boatmen from the back-country remarkable for their dissipated habits, unruly tempers, and lawless conduct." What was worse, "the white population bears so small a proportion to the black" that "the Blacks have already been guilty of two or three insurrections within a few years back." Another Federalist, Fisher Ames, had still less patience. "Otters," Ames wrote, were more capable of self-government than Louisiana's "*Gallo-Hispano-Indium omnimum gatherum* of savages and adventurers, whose pure morals are expected to sustain and glorify our republic."

As the Federalist Gouverneur Morris wrote in late 1803, soon after the Louisiana Purchase, "I had always thought that when we should acquire Canada and Louisiana it would be proper to govern them as provinces, and allow them no voice in our councils." Morris turned out to be right about Louisiana, however, even if the United States never added Canada: the inhabitants of Louisiana were placed under the direct rule of the U.S. government and initially, at least, denied a voice in the Congress of the United States.

Even President Thomas Jefferson did not want Louisiana to enter the Union on an equal footing with the existing states, at least not right away. The Creoles were "as yet incapable of self-government as children." Fewer than one in fifty "understands the English language." Liberty would be wasted on the Creoles, Jefferson told Congress, because "the principles of popular Government are utterly beyond their comprehension." In fact, the Creoles — and "Creoles" includes Louisiana residents of Spanish and African American descent, as well as French ancestry — preferred Spanish sovereignty to becoming a part of the United States. Jefferson used troops, then, to rule the new empire, and he created military governments to govern the territories of Orleans and Louisiana until the two regions could organize proper territorial governments in the manner of the Northwest Ordinance.

Nonetheless, according to Article III of the Louisiana Purchase treaty: "The inhabitants of the ceded territory shall be incorporated in the Union of the United States and admitted as soon as possible according to the principles of the federal Constitution to the enjoyment of all the rights, advantages and immunities of citizens of the United States, and in the mean time they shall be maintained and protected in the free enjoyment of their liberty, property, and the Religion which they profess." *Congress* could decide when the time was ripe to allow Louisiana inhabitants the right to fully participate in the government of the United States.

With the Louisiana Purchase, the United States for the first time absorbed other peoples *involuntarily* into the political system. The Spanish, French, Creoles, Cajuns, free blacks (many from Santo Domingo), and others in New Orleans had little choice in the matter — unlike white Americans or their predecessors, who chose to come to the New World. (African Americans and American Indians were also involuntary members of the United States, to be sure, but both were implicitly, and sometimes explicitly, parts of the political system since colonial times.)

But with the huge influx of persons into the vast new region and, in particular, into New Orleans and surrounding areas, the opposition of the Federalists and the unsuitability of the Creoles soon became irrelevant. The non-Anglo and non-Indian mix of persons living in the area of the Louisiana Purchase quickly became a minority within a new, dominant white majority emigrating from the eastern states and from northwestern Europe.

The scale and success of the Louisiana Purchase encouraged still more geographic growth, westward movement, feelings of nationalism, and thoughts of empire. It was the United States' "Manifest Destiny" (a phrase coined by the popular writer John L. O'Sullivan) to conquer the North American continent and become a great power; Providence had destined an American empire — and "empire" *was* the term of art that nineteenth-century writers used to describe the United States' mission in the world.

This view of the United States as an empire had a long history. Benjamin Franklin sought to acquire essentially all of British North America in the Paris peace negotiations of 1782 and 1783, and James Madison's view of an "extended republic" in *Federalist 10* is clearly consistent with expansionism. Madison thought that the United States might become "one great, respectable, and flourishing empire." As the New Englander Jedediah Morse wrote in 1789 in *American Geography*, "We cannot but anticipate the period, as not far distant, when THE AMERICAN EMPIRE will comprehend millions of souls west of the Mississippi . . . [which] was never designed as the western boundary of the American empire." And in 1811 John Quincy Adams wrote that he saw, after the Louisiana Purchase, "an assumption of implied power greater in itself and more comprehensive in its consequences than all the assumptions of implied powers in the twelve years of the Washington and Adams administrations put together."

As the United States expanded, it added still other non-Anglo populations to its domain. Florida had a small population of persons of Spanish and Spanish-Indian descent, Anglo-American immigrants from the existing states, and others, when Spain sold West and East Florida to the United States — knowing that it would be unable to hold on to Florida and fearing its outright seizure by U.S. forces or internal rebellion, as one had already occurred in 1812. As the text of the Adams-Onís Treaty of 1819 (also known as the Transcontinental Treaty) read: "The Inhabitants of the Territories which his Catholic Majesty cedes to the United States by this Treaty, shall be incorporated in the Union of the United States, as soon as may be consistent with the principles of the Federal Constitution, and admitted to enjoyment of all the privileges, rights and immunities of the citizens of the United States." But some of Florida's inhabitants may not have wanted to become part of the United States — just like some of the indigenous inhabitants of Louisiana — even if they did not want to return to Spain.

In contrast, the Treaty of Washington between the United States and Great Britain in 1846 over the Oregon Territory boundary dispute — an agreement needed by the Polk administration, which faced a likely war against Mexico — affected white Americans, a handful of British citizens, and, of course, Indians. Yet the Treaty of Washington with Britain, also known as the Oregon Treaty, had no provisions for any indigenous inhabitants. Article II merely noted that British subjects and their goods were to be treated equally for river navigation and portage purposes, and Article III noted that "the possessory rights of the Hudson's Bay Company and of all British subjects who may be already in occupation of land or other property, lawfully acquired within the said territory, shall be respected."

The terms of the Mexican Cession in 1848 echoed the terms of the treaties for the Louisiana Territory and Florida. The Treaty of Guadalupe Hidalgo held that the United States now ruled over a vast new area with an indigenous population of varied Spanish, Mexican, and Indian descent, and that Congress could decide when to admit these inhabitants as members of the United States: "The Mexicans . . . shall be incorporated into the Union of the United States and be admitted, at the proper time (to be judged by the Congress of the United States) to the enjoyment of all the rights of citizens of the United States according to the principles of the Constitution." The text of the treaty left it open for Congress to decide when that time was.

The nonwhite inhabitants of the Mexican Cession posed little threat to American society, the *New Orleans Picayune* reassured its readers: "In the annexation of New Mexico and California the United States will incur none of the dangers which have been predicted of admitting a race of men, differing from us in language, religion, descent, laws, manners, and social condition to an equal participation in the benefits and responsibilities of free government." The reason for the *Picayune*'s confidence was that the region being acquired was "comparatively unsettled," and "by the time it has a population enough to send a member to Congress [it] will be thoroughly Americanized. So all of the forebodings concerning the appearance in the Senate or House of Representatives of a thorough-bred Mexican or half-breed Mexican will be dissipated." Yet these persons, too, came under U.S. sovereignty involuntarily, through the actions of President Polk and the government of the United States, where the military, population, and resources of the United States of Mexico were greatly overmatched.

Whether these new areas of the United States were to be admitted "as soon as possible according to the principles of the federal Constitution," as the Treaty of Paris of 1803 (consummating the Louisiana Purchase) stated, "as soon as may be consistent with the principles of the Federal Constitution," as the Adams-Onís Treaty of 1819 had it, or "at the proper time (to be judged by the Congress of the United States)," according to the terms of the Treaty of Guadalupe Hidalgo, mattered little in practice. Congress could in every instance itself decide when and where to establish new territories, and when and where to annex new states as parts of the Union.

Texas stands out as an exception to this history of American expansion through treaty, since it was admitted as a state and incorporated into the Union in 1845 "on an equal footing with the existing states" by the terms of the congressional resolution — not treaty — that admitted Texas into the Union. But the political incorporation of the Mexicans residing within Texas's borders was a matter for the state of Texas to settle: so long as Texas had republican government, questions of citizenship were not the concern of the U.S. Congress.

Yet in the pursuit of geographic expansion, the United States did not get all that it wanted. Americans had long sought to add Canada to the United States, for instance, but Canadians would not support the United States during the Revolution or the War of 1812, contrary to the expectations of many Americans. The United States was also unable to buy Cuba from Spain, as Presidents Polk, Pierce, Buchanan, and, later, McKinley, tried to do (although we will see what happens when Fidel Castro dies). Then, too, the United States received much less of the Pacific Northwest from Britain in 1846 than many had hoped. Expansion was hardly a pre-scripted or predictable process.

Throughout this process, Congress had a deeply ambivalent relationship with the territories. On the one hand, Congress treated the territories and territorial citizens benignly; it followed the expectation that acquired areas would become organized as territories and then admitted as states, and it followed the liberal and progressive guidelines set down by the Northwest Ordinance. On the other hand,

Congress and the U.S. government had virtually full authority over the territories; the U.S. government wasn't only benign.

For one, Congress controlled the *timing* of new states' admission, just as it controlled when administrative districts were to be created in newly acquired regions and when territories were to have organized governments. The power to decide if and when to admit new states (Art. IV, Sec. 3, Cl. 1) was also, by implication, the power to *delay* the admittance of new states.

Congress delayed annexing states for partisan, sectional, and other reasons. The struggles for statehood for the thirty-seven nonoriginal states — to define "struggle" as the period between the first petition or bill for statehood and admission as a state — lasted an average of more than thirteen years, with Illinois the shortest, at eleven months, and New Mexico the longest, at sixty-two years; for seven states, the process took longer than twenty years. In the years leading up to the Civil War, for instance, Congress balanced the admission of free states with that of slave states for the purposes of the Senate (since the House of Representatives could not be balanced, given the North's population advantage over the South). So Congress balanced Maine (1820) with Missouri (1821), Arkansas (1836) with Michigan (1837), and Florida (1845) with Iowa (1846). Even before the Missouri Compromise, Congress balanced the admission of Illinois in 1818 (with 34,620 persons, well below the Northwest Ordinance's specification of 60,000 persons for statehood) with Alabama (1819).

Congress also set the *boundaries* of the territories and new states. It altered the boundaries of Michigan and Ohio (Michigan got the Upper Peninsula in compensation for an area in what had been southeastern Michigan, which went to Ohio) and it brokered the Compromise of 1850 under the leadership of Senators Henry Clay, Daniel Webster, and Stephen Douglas, which redrew the boundaries of the American Southwest. The Compromise of 1850 admitted California as a state; it organized New Mexico (which then included Arizona) as a territory; it reduced the size of Texas (which had to cede much of its northern and western land claims, or about one-third its area); and it shrunk the size of Deseret, the political community established by the Mormons in the intermountain West, by two-thirds from the original boundaries claimed by the Mormons.

Congress created a total of sixty-three separate territories over the history of continental North America, in fact, and altered the boundaries of eight states — five within the first year of their establishment and one, Nebraska, six years after its admission; only twice, with Texas and Alabama, did Congress reduce the size of a state.

Congress's authority extended, too, over the *number of delegates* each new state could send to the House of Representatives. Congress usually granted the minimum of one representative per state until a new census could be held to determine the correct number of representatives. But it disregarded the fact that Louisiana (1812) and Missouri (1821) each qualified for more than one representative on a census basis, and nonetheless assigned them only one representative each. Later, Congress allowed Iowa (1846), Wisconsin (1848), California (1850), and Minnesota (1858) two delegates each, before any census had been taken. And Congress granted Oklahoma (1907) five representatives, although Oklahoma qualified for just four.

In addition, Congress included *English-language requirements* when admitting Louisiana (1812), Oklahoma (1907), New Mexico (1912), and Arizona (1912) as states.

The most powerful instrument in Congress's hands, however, was its *authority over the land* lying within the territories — a provision also based on the Northwest Ordinance, which stipulated that "the legislatures of those districts, or new States [formed out of the Northwest Territory], *shall never interfere with the primary disposal of the soil* by the United States in Congress assembled, nor with any regulations Congress may find it necessary for securing the title in such soil to the *bona-fide* purchasers" (emphasis added). In other words, the U.S. government kept control of that portion of the public domain lying within a territory (or state) that had not already been sold, given away, or transferred to individuals, businesses, or the territorial government. Congress could dispose of this land as it wished.

Neither could the legislatures of the districts or states impose any taxes on U.S. government lands, "and in no case shall non-resident proprietors be taxed higher than residents." Not only could the U.S. government's lands not be taxed, then, but the Northwest Ordinance and all subsequent legislation that organized territorial and state governments prohibited territorial and state legislatures from taxing the sometimes vast landholdings of eastern speculators, foreign real estate investors, or other nonresident holdings at rates higher than those levied on resident farmers, merchants, laborers, artisans, or others.

Perhaps the most striking example of Congress's authority over the territories, though, was its particular treatment of the Mormons and Utah Territory. (Even the name that Congress bestowed on Deseret — "Utah," for the Ute Indians — was not one chosen by Brigham Young or the Mormon elders.) The 1862 Morrill Act for the Suppression of Polygamy prohibited bigamy in the territories, annulled the incorporation of the Church of Jesus Christ of Latter-day Saints by the Utah territorial legislature, and outlawed religious organizations — that is, the Mormon Church — from owning real estate valued at more than $50,000. Yet the Morrill Act was virtually unenforceable, since no grand jury would convict polygamists. In fact, the condemnation of antipolygamists in Washington only further motivated the Mormon faithful.

Congress then passed the Poland Act of 1872, which reduced the powers of the territory's probate judges, called for jury pools to be selected by U.S.-appointed territorial officials, and provided for polygamy convictions to be appealed to the U.S. Supreme Court. In 1882 Congress passed the Edmunds Act, which outlawed polygamy ("unlawful cohabitation"), disenfranchised polygamists, and prohibited polygamists from serving on juries. The combination of these three swamped the Utah criminal justice system with cases on sexual matters.

So Congress passed the Edmunds-Tucker Act of 1887, which served as the deathblow to the Mormon "Principle" (as the Mormon elders called polygamy). The Edmunds-Tucker Act required church corporations to forfeit their property — property that they received through the tithes of the Mormon faithful. The bill's sponsors and others believed that Congress, by shattering the church organization through the dissolution of church property, would cause the dissolution of the corporate nature of the Mormon Church, and thereby shatter the Mormon religion and eradicate polygamy.

Throughout the history of anti-Mormon legislation, the U.S. Supreme Court supported Congress and its policies destructive of polygamy (policies that received enthusiastic approval elsewhere in the United States). Despite the First Amendment's protection of religious freedom and despite the hopes of the Mormons, the Supreme

{ *Chapter 1* }

Court upheld the ban on polygamy in *Reynolds v. United States* (1878); it endorsed the ban on polygamists from voting in *Murphy v. Ramsey* (1885); and it legitimated the forfeiture of Mormon corporate property in the *Mormon Church Case* (*Late Corporation of the Church of Jesus Christ of Latter-Day Saints et al. v. United States* [1890]). The Supreme Court repeatedly upheld the plenary power of Congress to regulate the territories as needed.

Only when Mormon elders decided to abandon the claim to legally practice polygamy, faced as they were with an antagonistic U.S. Congress, federal government, and Supreme Court, did Congress then admit Utah as one of the states of the Union in 1896 — almost fifty years after it annexed Utah as a U.S. territory.

———

In sum, the U.S. government exercised considerable authority over the territories, authority that it exercised in different dimensions and for varying periods. Members of Congress and the American public nonetheless assumed that the territories and their inhabitants would become states and citizens of the Union. Even Utah eventually became a state, as later would Oklahoma, New Mexico, and Arizona.

But fewer than five years after Frederick Jackson Turner wrote of the closing of the American frontier in his famous essay, "The Significance of the Frontier in American History," the United States suddenly had Cuba, Puerto Rico, the Philippines, and Guam in its possession — islands that many, if not most, Americans wanted to keep as their newfound spoils from the war with Spain. Neither the imperialists or expansionists (such as President McKinley, the vice president and former assistant navy secretary Roosevelt, Massachusetts senator Henry Cabot Lodge, and most other leading Republicans, all of whom favored expansion) nor the anti-imperialists or anti-annexationists (such as former U.S. presidents Benjamin Harrison and Grover Cleveland, Andrew Carnegie, Mark Twain, William Jennings Bryan, and Massachusetts senator George Hoar, among others) wanted the new territories and their large populations to become part of the United States and the American polity.

Not only were Cuba, Puerto Rico, and the Philippines densely populated by non-Anglos and non-English-speaking inhabitants of mixed racial background, but many were Catholic and some, in the Philippines, Muslim rather than Christian. In addition, each of the three principal new island territories — Cuba, Puerto Rico, and the Philippines — posed distinct challenges for the U.S. government and major American political interests.

CHAPTER 2

The Spoils of the Spanish-American War

In 1789 the United States was a wilderness lying upon the outskirts of
Christendom; she is now the heart of civilization and the focus of energy.
The Union forms a gigantic and growing empire which stretches half round
the globe, an empire possessing the greatest mass of accumulated wealth, the
most perfect means of transportation, and most delicate yet powerful industrial
system which has ever been developed. By the products of that system she
must be brought into competition with rivals at the end of the earth.
The nation has to deal with problems domestic and foreign, more vast and
more complicated than were ever before presented for solution. In a word, the
conditions of the twentieth century are almost precisely the reverse of those
of the eighteenth and yet the national organization not only remains unaltered,
but is prevented from automatic adjustment by the provisions of
a written document, which, in practice, cannot be amended.
BROOK ADAMS, *The New Empire*, 1902

Events in Cuba caused the Spanish-American War. Cuba had a total
population of about 1.6 million persons, according to a U.S. census
of 1900 — more than a million whites, by the census count, and more
than 500,000 blacks and mulattoes. The island of Cuba is 740 miles
long — the equivalent of the distance between Washington, D.C., and
the Mississippi River — and lies less than 100 miles south of Florida.

The Cuban independence movement emerged following the death
of José Martí, the famous Cuban nationalist writer, artist, and poet, in
1895. With the Cuban army's destruction of cane fields and sugar mills
and with the Wilson Tariff replacing the free-trade McKinley Tariff,
Cuban sugar production plummeted, with sugar exports to the United
States falling by 75 percent between 1894 and 1896. As the Cuban
economy worsened over the course of the late 1890s, more and more
Cubans flocked to the independence movement, thereby accelerating
the decline of the Cuban economy. With the well-publicized struggles
of the Cuban independence movement and the stories of Cuban suf-
fering under the Spanish, led by General Valeriano Weyler y Nicolau,

many Americans supported the cause for Cuban independence — Cuba Libre — and contributed money, weapons, and sometimes their own services in the fight against Spain.

These "many Americans" did not include McKinley and his White House advisers, leading Republicans in Congress, or most financiers and businessmen. They wanted no part of Cuban independence if it meant the triumph of "the politically displaced, the socially dispossessed, the economically destitute," and other Cubans — many of them black. The armed revolution for an independent Cuba may have offered the Cuban poor a chance at a new start and a means to redress historic grievances, but Cuban independence also fundamentally threatened the political and economic interests of Cuban elites and American investors in Cuba. Property owners in Cuba feared independence, in fact, and preferred annexation to the United States.

With this turmoil in Cuba, several groups of leading planters, businessmen, lawyers, and merchants in Cuba met on different occasions with American political and business leaders to voice their hopes that the United States would intervene. Prominent among the voices were Edwin F. Atkins of Boston, who owned the 12,000-acre Soledad Plantation, valued at $1 million, and Henry O. Havemeyer, who had invested $600,000 in sugar-growing land and sugarcane mills. Atkins not only was one of Cuba's largest sugar producers but also was close to U.S. attorney general Richard Olney (in the Cleveland administration). Atkins lobbied actively against the rebellion and for continued Spanish rule. Havemeyer, for his part, ran the American Sugar Refining Company together with his brother Theodore, and treasurer and secretary John E. Searles; the American Sugar Refining Company, meanwhile, controlled the Sugar Trust. And Havemeyer and the American Sugar Refining Company had for a long time sought the annexation of Cuba.

U.S. politicians were therefore divided about Cuba, with some supporting Cuba Libre and others supporting Cuban property owners. But events quickly came to a head and forced President McKinley into action. On top of the Cuban army's growing success against Spain came the sinking of the USS *Maine* in Havana harbor in February 1898, and then the publication of the de Lôme letter (in which Enrique Dupuy de Lôme, a Spanish diplomat, ridiculed McKinley for his weakness and lack of will). Pressure for war steadily mounted among both Democrats and Republicans in Congress, in the press, especially the yellow press, and, finally, on the part of financial interests who sought an end to the uncertainty over whether there was to be a war.

With the growing likelihood of Cuban independence, the McKinley administration in March and early April 1898 again sought to buy or otherwise obtain Cuba — McKinley offered $300 million at one point, lesser amounts at other times — but Spain would not sell or transfer Cuba to the United States. But when Spain at the last minute agreed to surrender Cuba to the United States, the Cuban rebels refused to agree to a cease-fire. The McKinley administration, for its part, did not want to fight alongside the Cuban rebels — in fact, the president and his advisers did not even consult Cuban leaders Estrada Palma and General Máximo Gómez on how they would react to the United States' annexation of their island. Given that Cuban independence was unacceptable, the McKinley administration decided on military intervention.

Preventing the United States from annexing Cuba, however, was the U.S. Congress. Only days before the war began, Congress had unanimously passed the Teller Amendment as part of a joint resolution, named after Senator Henry M. Teller (R-Colo.). The Teller Amendment, signed by President McKinley on April 20, 1898, stated: "1. That the people of the island of Cuba are, and of right ought to be, free and independent," and "4. That the United States hereby disclaims any disposition or intention to exercise sovereignty, jurisdiction, or control over said island except for the pacification thereof, and asserts its determination, when that is accomplished, to leave the government and control of the island to its people." Members of Congress supported the amendment not only because they opposed expansion and because the popular cause of Cuba Libre made annexation politically difficult, but because they sought to protect existing agricultural interests within the states, especially sugar and tobacco growers, from Cuban competition. Were Cuba to be part of the United States, then its goods would come in duty-free and thereby undermine workers and producers in business that faced competition from (cheaper) Cuban goods.

With the success of the Cuban insurrectionists imminent, as the historian Louis A. Peréz points out, with businesses now supporting war so as to end the prolonged uncertainty, and with the clamor for war in Congress and the press, the McKinley administration moved into action. The United States put a blockade on Cuba on April 22; shots were fired the next day; Admiral George Dewey was ordered to the Philippines on April 24; and Congress on April 25 retroactively declared that the war with Spain had started on April 21. In a matter of weeks the United States defeated Spain at sea as well as on land, and occupied Spain's former colonies — Cuba, Puerto Rico, and the Philippines.

The title "Spanish-American War" is therefore a misnomer, since the war was as much about Cuba as it was about Spain. Indeed, the name does a disservice to the cause of the war (the success of the Cuban independence movement), to the victims of the war (where Cubans suffered losses easily matching those of Spanish and U.S. forces), and to the war's consequences (where the McKinley administration refused to recognize Cuban independence, and where Cuba would become a protectorate of the United States instead).

The U.S. military occupied Cuba from late 1898 to mid-1902 (and paid each Cuban soldier $75 to bring in and deposit his arms, spending a total of $2,547,750 to muster down the Cuban army). The U.S. military occupied Cuba until a "balanced" and "responsible" government could be formed in the judgment of the McKinley administration and the military governor of Cuba, General Leonard Wood. Cuba raised its own flag over the island on May 20, 1902.

If the war was about Cuba, the cause of the congressional and ultimately constitutional controversy caused by the Spanish-American War was over Puerto Rico. U.S. forces occupied Puerto Rico from October 18, 1898, until May 1, 1900. The island had about 950,000 inhabitants, 361,000 of whom were "colored," according to a U.S. Department of War census, and was as densely populated as New Jersey — the nation's most densely populated state at the time.

With annexation of Puerto Rico by the terms of the Treaty of Paris, ratified by the U.S. Senate on February 4, 1899, Congress began to draft legislation for setting up a local government in Puerto Rico — the Foraker Act, named for its sponsor, Republican senator Joseph Foraker of Ohio, a twice-elected governor of that state and an opponent of expansion. Foraker wanted to make U.S. citizens of all Puerto Ricans who wanted it; he sought to extend the U.S. Constitution to Puerto Rico; and he sought to establish an elected house of delegates for the island. But other U.S. senators would have no part of it.

The Senate committee's report recommended, instead, that Congress withhold "the operation of the Constitution and the laws of the United States" from "a people of wholly different character, illiterate, and unacquainted with our institutions, and incapable of exercising the rights and privileges guaranteed by the Constitution to the States of the Union." The subsequent bill recommended U.S. citizenship (at least in name), the establishment of an island legislature, the election of a delegate to the U.S. Congress, and — most controversial of all — the imposition of a tariff on goods traded between Puerto Rico and the states fixed at 15 percent of the rates specified in the Dingley Tariff Act of 1897.

But Foraker's bill received strong opposition from the White House and both parties in Congress. Opponents disagreed over the tariff provision, the granting of U.S. citizenship, the provision for a nonvoting delegate to Congress, the creation of a wholly elected Puerto Rican legislature, and the full extension of the Constitution. The largest sticking point, however, was the tariff. Although early versions of the Foraker bill provided for free trade with Puerto Rico — which was also the position of the McKinley administration — Democrats and Republicans from western states insisted on a tariff and were able to carry the day. Thus McKinley and his advisers, who had to maintain their working relationship with congressional Republicans and other high-tariff supporters, had to retreat from advocacy of free trade and accept a small tariff being imposed on trade with Puerto Rico — that is, the 85 percent reduction of the Dingley Tariff rates, which was the rate contained in the final version of the Foraker bill. But western Republicans and Democrats went further and included a provision in the Foraker Act to restrict landownership to parcels of 500 acres or less, thereby making business investments in sugarcane plantations in Puerto Rico less attractive to foreign investors. Again, McKinley and his advisers had to go along.

The Foraker Act, as passed by Congress and signed by McKinley, called for the U.S. president to appoint a governor and an eleven-man executive council (six members to be appointed by the U.S. president), and for a lower chamber of thirty-five delegates. Delegates were to be elected to two-year terms, had to be literate in English or Spanish, and had to own taxable property. Only if both chambers of the legislature and the governor agreed could all Puerto Rican males have the right to vote. The judicial power was vested in a Supreme Court of Puerto Rico, whose members were also to be chosen by the U.S. president and whose decisions could be appealed to the U.S. Supreme Court. Finally, Puerto Ricans were to be "citizens of Porto Rico," not citizens of the United States.

In sum, the Foraker Act's tariff provisions and other restrictions made Puerto Rico's political subordination to the U.S. government obvious. As Senate minority leader Augustus Bacon (D-Ga.) remarked with respect to Congress's discriminatory treatment of Puerto Rico, "every feature of a free territorial government has been sacrificed in order that a tariff may be enforced against Porto Rico."

By the terms of the Treaty of Paris the United States also annexed the Philippines, paying Spain $20 million for the islands. The Philippines consisted of 342 islands (Luzon and Mindanao being the two largest) with 7.6 million inhabitants of different ethnic backgrounds, according to a U.S. census. About 95 percent of Filipinos were Catholic, and 5 percent Muslim. The Philippines had little developed agriculture or manufacturing industry; most of the inhabitants were engaged in subsistence farming. One-half of the population could neither read nor write, the census found, and only one out of nine attended school (by comparison, one of six residents in the U.S. territory of New Mexico attended school).

But the same day that the U.S. Senate ratified the Treaty of Paris — on February 4, 1899 — the United States found itself at war in the Philippines, fighting against the independence movement led by Emilio Aguinaldo, the young Filipino nationalist. Although an aide to Admiral Dewey had told Aguinaldo that the United States would recognize Philippine independence, the United States would not in fact recognize any independent Philippine authority (just as it would not accept Cuban independence). So not long after the hostilities between the United States and Spain came to an end — with Aguinaldo fighting alongside the United States against Spain — U.S. forces and Filipinos began their own war over the political control of the Philippines.

What quickly became obvious was that the United States had much better trained and much better equipped forces than did the Philippine resistance. Aguinaldo and his forces therefore retreated into the villages and countryside, to wage guerrilla warfare against the U.S. occupation. The war in the Philippines (1899–1902) cost hundreds of millions of dollars and demanded 70,000 U.S. troops at the peak (the actual number of troops on the ground averaged about 24,000 soldiers at any one time, according to the historian Brian McAllister Linn). About 600,000 persons, or one-sixth of the population of the island of Luzon, died as either a direct or indirect result of U.S. military operations, according to U.S. general J. F. Bell in 1902; Linn and others estimate the number of deaths at less than half that figure. Because of the many islands, the rugged terrain, the fact that this was a guerrilla war, and the length of time that has elapsed, however, it is probably impossible to gauge the full measure of death and casualties that directly or indirectly resulted from the war.

But all recognize the relatively high number of Filipino deaths, many the result of the U.S. army's "very drastic methods," as General Arthur MacArthur (father of the World War II and Korean War general Douglas MacArthur) called them in 1902. The army herded hundreds of thousands of Filipinos into concentration camps, caused very high death rates among jailed Filipino prisoners, and slaughtered masses of civilians in the course of fighting the guerrilla war — not unlike the United States' later wars in Vietnam and twenty-first-century Iraq, where it was also difficult to tell combatants from non-combatants. The harshness of the U.S. methods is suggested by the ratio of dead to injured, which was about fifteen to one — almost a complete reversal of the typical dead-to-injured ratio in military combat. The Department of War and the Roosevelt administration also received a great deal of damaging publicity on the widespread use of tortures such as the "water cure" and the "rope burn."

With Manila and much of the surrounding island of Luzon secure, the McKinley administration set up a civilian commission under Jacob Schurman, president of Cornell University, to report on what kind of civilian government the United States should establish in the Philippines to replace military rule. The Schurman Commission did not itself govern, however. Rather, the transfer to civilian government fell to the second Philippine Commission, the "Taft Commission," chaired by William Howard Taft. This five-member commission, which built upon the practices of the previous Spanish administration and the U.S. military rule, established administrative and judicial districts throughout the Philippines. The Taft Commission also served as its own legislature to enact the policies and laws to apply in the Philippines as well as appointed judges to the courts as well — almost all of whom were Americans, a feature that displeased many Filipinos, especially with respect to the appointees to the Philippine Supreme Court.

On July 4, 1901, Taft became the civilian governor general of the Philippines, where, despite the war and the occupation, he succeeded beyond most expectations by virtue of his cultivation of good relations with the wealthy, educated, and politically influential Filipinos. One year later, in the Act of July 1, 1902, the U.S. Congress established civilian government in the Philippines. The organic act affirmed the government set up under President McKinley and the military government, and continued under President Theodore Roosevelt. The Act of July 1, 1902, contained a Philippine Bill of Rights, but it denied Filipinos the full set of rights guaranteed under the U.S. Constitution. It also explicitly excluded the Philippines from becoming a part of the United States for the purposes of political membership.

––––––

The situations in Cuba, Puerto Rico, and the Philippines thus posed three difficult and distinct challenges for the United States following the Spanish-American War. All three occupied islands — or, rather, island groups — were noncontiguous with the forty-five states, accessible only by sea, and, in the case of the Philippines, separated by thousands of miles from the Pacific coast — not unlike Hawai'i, which was annexed in 1898, and the islands of eastern Samoa, annexed in 1899 in a tripartite agreement with Great Britain and Germany. (Although neither the territory of New Orleans nor California was contiguous to the existing states when admitted into the Union, both could be reached overland, and the United States had claim on the area lying between them and the existing states.) Although each of the three new island possessions attracted its share of adventurers, speculators, miners, merchants, and others looking for opportunities, none attracted much in the way of settler colonies from the existing American states.

Hawai'i was different. In 1876, Hawai'i obtained a reciprocity treaty with the United States, allowing Hawai'ian sugar to enter the states duty-free. The whites in Hawai'i, who had been on the islands since 1820, viewed the reciprocity treaty as the first step toward annexation. The reciprocity treaty was subsequently extended in 1887 to include the United States' exclusive access to Pearl Harbor as a naval station. But the McKinley Act of 1890, by abolishing tariffs on *all* sugar imported into the United States, placed Hawai'i at a disadvantage relative to other sugar producers, whether foreign or domestic, in reaching the American market — despite the bounty Hawai'ian growers received at two cents a pound. Whites now believed that annexation was indispensable for their economic prosperity.

In January 1893, the white Hawai'ians — or "haoles" — seized power in a coup d'état against the Hawai'ian monarch, Queen Lili'uokalani, helped by 150 marines from the USS *Boston*, who were sent by the U.S. minister to Hawai'i supposedly to protect the interests of the U.S. government and the safety of American citizens. The whites quickly moved to disenfranchise nonwhites and restricted voting to just 2,700 persons — virtually all whites and substantial property owners. To qualify for the right to vote, whites had to pledge to support the Hawaiian Constitution, which in turn stipulated the annexation of Hawai'i to the United States.

The whites proceeded to establish English throughout the government and school system, impose an American legal system, follow American standards, and use the U.S. dollar as legal currency. Hawai'i was the "only true American colony," one congressman remarked in the debate on Hawai'ian annexation. And it was run by white Americans: "There is a government in the Territory which is centralized to an extent unknown in the United States and probably almost as much centralized as it was in France under Louis XIV," noted Edward P. Dole, the attorney general of Hawai'i, in 1903. Since whites controlled the economy, politics, and culture of the islands, Hawai'i was acceptable as a U.S. territory.

"The condition of the Sandwich Islands is peculiar," Abbott Lawrence Lowell wrote in the *Atlantic Monthly* in 1899. "A small faction of the population are Anglo-Saxon, and perfectly familiar with self-government . . . while of the remainder, fifteen percent are Portuguese, forty percent are Japanese or Chinese, nearly thirty percent are Kanakas [i.e., Hawai'ians], and eight percent more of partly of Kanaka blood. No one proposes to treat all these as political equals," Lowell wrote. "On the contrary, the Hawaiian commissioners have recommended that the islands be organized with a territorial government, but that the Japanese and Chinese shall not be made citizens at all, and that the Kanakas and Portuguese shall be virtually excluded from the suffrage by making the right to vote depend upon ability to read and write English and the payment of a tax." And this is what happened.

———

In sum, when the United States acquired its Caribbean and Pacific island territories it departed from the path of territorial development that had begun in the old Northwest. The text of the 1898 Treaty of Paris reflected the break in this historical trajectory. Unlike the treaties annexing Louisiana, Florida, and the Mexican Cession, which provided that the inhabitants of the new territories be "incorporated" and then "admitted" into the Union, Article IX of the treaty with Spain merely provided that "the civil rights and political status of the native inhabitants of the territories hereby ceded to the United States shall be determined by Congress." (The native Spanish who lived in the United States' new acquisitions, the "peninsulares," had one year in which to decide whether or not to return to Spain.)

How, then, were these tropical, even exotic, islands to fit into the existing territorial system, and what was their place in the U.S. Constitution?

Expert opinion showed little consensus on the question. The leading legal and political scholars of the period agreed that the United States had the right to acquire territory, whether by treaty, war, or discovery, and that with the right to hold territory came the right to govern or administer it. "The United States, having rightly acquired the territory, and being the only government which can impose laws on them, has the entire dominion and sovereignty, national and municipal, Federal and State," ruled the Ninth Circuit Court of Appeals in *Endleman v. United States* (1898). But experts differed over what place the island possessions had in the U.S. political system and how these new acquisitions should be governed.

Views on the constitutional status of the United States' new island possessions fell into roughly three camps. One view was that the

United States consisted of the states *alone*, a view taken by, among others, Christopher Columbus Langdell, the dean of Harvard Law School (incidentally, Langdell was personally responsible for introducing the case method to legal education); Harry Pratt Judson, president of the University of Chicago; Charles A. Gardiner of the New York Bar Association; and James Bradley Thayer of the Harvard Law School. Another view, held by Judge Simeon Baldwin, Carman Randolph, Paul Shipman, Edward Whitney, and others, was that the United States consisted of *both* the states and the territories. A third view, proposed by Abbott Lawrence Lowell, a lawyer and professor of government (and future president of Harvard University), was that the United States was neither exclusively the states nor necessarily inclusive of the states and the territories. Rather, the definition of the United States depended on the texts of congressional legislation and the phrasing of the nation's treaties.

Langdell, Judson, Gardiner, Thayer, and others argued that the United States *was* the states, consistent with Daniel Webster's argument as counsel in *American Insurance Company v. Canter* (1828). It was also the position of Thomas Cooley, the famous constitutional commentator and Michigan Supreme Court justice: "The Constitution was made for the States, not for territories," wrote Cooley in *General Principles of Constitutional Law*. "It confers power to govern territories, but in exercising this the United States is a sovereign dealing with dependent territory according as in its wisdom shall seem politic, wise and just, having regard to its own interests, as well as to those of the people of the territories." William Bradford Bosley, another attorney who took the first view of the United States, agreed that "the term 'United States,'" as used in the commerce clause, referred only "to the constituent members of the Union." This was also clearly "the sense in which the term 'United States' is used in the preamble, in Sections 1, 2, 3, 6 and 10 of Article I and in Section 1 of Article III."

The United States, for these experts, did not always or only refer to the states. There was also an "international sense," to be sure, a meaning that encompassed the entire scope of territory within the authority of the republic. In addition, there was a colloquial use that might well include the territories along with the states. But the international and colloquial uses of the idea of the United States were not to be confused with the meaning of the United States for the purposes of constitutional government: the United States of its collective member states, united under a single federal government and governed by institutions empowered to write laws, make treaties, and interpret the law. And these institutions "derive[d] their authority wholly from the will of the people within the narrower area," as Harry Pratt Judson put it. Furthermore, these political institutions, which represented the United States only in the narrow sense, have "every sovereign power not expressly prohibited by the constitution," Gardiner wrote. The plenary power of the federal government over U.S. foreign relations included the right to acquire, hold, and govern territory.

The U.S. government could thus treat the new territories according to what members of the legislative and executive branches decided was most appropriate. "It is for the political department of the government, that is, Congress or the treaty-making power, to determine what the political relation of the new people shall be," wrote James Bradley Thayer. "When a new region is acquired it does not at once and necessarily become a part of what we call the 'territory' of the United States," Thayer argued. Rather, the status of any new acquisitions had to be determined by the legislature, backed by the U.S. Supreme Court.

The history of the United States followed precisely such principles, Thayer remarked. "The Fourteenth Amendment did not make tribal Indians citizens of the United States," he noted; rather, the rights of the territories, like those of Indians, "are what Congress or the treaty-making power thinks it well to allow." Similarly, the "District of Columbia and the Territory of Utah" showed that the Constitution allowed the United States to acquire, hold, and permanently govern "territory of any sort and situated anywhere." In fact, "the power of the United States over the present-day territories" was little different "from that it exercised over past territories." The record of U.S. territorial administration was "exactly the process of governing a colony." The territories of the United States "are, and always have been colonies, dependencies," Thayer added. The United States had "been a colonial power without suspecting it" for more than a century, "only we choose to call them 'territories.'"

Thayer and the other experts who took this first, narrow view of the United States did not believe that the United States' territories had to become states. "What was appropriate in the case of some territories might not be in others. A cannibal island and the Northwest Territory would require different treatments," Thayer wrote. The "political theory" — as Thayer called it — that American government has, underlying it, the principles of self-government, universal suffrage, and republican government was abstract and idealistic. The truth, instead, was that Congress had the liberty to govern possessions as it thought best. For the proponents of this first view, the U.S. government's authority over the territories rested on the sovereign powers that the United States had had since the Declaration of Independence and that were implicit in the Constitution, especially in the territory clause.

The Constitution's territory clause, which referred to Congress's authority over the territory and property "belonging to the United States," gave Congress "great liberty" over territorial policies, Harry Pratt Judson pointed out. "Notice," Judson wrote, "*belonging to* the United States, not a *part of* the United States." Furthermore, the power to "dispose of territory" in the clause was not mutually exclusive from "the power to rule and regulate" the territories, Charles Gardiner observed; "*both powers are granted and are unlimited*" (emphasis added). Under the power of the territory clause, then, the United States could administer the unpopulated guano islands in the Caribbean and Pacific and, at the same time, maintain provisional governments in Cuba, Puerto Rico, and the Philippines — just as it did "after the Mexican War, in Tamalipas and California; and after the Rebellion [i.e., the Civil War], in Florida, Alabama and Arkansas from 1865 to 1868, in Mississippi and Georgia from 1865 to 1869, and in Virginia and Texas from 1865 to 1870," Gardiner remarked. Again, it was for *Congress* to determine how it wanted to govern its new "acquisitions, whether 'organized' or 'unorganized,' directly or indirectly, temporarily or permanent."

The proponents of this first view of the United States emphasized the significance of organized as opposed to unorganized territories (a distinction that the historian Max Farrand and others draw between "districts" and "territories"). "Organized territories," Gardiner wrote, were the areas of the public domain in "which Congress has extended our constitution and laws, and has established a system of organized local government; such are Arizona, New Mexico, and Oklahoma."

" 'Unorganized' territories," in contrast, "possess no organized local government, are usually not subject to our constitution and laws, and are ruled directly by Congress. Such are Alaska and Indian Territory." (Gardiner allowed that "Hawaii, Cuba, Porto Rico and the Philippines" should be called "territories," though, since "it would be more in harmony with American institutions" than to call them "colonies.") But the label itself did not matter, since the reality was the same: the "civil rights and political status of ceded territory are those guaranteed by treaty and conferred by Congress. They acquire no rights under our constitution and Federal statutes *ex proprio vigore.*"

By extension, "Statutes possess no innate power of expansion," Gardiner wrote, whether with respect to the tariff or to any federal law, since the determination of what laws or what constitutional provisions are to apply to the territories depends wholly on the decisions made in Congress. Neither did inalienable rights extend to the territories unless Congress legislated for it to be so, per the U.S. Supreme Court's ruling in the *Mormon Church Case* (1890).

Following this logic, the uniformity clause ("all duties, imposts and excises shall be uniform throughout the United States") referred to the states only. To interpret the Constitution as though it required "duties, imposts and excises laid and collected in the territories to be uniform with those laid and collected in the States," William Bradford Bosley agreed, would be to deny Congress and territorial legislatures the authority "to impose license taxes and any other kind of excises within the territories without imposing the like license tax upon the people of the United States." Similarly, the prohibition on Congress's power to tax exports, that "no tax or duty shall be laid on articles exported from any state" (Art. 1, Sec. 9, Cl. 5), was "not a prohibition to lay duties *on exports*," Judson argued, "but on articles exported *from any State.*"

Gardiner and his colleagues pointed out that precedents already existed for the imposition of tariffs between U.S. territories and the states. The United States had imposed lower tariffs by 25 percent on goods imported on American ships into the territory of Louisiana between 1804 and 1812, and it had made goods imported from Florida after its acquisition in 1819 liable to duty ("its ports must be regarded as foreign until they are established as domestic by an act of Congress," Marshall wrote in *American Insurance Company v. Canter*).

And in *Fleming v. Page* (1850) the Court established that cargo shipped to the states from Tampico, Mexico, could be treated as foreign imports for the purposes of the Polk administration's imposition of taxes on goods shipped to the states from U.S.-occupied areas. The U.S. government had never "recognized a place in a newly acquired country as a domestic port," Chief Justice Taney wrote in his opinion in *Fleming v. Page*, "unless it had been previously made so by an act of Congress."

As with the tariff, so too with the right to a jury trial and to the other guarantees under the Bill of Rights; these also fell under Congress's plenary authority for those holding the minimal view of the United States. "The federal bill of rights is no bar to suitable government of tropical territories," Judson explained. "After all . . . a jury is merely a means of inferring facts from evidence, and it is not the essence of the system that jurymen should themselves be uncivilized." Gardiner similarly observed that Article IV, Section 2 guarantees to the "citizens of each *State* all the privileges and immunities of the citizens of the several States"; Article IV said nothing about the citizens of the territories. Neither were these persons U.S. citizens under the Fourteenth Amendment (which stated that "all persons born or naturalized in the United States and subject to the jurisdiction thereof are citizens of the United States and of the States wherein they reside"), since the Fourteenth Amendment "contemplates two sources of citizenship and two sources only, birth and naturalization." So citizens of Puerto Rico and the Philippines, Gardiner pointed out, could "only become citizens by specific act of [C]ongress as was pending in the case of legislation for Hawaii that contained provisions for naturalization." To acquire citizenship by birth meant that the birth had to "be within American territory, *over which the constitution and laws shall have been specifically extended*" (emphasis added). Nor, for that matter, did territorial inhabitants have any right to immigrate to the United States, since they were not U.S. citizens.

According to the treaty power, however, the U.S. president and Senate had the authority to decide which territorial inhabitants could become citizens of the United States, and under what terms. But none of the previous U.S. treaties annexing areas and their inhabitants, Gardiner pointed out, included "wild Indians, or negroes, or any other persons" as "inhabitants" who "were incapable of becoming citizens." So the president and Senate had to decide what was best for the United States, and it was up to the Senate to "ratify, reject or modify any treaty," and there "is no limitation upon its treaty-making powers." Gardiner pointed out that the Senate had "modified a draft treaty with England in 1795, with France in 1801, with Norway and Sweden in 1818, with Mexico in 1848, and with Bolivia in 1868," in fact, just as it had rejected other treaties and ratified others without any alterations.

The U.S. government could also extend or limit the constitutional sphere through duly passed legislation. The legislative and executive branches had the authority to determine political rights, as they did with respect to suffrage. In *Murphy v. Ramsey* (1872), for instance, the U.S. Supreme Court established that the United States could disenfranchise persons in the territory of Utah who were found guilty of polygamy. Earlier, in *American Insurance Company v. Canter*, Marshall ruled that inhabitants of Florida could not "participate in political power" until Congress admitted Florida as a state; until that time, Congress could govern Florida with its power under the territory clause. Neither did the Fifteenth Amendment ("The Right of citizens of the United States to vote shall not be denied or abridged by the United States or by any State on account of race, color, or previous condition of servitude") automatically apply to territorial inhabitants, since these persons were not U.S. citizens. Meanwhile, the U.S. Supreme Court had already ruled that Congress could put qualifications — such as educational or property requirements — on the right to vote, without being in violation of the Fifteenth Amendment.

In other words, the United States could extend its "constitution and laws" both by treaty and by legislation. The political and legal experts who held the minimal view of the United States recognized that some fundamental rights *did* apply to the inhabitants of the United States' new island territories — such as the right to contract, habeas corpus, freedom of speech, and freedom of religion. The recognition of these rights was consistent with natural law, inhering in persons as their natural rights.

———

The second, broader view of the United States encompassed both the territories and the states. As Chief Justice Marshall had stated in *Loughborough v. Blake* in reference to the uniformity clause: "The District of Columbia, or the territory west of the Missouri, is not less within the United States than Maryland or Pennsylvania; and it is not less necessary, on the principles of our Constitution, that uniformity in the imposition of imposts, duties, and excises, should be observed in the one, than in the other." This was also the position taken by Chief Justice Roger Brooke Taney in *Dred Scott v. Sandford.*

Taney argued that the Constitution limited Congress in all respects vis-à-vis the territories, just as it did the states; the Bill of Rights applied no less to the people of the territories than it did to the people of the states. And Congress could not deny these rights: "The rights of property are united with the rights of persons, and placed on the same ground as the Fifth Amendment to the Constitution, which provides that no person shall be deprived of life, liberty, and property, without due process of law." In Taney's words, "There is certainly no power given by the Constitution to the Federal government to establish or maintain colonies bordering on the United States or at a distance, to be ruled and governed at its own pleasure; . . . and if a new State is admitted, it needs no further legislation by Congress, because the Constitution itself defines the relative rights and duties of the State, and the citizens of the State, and the Federal government. But no power is given to acquire a territory to be held and governed permanently in that character."

A number of political and constitutional experts agreed with this fuller definition of the United States. "The Constitution does not need to be extended," Paul Shipman wrote in the *Yale Law Journal.* Though the Constitution is not "self-executing," Shipman wrote, since its provisions need to be implemented and interpreted, it "is self-extending; it goes with the land of which it declares itself to be supreme law, as the form goes with the substance." The Constitution was "co-extensive with the political jurisdiction of the government it creates." Although the Constitution required Congress's action "to carry its powers into effect," it required "no extraneous agency to extend it." Indeed, the sovereignty of the United States could not be exercised *without* coming under the provisions of the U.S. Constitution and the laws of Congress. The U.S. government had to abide by its fundamental law, and Congress, in any event, could not act outside the Constitution; it could "not infringe, directly or indirectly, any provision of the Constitution, express or implied."

Congress's authority over the territories, which combined the power of the federal government and that of a state government, was therefore "limited by the constitutional prohibitions on both." There were "no unlimited powers" in the American constitutional system, Shipman wrote. "A limited government having unlimited powers [was] a contradiction in terms. . . . Extraconstitutionality is unconstitutionality." If the United States were to expand, then the provisions of the Constitution and the laws of Congress likewise extended to any new parts of the United States.

These scholars certainly recognized that the United States had the right to expand. Cuba, Puerto Rico, and the Philippines could simply become states of the Union, some thought. The island territories would pose no more of a challenge to political education for emigrating Americans and the U.S. Congress than had "the cowboy civilization of Wyoming, Nevada and Montana," as Elmer Adams put it in the *Yale Law Journal.*

The tariff issue, in particular, raised important constitutional questions with respect to the island territories. These involved the uniformity clause, the prohibition of taxes on exports (the export clause), the U.S. government's powers to regulate commerce (the commerce clause), and its authority to raise revenue (the revenue clause). Specifically, the New York attorney Edward Whitney asked: (1) Could goods shipped *into Puerto Rico from other countries* be taxed at different rates than goods imported into the states? (2) Could goods shipped *from Puerto Rico to the states* be subject to duties paid into the U.S. Treasury? (3) Could goods shipped *from the states to Puerto Rico* be subjected to duties? (4) And if such goods could be taxed, were the duties *valid,* since the proceeds would go into the local (Puerto Rico) treasury rather than general (U.S.) treasury?

Whitney answered no to all four questions. He observed that ever since "the territories had begun to be commercially important, the machinery for collection of duties was extended to include them; and they have been included practically, as well as theoretically, in the operation of the uniformity clause ever since." He thought that *Fleming v. Page* (which held that goods shipped from areas under U.S. occupation were to be treated as goods being shipped from foreign ports) had been rightly decided, but that Taney had made some "plainly erroneous" remarks about Florida and taxation. But in *Cross v.*

Harrison (1853), a California case involving recovered duties between the date of the treaty of the cession of California and the date when the customs collector took office, a unanimous Court held that California was "part of the United States" because of the ratification of the Treaty of Guadalupe Hidalgo, and that the uniformity clause therefore applied.

If exports from territories were to be taxed for the benefit of the local island government — in violation of the uniformity clause — then there had to be a constitutional amendment to that effect: "We the People, acting in the prescribed form, may tax exports, attaint unpopular politicians, grant titles of nobility, or establish empires in the South Seas," Whitney argued. "I do not understand that our rulers can do any of these things without consulting us." And "if they wish to do them," they had to go through the proper amendment process: "They must secure two-thirds of our representatives in each House of Congress, and then secure the assent of at least thirty-four States, either by application to their Legislatures or by direct appeal to their voters; for Congress may call together state conventions if it pleases." Not to limit Congress's taxing power was to take a "long step toward transforming the great Democracy into a great Oligarchy."

Carman Randolph, another prominent New York attorney, agreed with Marshall's ruling in *Loughborough v. Blake:* the territories of the United States could not be treated as foreign — at least not on a lasting basis — without violating the Constitution's requirement of uniform duties throughout the United States. The president *could* control a territory during a period of "belligerent occupation" until the war came to an end, Randolph argued, and such control could last until a normal government could be established. And Congress could use its own powers to extend such provisional control "after the territory has been annexed to the United States." During this transitional phase, the U.S. president could "withdraw the forces and leave the country to its fate; recognize a local government; make a disposition of the islands by diplomatic arrangement or, with the consent of the Senate, by treaty; or continue his rule." But the president's near-despotic authority "is only reconcilable with the principles of the Constitution as a temporary arrangement made advisable by the results of war." This is how Randolph explained the Court's decision in *Fleming v. Page:* the imposition of tariffs on goods shipped from Mexico took place in a "transitory condition," during U.S. occupation and before Congress acted to establish new authority.

As to other constitutional provisions, besides the tariff, Randolph noted that even the two dissenters in *Dred Scott v. Sandford*, Justices Curtis and McLean, recognized that legislation on the territories was subject to fundamental limitations with respect to the personal rights contained in the Constitution and its amendments. And in *Murphy v. Ramsey*, Randolph remarked, the Supreme Court had held that "*The personal and civil rights of the inhabitants of the Territories are secured to them, as to other citizens*, by the principles of constitutional liberty which restrain all the agencies of government, State and National" (emphasis added). But Randolph added — in an argument more consistent with the minimal view of the United States and inconsistent with other experts who took the second, full view of the United States — that "their political rights are franchises which they hold as privileges in the legislative discretion of the Congress of the United States."

Randolph, like the other experts who agreed with the second view of the United States, certainly recognized the challenges posed by the new territories and their inhabitants. But Randolph and others merely pointed out that the United States should not "annex a country evidently and to all appearances irredeemably unfit for statehood because of the character of its people and where the climactic conditions forbid the hope that Americans will emigrate to it in sufficient numbers to elevate its social conditions and ultimately justify its admission as a State." And if there is no "intention of admitting [a territory] as a State now or hereafter, . . . [then] the project is opposed to the spirit of the Constitution."

Neither did the United States need to have absolute control over its territories for the simple reason that the United States had no need of colonies in imitation of the other great powers. The United States was different from Great Britain, France, Russia, or Germany; its sovereignty was restrained by a written constitution interpreted by an independent judiciary. In the Philippines, for instance, the United States had a number of options, one expert observed. It could recognize a local government; it could recognize Spanish titular sovereignty but transfer the administration of the Philippines to another power (as with Cyprus and Bosnia, nominally part of the Ottoman Empire but administered by Great Britain and Austria, respectively); or it could

{ *Chapter 2* }

simply transfer the Philippines to another power. The U.S. Senate did not have to ratify the Treaty of Paris as it had been drafted; instead, the peace treaty could be renegotiated between the United States and Spain, redrafted, and sent back to the Senate for ratification.

———

The two views of the United States were both in evidence in the fierce Senate debates over the ratification of the Treaty of Paris. The second, full view of the United States formed the premise of the resolution proposed by Senator George Vest (D-Mo.) on December 10, 1898. The Vest Resolution denied the United States the authority to acquire and hold territory for any purpose other than statehood: "Under the Constitution of the United States no power is given to the Federal Government to acquire territory to be held or governed permanently as colonies. The colonial system of European nations cannot be established under our present Constitution, but all territory acquired by the Government . . . must be acquired and governed with the purpose or intent of organizing such territory into States suitable for admission into the Union."

The opponents of the Vest Resolution, who supported the Treaty of Paris, held the narrow definition of the United States. Senator Orville Platt (R-Conn.) remarked that the rights to acquire and govern territories were sovereign rights that the United States shared in common with other sovereign nations. And the right to govern was the right to establish whatever form of government fit the condition of the territory and the character of the inhabitants, whether they be savages, barbarians, or civilized persons. Senator Pratt agreed that the government to be provided by the United States should be "the most liberal, just, and beneficent government" possible. But to contend "that we should legislate otherwise" — that is, to entrust government to those who Pratt and others thought to be incapable of governing themselves — "is to hold that we are bound to perpetuate folly and invite disaster."

The Senate ratified the Treaty of Paris by a narrow margin, barely over the minimum two-thirds vote needed.

There was also a third view of the United States, one proposed by Abbott Lawrence Lowell in an article in the *Harvard Law Review*. Lowell argued that it was neither the case that "the power of Congress over the territories is absolutely unqualified by any constitutional restriction [the first view], nor the opposing doctrine that the limitations imposed by the United States Constitution upon the federal government apply wherever the jurisdiction of that government extends [the second view]." Instead, the United States had two options. One was that it could annex territory and make it part of the United States. "If so, all the general restrictions of the Constitution apply to it, save those on the organization of the judiciary." The second option was that "possessions may also be so acquired as *not* to form part of the United States, and *in that case constitutional limitations, such as those requiring uniformity of taxation and trial by jury, do not apply*" (emphasis added). What precise provisions of the Constitution applied depended on the provisions of the particular treaty and on congressional legislation. But the Constitution *always* applied if there were U.S. sovereignty; it did not have to be extended, in Lowell's view. And the territory clause gave the Congress the power to act with plenary authority over any U.S. possessions acquired "not to form part of the United States."

The United States' territorial history was one of the U.S. government exercising the first option, as Lowell saw it. "All the treaties for the acquisition of territory on the continent of North America have therefore provided that the people *should be incorporated into the Union,* or admitted to the rights of citizens, and some of them have professed in terms to extend the limits of the United States. The joint resolutions for the annexation of Hawaii may, perhaps, have the same effect, for they declare that the islands 'be and they are hereby annexed as part of the territory of the United States'" (emphasis added). Lowell pointed out, however, that "*the recent treaty with Spain makes no such provision. It merely cedes Porto Rico and the Philippines to this country without any stipulation in regard to the relations in which the islands or their inhabitants shall stand towards the United States*" (emphasis added). All depended on the wording. And U.S. presidents and senators over the course of American history had shown precisely such sensitivity to language when they had previously drafted and ratified treaties.

Lowell recognized that some constitutional provisions "have a universal bearing because they are in form restrictions upon the power of Congress rather than reservations of rights." Examples of such provisions were "that no bill of attainder or ex post facto shall be passed, that no title of nobility shall be granted, and that a regular statement and account of all public moneys shall be published from time to time." But such restrictions on congressional authority stood "upon a different footing from the rights guaranteed to the citizens, many of which are inapplicable except among a people whose social and political evolution has been consonant with our own." Examples of such rights for Lowell, as noted earlier, were the rights to uniform taxation and trial by jury.

Other political experts agreed with Lowell on the existence of a middle ground, although they were less specific on constitutional issues. (And there were dozens of books, popular articles, and scholarly writings that introduced the exotic new island territories to American readers, many of them with photographs and separate sections on each tropical territory.) Horace Fisher argued in *Principles of Colonial Government* (1899) on behalf of the creation of a new constitutional status, that of "colonial dependencies," to be distinguished from "our territories." Fisher, like Lowell, wanted to distinguish among the territories in U.S. possession: "We cannot incorporate in our Union, as Territories (much less as States), on terms of political equality and with the promise of statehood, any territory with a dense native population which has not attained [the necessary attributes] of self-government, without hazarding the welfare of the Union." The Constitution was "Imperial," as Fisher saw it, and the United States had now reached its "Imperial stage of National Development."

James Fernald took up the same theme in *Imperial Republic* (1899). Fernald hoped that "the American people . . . will find a way to make large public liberty consist[ent] with vast domain. At all events, this is the problem set before us, with the stern necessity to solve it or die." Fernald added, "It is for Americans to do that new thing among the nations — to make an imperial domain a republic." With its navy and its commerce the United States now *could* become the leading world power, Fernald argued, not unlike that of the Roman Empire (a common metaphor at the time, in fact). The duty of the United States, for Fernald, was to retain and govern the Pacific islands until "we may trust them to govern themselves." But the United States certainly could not "abandon lands to which we can now give civilized government, and leave them prey to warring factions of barbarians." In order for the United States to govern its newly acquired "vast domain," Fernald recommended the formation of a "department of the

Territories," where the "whole purpose of our occupation, civil or military, must be everywhere just what we have proclaimed it to be in Cuba — to enable the people "to establish and maintain a stable government of their own at the earliest possible moment." Trade and education would do the rest.

The United States could learn about colonial administration from England, which "does not attempt to govern the continental domain of Canada just as she does the two miles square of the rock of Gibraltar." "But we in our green youth — little more than a hundred years old — think there can be only one territorial system, and that the very one we have had heretofore." The Declaration of Independence gave the United States the right to "do all other acts or things which independent states may of right do," even if, as Fernald observed, "the Constitution is absolutely silent as to methods of territorial government."

Fernald was optimistic that the United States could govern its new dependencies benignly, such that they would be able to become more or less independent U.S. protectorates. Eventually, "With proper engineering and sanitation, and due use of inventive skill, Americans can live in Cuba, Porto Rico, Luzon, and Mindanao, as they have lived and become the ruling power in Hawaii." There was a natural progression toward Western civilization: "All that American rule has done for Florida and Louisiana, for Texas and California, which within this century were languishing under Spanish rule, the same American supremacy may do for the new lands that have come under the shelter of our flag."

Other political observers agreed with Lowell, Fisher, and Fernald about finding a constitutional solution so the United States could keep its new islands. Charles Morris, in his primer on the United States' new possessions, *Our Island Empire* (1899), described how the United States has "taken a new and radical step forward" by adding "to its dominions a large number of tropical islands, situated on opposite sides of the earth." For Morris, "only time and experience" could answer the question of what to do with them. In the meantime, Americans had "primitive populations to civilize, indolent populations to stimulate, hostile populations to pacify, ignorant populations to educate, oppressed populations to lift into manhood and teach the principles of liberty and the art of self-government." Other experts such as James Young, Judge Lebbeus Wilfley — later appointed attorney general for the Philippine Islands — and Alleyne Ireland of the University of Chicago were concerned that the United States develop the governing capacity to keep and administer its new colonies. But they all believed that the *fact* of colonies was a part of the contemporary world, and that it was time for the United States to adapt its political system to that worldly reality.

———

The matter of the political status of the United States' new Pacific and Caribbean territories did not remain hypothetical for long. In 1900 the firm of D. A. De Lima & Co. sued the U.S. government for the recovery of its payment of $13,145.26 in taxes on three shipments of sugar from Puerto Rico to New York. It was the idea of Frederic Coudert, the son of the founder of the international law firm Coudert Brothers, to file suit in federal courts against George R. Bidwell, the New York customs officer, to determine whether the sugar cargoes were, in fact, "imported." Other trading companies had sued to recover the duties collected on trade between the states and the new island territories, but by using the customs courts to file suit, the plaintiffs were implicitly conceding that the duties were being collected on imported goods. It was Coudert's innovation to directly confront the constitutionality question by suing in the New York Second District Court of Appeals on the basis of the uniformity clause — that "all duties, imposts, and excises shall be uniform throughout the United States."

But because *De Lima v. Bidwell* concerned duties on Puerto Rican trade imposed by the McKinley administration *before* the passage of the Foraker Act, which went into effect on May 1, 1900, Frederic Coudert also sought to make the more important challenge to the constitutionality of the tariffs being imposed on Puerto Rican trade *after* the passage of that act — that is, to challenge the *present* tariff policy of the United States. So Coudert, with the help of Elias De Lima of De Lima & Co., located a case that involved the payment of duties on trade taking place after April 1900 — S. B. Downes & Co.'s payment of $659.35 in duties on a shipment of oranges sent from Puerto Rico to New York. This was the case of *Downes v. Bidwell*.

Several other tariff cases involving the new island territories came up on appeal to the Supreme Court around the same time (see chapter 5): *Goetze v. United States; Fourteen Diamond Rings v. United States; Armstrong v. United States; Crossman v. United States; Huus v. New York and Porto Rico Steamship Co.*; and two cases with the name of *Dooley v. United States.*

Reasons for Empire

"What's all this about Cubia an th' Ph'lippeens?" asked Mr. Hennessy.
"What's beet sugar?"
"Th' throuble about Cubia is that she's free; th' throuble about beet sugar is
we're not; an' th' throuble about th' Ph'lippeens is the Ph'lippeens throuble," said
Mr. Dooley. . . . "We f'rgot about the' Beet. Most iv us niver thought about
that beautiful but fragile flower except biled in conniction with pigs' feet or
pickled in its own life juice. We didn't know that upon th' Beet hangs th' fate
iv th' nation, th' hope of th' future, th' permanence iv our instichoochions an'
a lot iv other things akelly precious. Th' Beet is th' naytional anthem an',
be hivins, it looks as though it might be th' naytional motto before long."
"Cuba v. Beet Sugar," FINLEY PETER DUNNE,
Observations by Mr. Dooley, 1902

It was a conservative Supreme Court that heard the arguments on *De Lima v. Bidwell, Downes v. Bidwell,* and the other *Insular Cases* in the weeks from early December 1900, to mid-January 1901. The nine justices on the Supreme Court deciding the *Insular Cases* lived in a white-dominated, racially divided United States. And it was under Chief Justice Melville W. Fuller (1888–1910) that the Court had earlier established the "separate but equal" doctrine for African Americans in *Plessy v. Ferguson* (1896) — a legacy that lasted until the Warren Court's decision on racial integration in *Brown v. Board of Education of Topeka, Kansas* (1954). Furthermore, most white Americans and political elites did not want the new islands and their inhabitants to become full members of the American political society, as noted earlier; they did not want millions of Filipinos, Puerto Ricans, and Cubans as their fellow citizens — not right away, and perhaps not ever.

The justices also shared a second view with many politicians, businessmen, military strategists, journalists, and the politically attentive public: that the United States was destined to be a world power, especially after the victory over Spain. Accordingly, the United States needed to — and should — keep its new war-earned possessions.

Yet to understand the thinking of political leaders and the American public on race and grand strategy is not enough. A basic, underlying issue remains: why the cases even came up before the Supreme Court — a question that brings in the American political economy and the role of the tariff. It was the *tariff*, after all, that the attorneys from Coudert Brothers, from Curtis, Mallet-Prevost and Colt (now Curtis, Mallet-Prevost, Colt, and Mosle), and from other law firms were challenging in the *Insular Tariff Cases*. The Fuller Court, meanwhile, was especially renowned for its pro-business decisions in the *Income Tax Case* (*Pollock v. Farmers' Loan & Trust Co.*, 1895), the *Sugar Trust Case* (*United States v. E. C. Knight*, 1895), and, later, *Lochner v. New York* (1905): in the *Income Tax Case*, Fuller wrote the Court's opinion that overthrew the federal tax on incomes above $4,000 a year (a large amount at the time, of course); in the *Sugar Trust Case*, Fuller again wrote the lead opinion that emasculated the antitrust provisions of the Sherman Act; and in *Lochner*, Fuller sided with the seven-to-two majority that overthrew a New York law restricting bakeshop-employee working hours.

Although we might think of the Fuller Court's near-absolute protection of economic liberty as "economic conservatism," given its defense of the rights of persons to do business with minimal interference from the government, the Court was, in fact, radical for its time with its judicial activism. It was willing to overthrow arguably reasonable and duly passed legislation at the state and federal levels of government for the sake of absolute economic liberty. And the tariff imposed by the Foraker Act was a government-imposed restriction on the free movement of goods in areas under U.S. sovereignty.

———

Race, religion, and political greatness were intertwined in the realization of a prospering, growing United States. "By 1850," the historian Reginald Horsman points out, "the natural inequality of races was a scientific fact which was published widely. One did not have to read obscure books to know that Caucasians were innately superior, and that they were responsible for civilization in the world, or to know that inferior races were destined to be overwhelmed or even to disappear." Novels by Sir Walter Scott — and some 500,000 copies of his novels were published in the United States — reinforced the idea that the American people represented the continuation of their English kinfolk. Thomas Carlyle, the English essayist, also exalted the Germanic and Saxon roots of the American people and was widely read from the 1820s to the 1840s. So, too, were many other writers both European and American.

For Scott, Carlyle, and others, African Americans, Indians, Mexicans, and all other races and ethnic groups were inferior to the Teutonic or Anglo-Saxon people. (Horsman points out the artificiality and inaccuracy of the term "Anglo-Saxon" to describe the mix of races, languages, cultures, and nationalities of the United States, but the term stuck.) In the last years of the nineteenth century Theodore Roosevelt, Henry Cabot Lodge, and other white, Protestant Republicans articulated the vision of an American empire, one where Anglo-Saxon Americans "could bring Christian civilization and progress to the world as well as infinite prosperity to the United States. . . . American and world economic growth, the triumph of Western Christian civilization, and a stable world order could be achieved by the American economic penetration of underdeveloped areas." The redeeming penetration of the world for the sake of its transformation would, of course, be led by the superior race.

Race thus repeatedly came up as a topic in the debates over the annexation of the United States' new island territories. Race, most white Americans believed, was intrinsically and ineluctably connected to the quality of American culture. Yale law professor Simeon E. Baldwin opposed U.S. expansion precisely because of racial concerns, just as did former U.S. presidents Harrison and Cleveland, and as did the reformer and former Interior secretary Carl Schurz. "To give the half-civilized Moros of the Philippines, or the ignorant and lawless brigands that infest Puerto Rico, or even the ordinary Filipino" the "guarantees of personal security" contained in the Constitution, in distinction "from the sharp and sudden justice — or injustice — which they have been hitherto accustomed to expect would," Baldwin wrote, "of course, be a serious obstacle to the maintenance there of an efficient government." Because the operation of the Constitution was coextensive with the scope of U.S. sovereignty, Baldwin opposed the territorial expansion of the United States over "half-civilized" island inhabitants.

The political scientist John W. Burgess of Columbia University similarly believed that "the Teutonic nations are the political nations of the modern era, . . . the duty has fallen to them of organising the world polit- ically." It was because of "the manifest mission of the Teutonic nations," Burgess wrote, that Western nations were justified in interfering "in the affairs of populations not wholly barbaric, which have made some progress in state organisation, but which manifest incapacity to solve the problem of civilisation with any degree of completeness."

U.S. Solicitor General John K. Richards likewise recognized that "the acquisition of these territories, situated in distant tropical seas, and inhabited by alien races, savage or semi-civilized, strangers to our system of law and mode of government, with the accompanying obli- gation of so governing them so as to secure and preserve peace and order and protect life and property, has brought us face to face with problems." Richards accordingly wanted to confine the United States to the states themselves.

Abbot Lawrence Lowell wrote at length in the *Atlantic Monthly* of the difficulties of democratic government in the United States' new territories:

> The art of self-government is one of the most difficult to learn; for it requires perpetual self-restraint on the part of the whole people, which is not really attained until it has become unconscious. The Anglo-Saxon race was prepared for it by centuries of discipline under the supremacy of law; . . . The vast numbers of immigrants coming to America might indeed have made the experiment a failure here, had it not been that many of them came from countries where self- government was practiced, and the rest were so distributed through- out the land that, like recruits in a regiment, they quickly learned the drill and took their place in the ranks. Now, these conditions are not true in our new possessions. . . . Every unprejudiced observer must recognize that to let the Filipinos rule themselves would be sheer cruelty both to them and to the white men of Manila. Even in the case of Porto Rico . . . self-government must be gradual and tenta- tive, if it is to be a success. They must be trained for it, as our fore- fathers were trained, beginning with local government under a strong judicial system, and the process will necessarily be slow.

This was the United States' paternalistic civilizing mission.

McKinley's men in the islands confirmed such racial stereotypes. "The municipalities are as ignorant as children," General Wood wrote

McKinley from Cuba on April 12, 1900. Wood, who administered the U.S. occupation of Cuba after the Spanish-American War, found that the people of Cuba "know that they are not ready for self government and those who are honest make no attempt to disguise the fact." Wood's assessment was that "the great mass of public opinion is perfectly inert; especially is this true among the professional classes. The passive inactivity of one hundred and fifty years has settled over [the Cubans] and it is hard to get them out of old ruts and old grooves." Major George M. Barbour, stationed in Santiago, was harsher yet. Cubans were "stupid, given to lying and doing all things in the wrong way," Barbour was quoted as saying in a story in *Outlook* magazine of December 1899. Under the supervision of the United States, however, "the people of Cuba may become a useful race and a credit to the world." But for the United States to make them independent "during this generation, would be a great mistake." Major Barbour, General Wood, and other Americans simply believed that Cubans' racial and colonial heritage made them unfit to be members of the United States.

Puerto Ricans, for their part, had an "extremely low" standard of living, Henry R. Burch wrote. They had "deplorable" education with "enormous" illiteracy, lacked "energetic motive," and were "ignorant, but polite, kind-hearted and sociable." Secretary of War Elihu Root opposed granting citizenship to Puerto Ricans on similar grounds; Congress was "chuckle-headed," moreover, for suggesting that they be allowed to be American citizens. Root's letter of December 24, 1908, reveals his distaste for Puerto Rican self-rule:

Citizenship in a democracy means something more than a decorative title. It means the right to share in government. What Porto Rico needs and really wants is not to take part in the government of the United States, but to be protected in governing herself. . . . Her people cannot really be citizens of the United States, and, calling them so only delays the real liberty Porto Rico should have.

If we give citizenship to the Porto Ricans the next step inevitably would be a demand for statehood with the same kind of pressure which New Mexico and Arizona are now exerting. It would be more difficult because more illogical to resist that claim on the part of the more than a million American citizens than it will be to resist the claim to citizenship on the part of a people who differ so widely from the people of the United States. The true policy I am confident is to give to Porto Rico the greatest possible measure of self government which she is competent to exercise, increasing the measure as she increases in competency until finally our relations to her approximate to our relations to Cuba, with a protectorate perhaps stronger in its character than that which we virtually have over Cuba, but stronger because the interests of the Porto Ricans themselves will demand it, and they will be unwilling to give up the benefits which they receive from the close relations.

In fact, when Root was first appointed secretary of war under McKinley — and Root was as much as anybody the architect of the United States' territorial policy — he joked to his friend U.S. Attorney General John Griggs, "I think the main feature of the change I am making is the formation of a new law firm of 'Griggs and Root, legal advisors to the president, colonial business a specialty.'"

William Howard Taft, the head of the Taft Commission in the Philippines, regarded Filipinos as also being inferior. Taft wrote Root of the undesirable characteristics of Filipinos in a letter of July 14, 1900:

> The population of the Islands is made up of a vast mass of ignorant, superstitious people, well-intentioned, light-hearted, temperate, somewhat cruel, domestic and fond of their families, and deeply wedded to the Catholic church. They are easily influenced by speeches from a small class of educated meztizos [sic], who have acquired a good deal of superficial knowledge of the general principles of free government. . . . They are generally lacking in moral character; are with some notable exceptions prone to yield to any pecuniary consideration, and are difficult persons out of whom to make an honest government. We have to do the best we can with them. They are born politicians; are as ambitious as Satan, and as jealous as possible of each other's preferment.

Taft repeatedly remarked to listeners that only 7 or 8 percent of Filipinos were educated, and that "over 90 percent were so ignorant that they could not be trusted."

McKinley, U.S. military officers, and others often referred to the Filipinos as constituting various "non-Christian" tribes, much like the

{ *Chapter 3* }

American Indians. (In fact, the United States established two provinces, the Moro and Mountain provinces in the Philippines, in which it allowed "considerable political autonomy" — not unlike American Indian reservations. The local autonomy in these areas depended on the administration of the officials appointed to local and municipal governments, however, whereas the limited local autonomy of American Indian reservations depended on the chiefs selected by the tribe members themselves.) As the *Santa Fe New Mexican* summarized — New Mexico was a U.S. territory at the time — the Philippines "are not the land for the American or the European." But "they are," the *New Mexican* added, "an almost ideal country" for "the Filipinos and the Chinese."

Members of Congress had their own opinions of the racial fitness of the inhabitants of the newly acquired territories. As Senator Albert Beveridge (R-Ind.) stated, "God has not been preparing the English-speaking and Teutonic peoples for a thousand years for nothing but vain and idle self-contemplation and self-admiration. No! He has made us the master organizers of the world to establish a system where chaos reigns. He has made us adept in government that we may administer government among savage and servile peoples."

Representative James Vardaman (D-Miss.), writing a few years later, called Cubans "a class of people that could cause hell itself to deteriorate. . . . [O]f all the weak, weary and altogether worthless people that I have ever had the misfortune to come into contact with the Cuban is . . . the most terrifying." And House Speaker Thomas Reed (R-Me.) dismissed Filipinos as "naked Sulus" and "yellow bellies." Meanwhile, Senator George Vest — the anti-imperialist — condemned "the idea of conferring American citizenship upon the half-civilized, piratical, muck-running inhabitants of 2,000 islands." Senator John W. Daniel (D-Va.), too, referred to the Philippines as a "witch's cauldron." As the historian David Fry reports, Daniel worried that were the Philippines annexed and Filipinos made full U.S. citizens, then "all the various inferior tribes of the country" would be able to move to the states themselves, vote, and get elected to office. President Theodore Roosevelt, for his part, referred to the Filipinos as "a jumble of savage tribes." The Democrats were no better: one of the planks of the 1900 Democratic platform stated, "Filipinos cannot be citizens without endangering our civilization."

Not only was this a racist America, it was an overtly racist society — even among the nation's leading politicians, U.S. presidents included.

Booker T. Washington identified the hypocrisy in the United States' imperialism when he asked "whether this country can do for the millions of dark-skinned races to be found in Cuba, Porto Rico, Hawaii, and the Philippine Islands that which it has not been able to do for the now nearly 10,000,000 negroes and Indians" residing in the several states.

For all the salience of race and racism in the United States of the late nineteenth and early twentieth centuries, however, race does not itself explain why the United States acquired these Caribbean and Pacific islands in the first place. For if race and racism were decisive, then the McKinley administration, Congress, and the American public would have had no interest in annexing tropical islands already well populated by non-Anglo inhabitants.

So why *did* the United States annex Puerto Rico, considering that Puerto Rico was not even a belligerent in the war against Spain? Why *did* the United States seize the Philippines, and not other areas controlled by Spain — such as Spanish Morocco in northern Africa, Spanish Guinea in sub-Saharan Africa, or other islands in the Marianas archipelago, besides Guam? And why did the United States *not* annex Cuba, the proximate cause of the war and lying only eighty-seven miles from Key West, Florida?

————

Theodore Roosevelt, Lodge (R-Mass.), other Republican politicians, military men, publishers, editors, academics, and others were nationalists writ large: they pursued the United States' achievement of economic, political, and military power — and ultimately its superiority — around the world. As Senator William Seward had declared in the 1850s — and Seward would become a future secretary of state and initiate the purchase of Alaska — "Multiply your ships, and send them forth to the east. The nation that draws most materials and provisions from the earth, and fabricates the most, and sells the most of productions and fabric to foreign nations must be, and will be, the great power of the earth."

The proponents of expansion in the late nineteenth century — or "imperialists," as they were also called — agreed with the economist Charles C. Conant, who in 1901 argued that the United States needed to promote its own businesses and secure access to foreign markets through political and military means so as to be able to use its excess capital and "to overcome the limitations of U.S. markets." (Englishman John A. Hobson would make a similar argument in 1902, as later would V. I. Lenin.) Many leading bankers and businessmen shared Conant's view, one that the severity of the depression of 1893 reinforced. The imperialists' vision extended south, to Central and South America, and west, to the Far East, especially China. East Asia, after all, was "the prize for which all energetic nations are grasping," wrote Brooks Adams, a direct descendant of John and John Quincy Adams. Alfred Thayer Mahan, too, wrote in *The Problem of Asia and Its Effect upon International Policies* of China's importance in the new century.

The United States' newly acquired island territories were indispensable parts of this global vision of increased overseas trade and decreased reliance on the domestic economy for both demand (i.e., the territories as a source of additional consumption) and supply (i.e., the territories as a source of low-cost, stable production). The value of goods sent from the states to Puerto Rico, to use one indicator, tripled in ten years, from $2.8 million in 1892 to $8.7 million by 1901. And whereas Puerto Rico was the fifth-largest market for U.S. products in Latin America in 1900 (and twenty-seventh-largest in the world), it became the fourth largest in Latin America by 1910 (and eleventh in the world). Likewise, American overseas investments grew from $700 million in 1897 to $2.5 billion in 1908. U.S. corporations dominated world markets in several industrial sectors, the historian Walter LaFeber points out — petroleum, agricultural equipment, cameras, and sewing machines.

The emphasis on trade and foreign investment demanded that the individuals and businesses trading and investing be protected militarily. Alfred Thayer Mahan, who was at the center of the movement calling for a stronger navy, wrote that the rise of the United States as a commercial, seagoing power depended on a larger navy, on more coaling stations (needed for refueling coal-burning steamships), and on new naval stations (i.e., naval bases).

The Harrison administration began the push for a newer, larger navy in 1890, the same year that Mahan came out with his influential book, *The Influence of Sea Power upon History*. Republicans continued their push for a stronger navy throughout the 1890s and early 1900s. Roosevelt, Lodge, and other Republicans, particularly those from the

Northeast and upper Midwest, were committed to increasing the size of the naval fleet and securing more congressional funding for building new ships. Another military strategist, W. V. Judson, remarked: "All authorities agree on this one point, neither fortifications nor men can hold for more than a short time any possession distant from the primary base, unless the line of communications be kept open. And to keep the line of communications open means to obtain and retain the command of the sea." This meant more and better ships, coaling stations, and naval bases.

An open line of communication meant one more thing to Mahan, Roosevelt, Lodge, Judson, and the other visionaries of a new U.S. grand strategy: the construction of an isthmian canal — whether across Panama or Nicaragua — to connect the Atlantic and Pacific oceans. As early as 1894, in fact, Roosevelt had written of the interrelationship of an isthmian canal, a great navy, and U.S. expansion into Samoa and Hawai'i. And it was President McKinley who in July 1897 initiated the engineering studies and negotiations for the construction of an isthmian canal. After 1898, moreover, the need for the canal only increased, since the United States' new overseas possessions spread out the U.S. Navy defensively. A canal across the Central American isthmus would thereby give U.S. policymakers additional flexibility in how they deployed the fleet.

Commercial and strategic goals were thus deeply interrelated. But the pursuit of these foreign-policy goals created dangers of their own. Although President Roosevelt was not personally worried about the German threat — Germany at the time was a growing rival to the United States geopolitically, economically, and technologically — others in his administration, the Navy and War Departments, and Congress were. "If we have a strong and well equipped navy," Lodge wrote "Theodore" on March 30, 1901, "I do not believe Germany will attack us. At the same time there is a fundamental danger which arises from our rapid growth economically. We are putting terrible pressure on Europe, and this situation may produce war at any time. The economic forces will not be the ostensible cause of trouble, but they will be the real cause, and no one can tell where the break will come."

With the plans for a canal, with the growth of trade and foreign investment, and with the larger navy, the United States needed naval stations in both the Pacific and the Caribbean. "There are only three places that are of value enough to be taken," Secretary of State James G. Blaine wrote President Harrison in 1890. "One is Hawaii and the others are Cuba and Puerto Rico." As Mahan explained a few years later, in 1897: "the pre-eminent intrinsic advantages of Cuba . . . only if naval supremacy in the West Indian waters could be asserted. Assuming the latter condition, Porto Rico, with the fortified port of San Juan, 1,000 miles from Havana and 5,300 miles from Cadiz [the Spanish seaport], was also a strategic point of importance."

Cuba offered several excellent harbors, among them Havana, Cienfuegos, and Santiago. The eastern tip of Cuba also made up the northwestern half of the Windward Passage, one of only a few key entryways into the Caribbean. In fact, the U.S. Navy was looking at the Cuban ports of Guantánamo and Cienfuegos, as well as at sites in Puerto Rico, U.S. Navy secretary Long wrote Secretary of State Hay on December 21, 1900, given that Puerto Rico was located on the eastern side of the Mona Passage, which ran between the Dominican Republic and Puerto Rico. Control of the Mona Passage, another of the few ways to approach the Caribbean from the North Atlantic, was especially important to the McKinley and later Roosevelt administrations' plans for an isthmian canal. Thus did McKinley on June 26, 1898, authorize the invasion of Puerto Rico.

The Philippines, for their part, were considered a gateway to China and were desired for their minerals, timber resources, and fertile soils. The Philippines could also supply the U.S. domestic market with hemp and unrefined sugar (the Philippines was the third-largest exporter of sugar to the United States, behind Cuba and Java). Before the Spanish-American War began, Lieutenant William W. Kimball, a navy intelligence officer, had drawn up war plans for the U.S. Navy to engage Spain in the Philippines so as to deprive Spain of a naval base and source of revenue, as well as establish a U.S. presence in the Far East. The plans were delivered to Admiral Dewey shortly before the war started, and Dewey carried them out.

Guam, for its part, was the southernmost island in the 420-mile Marianas (or Ladrones) archipelago, some 8,000 miles from Washington, D.C., and 3,000 miles from Hawai'i. On May 9, 1898, shortly after the U.S. victory in the Spanish-American War, the Naval War Board recommended that the United States seize Guam as "a strategic point between Honolulu and Manila," because of its value as a coaling and water station in the western Pacific. Thus the McKinley administration obtained Guam in the peace settlement with Spain and established a naval station on the island in August 1899.

Hawai'i, too, had been used by the U.S. Navy as a coaling and watering station since 1875, of course, but it was only three days after the end of fighting in the war against Spain, propelled by the momentum for expansion following the United States' victory, that Congress passed the controversial Newlands Resolution in mid-1898 to annex Hawai'i. Hawai'i had not only good harbors (e.g., Pearl Harbor) and a white Anglo ruling class but also extensive ongoing trade with the states.

The promotion of trade and foreign investment, on the one hand, and the acquisition and construction of naval stations, on the other, were interrelated in practice, of course, and reinforced each other. They converged on the policy of acquiring colonies, since naval bases and coaling stations could not be protected, according to the conventional wisdom of the day, unless the surrounding areas and hinterlands were themselves secured. This meant acquiring entire islands rather than just strategic ports. So if the United States were to increase its wealth, establish new areas of influence and control, and shelter and support naval vessels — or possibly station troops — then it, too, needed to possess colonies like those in the possession of other great powers.

The United States' new offshore islands thus played critical parts in the nation's new grand strategy — hence the acquisition of these islands and not other places under Spanish control, such as Spanish Guinea, northern Morocco, or others of the Mariana Islands. In fact, for the United States to acquire additional territories would have stretched the U.S. Navy only further and made American trade and the existing U.S. territories that much more vulnerable to hostile navies.

In short, a look at the strategic ambitions of the McKinley administration and others goes far toward explaining the United States' acquisitions following the war with Spain. Planners in the McKinley administration, the War, Navy, and State Departments, and Congress wanted Cuba, wanted Puerto Rico, wanted the Philippines, and wanted Guam. In addition, expansionists had for some time wanted Hawai'i. As President McKinley told William M. Laffan, editor of the *New York Sun*, on July 13, 1898: "While we are conducting war we must keep all we can get; when the war is over we must keep what we want." The United States did not acquire its new empire by accident, in a fit of absent-mindedness, or "blindly, unintentionally, accidentally and really in spite of ourselves," as Henry Luce, the founder and publisher of *Time* magazine, wrote. Neither did the United States achieve its empire through "the sheer genius" of Americans and "not because we chose to go into the politics of the world," as Woodrow Wilson stated. Nor was it the case, as Theodore Roosevelt characterized the rise of the United States as a world power, that "America, like it or not, would have to play a large part in the world."

Rather, Roosevelt, McKinley, their advisers, Lodge, Mahan, and other Republican expansionists *did* want an overseas empire, *did* want "to play a large part in the world," and *did* want the United States to be able to compete with its European counterparts, as the historian Matthew Frye Jacobson comments. Roosevelt knew the facts of the matter — that the expansionists sought to have a globally dominant United States — perhaps better than anyone else.

And the great powers of Europe had been rapidly acquiring territory. Germany added 1 million square miles to its territorial holdings between 1870 and 1900; France added 3.5 million square miles to its possessions over the same period; and Britain added almost 5 million square miles to its empire over those same years, an area several times larger than all of the United States. "The lesson of history is singularly clear," wrote Alleyne Ireland, the colonial commissioner of the University of Chicago: "For three thousand years there has not been a single nation of any importance which has not had colonies."

It went without saying that white Americans would oversee the United States' rise in the world, whether they were referred to as "Anglo-Saxon," "Aryan," or "Teutonic." The United States was now to rule over the less advanced societies and to educate their less civilized, nonwhite inhabitants in Western ways.

———

But if Puerto Rico, the Philippines, and Guam were annexed as part of the U.S. grand strategy, why not Cuba? Cuba had obvious strategic value, as we have seen. It had attracted considerable American investment. And it was the cause of the war. U.S. presidents and leading politicians from Benjamin Franklin on had long sought to annex the island, in fact. "I candidly confess that I have ever looked on Cuba as the most interesting addition which could ever be made to our system of states," Thomas Jefferson wrote James Monroe on October 24, 1823. "The controul [*sic*] which, with Florida [and] this island would give us over the Gulph of Mexico, and the countries and the Isthmus bordering on it, as well as all those waters flow into it, would fill up the measure of our political well-being." Secretary of State John Quincy Adams, also in 1823, called Cuba and other islands of the West Indies the "natural appendages" of the United States. Later, Presidents Polk, Buchanan, and Pierce — with the 1854 Ostend Manifesto — had all tried to buy Cuba from Spain and were rebuffed, just as was the McKinley administration in its attempts just before the outbreak of the war.

The answer is that the potential annexation of Cuba, the most important possession in the Spanish-American War, threatened important American business interests. These business interests, together with their congressmen and senators, opposed the United States' annexation of Cuba (as manifest in the passage of the Teller Amendment resolving that the United States would honor Cuba's independence). And it was the tariff issue that evoked the controversies over Cuba.

———

American businesses clashed loudest and most forcefully over the tariff. The tariff was the most important political issue of the late nineteenth and early twentieth centuries; the only political issues possibly rivaling the tariff in importance at the time were the money issue — whether the United States would have a gold-based or a silver-based currency — and the regulation of business monopolies (i.e., the "trusts") in the steel, oil, coal, canning, beef, farming machinery, linseed oil, whiskey, tobacco, and other industries. The tariff provided almost half of U.S. government revenues throughout the 1890s, and more than half of U.S. government revenues in the previous and succeeding decades (the 1880s and the first decade of the twentieth century). With the size of the government revenues and business incomes (and profits) at stake, congressional debate over tariff legislation pitted manufacturers against manufacturers, manufacturers against farmers, farmers against other farmers, region against region, and the Democratic Party against the Republican Party.

The Republican Party had historically been the high-tariff party, consistent with the policies of its predecessor, the Whig Party. The

Republican Party believed in encouraging U.S. manufacturing and raising government revenues for funding internal improvements — later, pensions for Union veterans and their survivors, a bigger navy, and other programs — by taxing imported goods. Most Democrats and southern politicians, for their part, opposed the tariffs, since they hurt cotton growers and other exporters, given that countries importing from the United States typically retaliated with tariffs of their own. Furthermore, the South did not have the North's and Midwest's industrial base to offset the tariff's adverse effects on exports and consumer prices.

William McKinley had made his political career as a high-tariff man. It was his principal issue as an Ohio and then a national politician, and he received crucial support early in his career from the pro-tariff steel industry. McKinley himself proclaimed, "I am a Tariff Man" and "I stand on a Tariff platform." It was no accident that the controversial McKinley Tariff of 1892 had the title it did. This tariff raised import duties to among the highest rates in U.S. history and, for the first time, made it possible for the U.S. government to combine high tariffs with the negotiation of reciprocity treaties with other nations. Other countries could, as a consequence, obtain access to the U.S. market in return for opening up their own markets.

Despite the controversy caused by the McKinley Tariff, President Cleveland was unable to much alter its rates with his own Wilson-Gorman Tariff of 1895. Then, with Republicans back in control of both houses of Congress and the White House after the 1896 elections, Congress passed new tariff legislation, the Dingley Tariff of 1897. Although the Dingley Tariff kept the high tariffs, it contained fewer contradictions and had "less quackery" in it than did the McKinley Tariff, as the muckraker Ida Tarbell characterized the bill.

To better understand the tariff issue, however, we also need to look at the sugar industry. Sugar was by far the United States' single largest import at the time: sugar imports amounted to $100 million in 1900. (Domestic sugar producers in Louisiana and other states produced only about 12 percent of what American consumers and manufacturers demanded.) As *Our Island Empire: Handbook of the United States' New Island Empire of Cuba, Porto Rico, Hawaii, and the Philippine Islands* pointed out, "In gaining these tropical islands, the United States has entered into a new and important business and political relation with the nations of the world. Widely separated as they are they possess a remarkable similarity in production. . . . Sugar is the leading product of most of them and an important product of them all." And the sugar industry was the virtual monopoly of the American Sugar Refining Company under the Havemeyers, which ran the Sugar Trust.

In 1892 the Sugar Trust under the Havemeyers controlled 98 percent of the domestic sugar market, and in 1895 it still controlled more than 95 percent of the U.S. sugar market. The American Sugar Refining Company obtained its stranglehold on the sugar industry by buying out smaller firms or forcing them to merge, often using its market power to lower sugar prices to the point that smaller competitors and new companies had little choice but to cooperate with the trust if they wanted to survive. In other words, domestic competition among sugar manufacturers played only a small part in setting the price of sugar for American consumers.

The Sugar Trust made its money on the difference between what it paid for raw and partially refined sugar, on the one hand, and the price it received from selling more refined grades of sugar in the U.S. market, on the other. The price that the trust got for its sugar depended on two things, in essence: the initial cost of the sugar according to grade (a 100-point scale that ranged from molasses to highly refined, white sugar); and the tariff levels imposed on each of the different grades of sugar being imported. The initial cost of sugar was thus a function of location — where the sugar was being imported from, with the attendant land and labor costs — and the tariff duties being set by Congress and the White House.

The specifics of the tariff law were therefore critical to the Sugar Trust's profitability, since the exact schedule of tariff rates that applied to each grade of sugar and the existence of a reciprocity treaty would have great impact on the trust's bottom line. In general, the higher the tariff rate, the less the difference between the Sugar Trust's costs from buying imported sugar and domestic sugar producers in the states and Hawai'i.

Although the tariff was "sacred" for McKinley and his political manager, Mark Hanna, McKinley's position on the tariff depended on the industry in question. A chief attribute of the McKinley Tariff, apart from its overall high rates — especially the high duties that the

McKinley Tariff placed on steel and other manufactured goods — and the possibility it allowed for reciprocity treaties, was that it set *no* duties on imported sugar. Thus the McKinley Tariff particularly benefited the Sugar Trust, given the trust's near monopoly of the sugar industry. And the Sugar Trust enjoyed low costs and correspondingly high profits in the early and mid-1890s.

In fact, McKinley owed his political career to the Havemeyers. The Sugar Trust had previously invested large sums in McKinley's congressional election campaigns, it had contributed heavily to the 1900 election, and it had been the largest single contributor to McKinley's 1896 presidential campaign. In addition, McKinley's secretary of war, Elihu Root, was a close ally of the Havemeyers. Root had served as counsel for the American Sugar Refining Company in the early 1890s, at which time he had reorganized the company after the New York Court of Appeals in 1890 had ruled that the trust deed under which the American Sugar Refining Company was able to control other corporations refining sugar was invalid. Root proceeded to make changes in the American Sugar Refining Company's charter and to move the company to New Jersey — then the home of the least restrictive rules for corporate charters. Root also served on the company's board of directors and was a large shareholder. Because of Root's abilities as an attorney and his well-earned reputation for discretion, the Havemeyers trusted him completely. And so it turned out that Secretary Root and the War Department had responsibility for the administration of the United States' insular territories until such time that civilian governments could be set up.

In the Senate, the Sugar Trust worked closely with Senator Nelson Aldrich (R-R.I.), who ran the Senate with a handful of other Republicans — William Allison (R-Iowa), Orville Platt (R-Conn.), and John Spooner (R-Wis.). Aldrich not only was the master of the intricate tariff schedules but also supported "this great industry," as he called the sugar industry when he arranged for the passage of the McKinley Tariff. And he ensured that the Sugar Trust got "fair treatment in Congress." Because of Aldrich's expertise on the tariff and his control of the Senate, historians credit Aldrich with having probably more influence over the late nineteenth-century and early twentieth-century political economy of the United States than anyone else, U.S. presidents included.

The Supreme Court's decision in the *Sugar Trust Case* was suggestive of the American Sugar Refining Company's political influence and the laissez-faire politics of the period. When the Sugar Trust effectively cornered the sugar market in the early 1890s, political considerations forced President Harrison to act. The Harrison administration prosecuted E. C. Knight, a Philadelphia sugar company and a partner in the Sugar Trust, for violating the antitrust provisions of the Sherman Act. But the Supreme Court ruled against the U.S. government. Chief Justice Fuller argued that the consolidation of the Philadelphia sugar industry did not pose a threat to the national sugar market. Fuller held for the Court majority that the control of manufacturing "bore no direct relation" to interstate commerce. Following the decision in the *Sugar Trust Case* in 1895, there were no more prosecutions against U.S. companies under the Sherman Act until Roosevelt became president in 1901, after the assassination of President McKinley.

The more serious lesson of the *Sugar Trust Case* was that the U.S. government made a lackluster effort to prosecute the American Sugar Refining Company. Neither President Harrison and his attorney general, William Miller, nor President Cleveland and his attorney general, Richard Olney (who took over the case), prosecuted the American Sugar Refining Company and the Havemeyers with any vigor. It further appears that the U.S. government's attorneys sabotaged their own efforts through shoddy argument and missed opportunities.

Soon after the decision in the *Sugar Trust Case*, U.S. attorney general Olney confided to a friend: "You will observe that the Government has been defeated in the Supreme Court on the trust question. I always supposed it would be, and *have taken the responsibility of not prosecuting under a law I believe to be no good*" (emphasis added). Circumstantial evidence indicates that this is what happened. Olney had earlier worked with Root to defend the Distillers and Cattle Feeding Company (the "Whiskey Trust") against prosecution under the Harrison administration; before that, he had made a successful career as a corporate attorney defending questionably legal business practices. Olney would later become a director of the American Sugar Refining Company and in 1910 defended the Sugar Trust against antitrust prosecution initiated by the Taft administration.

This history of the Sugar Trust and its political influence on the McKinley administration takes us back to Cuba and the question why the United States did not annex Cuba at the turn of the twentieth century: both the Sugar Trust and the McKinley administration wanted the United States to annex Cuba or, at minimum, secure free trade with the island, since it was the source of most of the trust's sugar. In fact, the White House sought free trade with *all* the new island territories, consistent with interests of the Sugar Trust and the McKinley administration's alliance with the trust, although inconsistent with the McKinley administration's and the Republican Party's traditional protectionism.

Secretary Root advocated immediate free trade with Puerto Rico in the summer of 1899, "either by executive order or special session." In December 1899 President McKinley announced: "Our plain duty is to abolish all customs tariffs between the United States and Porto Rico and give her products free access to our markets." Free trade between the U.S. territories and the states would mean that the Sugar Trust would be able to secure tariff-free imports of sugar from areas with low production costs.

Blocking the designs of the Sugar Trust and the McKinley administration were the producers of beet sugar (as Mr. Dooley tries to explain to Mr. Hennessy in the chapter epigraph). Although beet sugar provided only about 12 percent of the sugar consumed in the United States in 1900, and although it was a relatively new development (scientists had only recently increased the sugar content in the beets so that they were economically viable), the sugar beet industry enjoyed support across the United States and particularly in California, Michigan, Utah, and Colorado after the depression of 1893; the Sugar Trust, in contrast, was centered in New York City, under the control of the American Sugar Refining Company. Sugar beet growers were further helped by U.S. government subsidies (in return for their support of tariff legislation) and by the U.S. Department of Agriculture's distribution of promotional literature for the cultivation of sugar beets. Meanwhile, a 40 percent import duty kept European beet sugar out of the U.S. market. In a short time, the sugar beet industry had become a formidable political actor.

Little wonder, then, that the sugar beet industry opposed free trade with Puerto Rico (and other U.S. territories) in the early versions of the Foraker bill. Little wonder, too, that the sugar beet industry and a few other interested producers took the further step of filing an amicus brief in support of the constitutionality of the Foraker Act in *Goetze v. United States*, one of the first *Insular Cases* of 1901.

———

A review of the racism and ethnocentrism of the early twentieth century, of the United States' shift to an overseas commercial empire, and of the politics of the tariff and the sugar industry reveals that the Supreme Court's decisions in the first set of *Insular Cases* of 1901 were not simply about race, naval strategy, or even duties being imposed on Puerto Rican oranges — or, for that matter, on coffee, tobacco, or other goods. Rather, the Court's decisions had particular implications for the sugar industry: *sugar* was the cargo being shipped by De Lima & Co., and the prohibition of duties on trade between the insular territories and the states would be especially profitable to the Sugar Trust, given its refining capacity and market control. And Coudert Brothers, counsel for De Lima & Co. and Downes & Co., had the American Sugar Refining Company as a client.

Conversely, the imposition of a tariff on Puerto Rican trade and other trade with the new island territories, including restrictions on foreign investment in and foreign ownership of cane-growing land, would benefit the beet-sugar growers located among the states and the cane-sugar producers in Louisiana and Hawai'i (in 1892, however, Havemeyer made a deal with Claus Spreckels, who had personally developed and controlled the Hawai'ian sugarcane industry, for the coordination of sugar prices and the distribution of sugar in the states). Although Puerto Rican sugar production came to less than 400,000 tons a year and did not threaten the profitability of domestic cane-sugar or beet-sugar producers (and neither did other Puerto Rican goods, such as coffee and tobacco, given the vast American demand), trade policy with Puerto Rico would set an all-important precedent for the Philippines, Cuba, and possibly other (new) U.S. territories.

Were Congress to be prohibited from allowing trade restrictions with Puerto Rico, then by the terms of the Treaty of Paris, the Philippines would also get free trade, and Spanish goods would be able to enter the United States duty-free (since free trade between Spain and the Philippines was protected for several years under the Treaty of Paris). Other nations, through trade with Spain or through their "most favored nation" status with the United States, could thereby obtain unrestricted access to the Philippine Islands and, from the Philippines, the United States. Agricultural interests, organized labor, and other protection-minded producers in the states therefore understandably feared that the Philippines, and possibly other future U.S. territories, would then swamp the United States with cheap products and inexpensive labor.

Whereas the imperialists and anti-imperialists of the day both supported the annexation of Puerto Rico, with its population of 950,000, its ready market for U.S. goods, and the lack of competition it posed to American producers, neither group wanted to annex the Philippines. Nor did the McKinley administration, most Republicans, or the majority of Americans wish to give up possession of the Philippine Islands. But as Senator Orville Platt remarked in reference to Puerto Rico, "It is the first step that counts, and it is the establishment of a precedent that gives trouble." Puerto Rico would thus not only set a precedent for the Philippines but also one for Cuba, since it was by no means clear in 1900 that the United States would not annex Cuba in the near future. Even after the passage of the Platt Amendment in March 1901 (see chapter 9), many individuals and companies located to and invested in Cuba with the expectation that it would soon become annexed to the United States.

If the United States were to annex Puerto Rico as a territory, policymakers would be forced to choose between two unacceptable alternatives: to also annex the Philippines (and possibly still other areas), given the parallel situations of the U.S.-controlled islands; or to release the Philippines, which the McKinley administration and its political supporters also did not want to do, given the Philippines' strategic importance and commercial possibilities. Congress and the White House resolved their bind by agreeing to an imperfect political compromise: the controversial Foraker Act.

It was this imperfect settlement that Coudert Brothers challenged in New York's Second District Court of Appeals, and that De Lima, Downes & Co. and the other trading companies appealed to the Supreme Court. The decisions in the *Insular Cases* held serious implications for the McKinley administration, for the Sugar Trust, for protectionist interests within the states, and for the political and economic development of Puerto Rico, the Philippines, and potentially other areas — Cuba, in particular — that might be later annexed by the United States.

———

In January 1901 Philippine governor Taft wrote his friend Justice Harlan that if the Supreme Court were to rule the tariff on insular trade unconstitutional, it would "result in a very narrow colonial policy for the islands." Taft again wrote Harlan a few months later, shortly before the Court would issue its decisions in the *Insular Cases*, to emphasize the undesirability of applying the "uniform tariff clause" to the Philippines: "If there is room for two constructions . . . take the one that avoids such a result."

The day of the decisions, Monday, May 27, 1901, newspapers around the country reported on the Supreme Court's upcoming rulings. The common line on the story, exemplified in the *New York Daily Tribune*, was that "in official circles there is scarcely any doubt that the court will sustain the government's contention, which reduced to popular parlance, is that 'the Constitution does not follow the flag' ex proprio vigore." Early reports also predicted a divided bench, based on the observation that some of the justices had made remarks in public speeches "against the government's colonial policy," and that some of the justices' questions to the U.S. government's counsel during oral argument suggested an opposition to the McKinley administration.

One case occupied front and center: *Downes v. Bidwell*, which challenged the constitutionality of the Foraker Act. "No case ever attracted wider attention," Joseph Pulitzer's *New York World* reported on May 27. "Legal and political opinion was never so divided. A momentous political and legal question hinged on the decision. The Administration watched the case eagerly." And the *New York World* wondered too, as did many other newspapers and political commentators, if the Supreme Court would uphold the "McKinley policy of imperialism."

CHAPTER 4

Downes v. Bidwell

"I see," said Mr. Dooley, "th' Supreme Coort has decided th' Constitution don't follow th' flag."

"Who said it did?" asked Mr. Hennessy.

"Some wan," said Mr. Dooley. "It happened a long time ago an' I don't raymember clearly how it come up, but some fellow said that ivrywhere th' Constitution wint, th' flag was sure to go. 'I don't believe wan wurrud iv it," says th' other fellow. 'Ye can't make me think th' Constitution is goin' thrapezin' around ivrywhere a young liftnant in th' army takes it into his head to stick a flag pole. It's too old. It's a home-stayin' Constitution with a blue coat with brass buttons onto it, an' it walks with a goold-headed cane.' . . . 'But,' says th' other; 'if it wants to thravel, why not lave it?' 'But it don't want to.' 'I say it does.' 'How'll we find out?' 'We'll ask th' Supreme Coort.'"

"The Supreme Court's Decisions," FINLEY PETER DUNNE,
Mr. Dooley at His Best, 1938

Justice Harlan sensed the importance of what would become known as the *Insular Cases* as early as the summer preceding the decisions. On July 16, 1900, Harlan wrote Taft: "Our next term is likely to be a most important one; chiefly because we may be called on to declare the extent of the power of Congress, over our new possessions. I hear there is a case on the docket which will compel us to face the issue. It is a great question, and worthy of serious, deliberate consideration."

Taft replied: "You can be sure that we shall look with great interest to the consideration of constitutional features of the extension of American rule to these Islands. . . . The question of a right of trial by jury and by indictment, and the question of extending the United States tariff laws to these Islands are of course the two points which will most affect us in our work." Taft was alarmed at the prospect of "administering justice in a culture where people were habituated to bribery and were largely uneducated peasants." Harlan, for his part, feared a potentially "radical departure from the principles underlying our [political] system."

Although more than one case on the docket involved the territories, *Samuel B. Downes v. Thomas G. Bidwell* stood out as the seminal case of the *Insular Cases* — just as Taft, Harlan, the other justices on the bench, several attorneys, many businessmen, and some politically attentive observers anticipated: *Downes* brought the constitutional question of congressional authority into sharp relief — whether Congress could, under the authority of the Foraker Act, impose tariffs on trade with Puerto Rico consistent with the Constitution's uniformity clause.

In other words, the Supreme Court had to decide what was "domestic" and what was "foreign" for the United States with respect to the existing Dingley Tariff of 1897. The Dingley Tariff set the rate of duties to be "levied, collected, and paid upon *all articles from foreign countries*" (emphasis added). So if Congress could tax oranges (and other goods) being shipped from Puerto Rico to the several states or from the states into Puerto Rico, then Puerto Rico would effectively be a foreign country. Or, if the Supreme Court decided that Puerto Rico *was* part of the United States for the purposes of the tariff, then the Foraker Act had to be struck down as being unconstitutional.

———

Frederic Coudert and Paul Fuller of Coudert Brothers argued for Downes & Co. and against the constitutionality of the Foraker Act: Puerto Rico was not a foreign country, since the 1898 Treaty of Paris clearly made it part of the United States. Treaties become operative by their own force, the two attorneys argued, just as Secretary Root recognized in his 1899 annual report for the War Department, in which he wrote that Puerto Rico "is fully and without question under the sovereignty of the United States." And if Puerto Rico were under U.S. sovereignty, then the uniformity clause had to apply to trade between Puerto Rico and the several states. The payment of import duties on goods shipped from Puerto Rico to the states therefore contravened the constitutional provision that taxes had to be uniform "throughout the United States."

Coudert and Fuller recognized that Puerto Rico was a territory, and therefore in an intermediate position between being "foreign" and "national." As a territory, Puerto Rico was "subject exclusively to Federal control, exercised by the Congress." But Congress's exercise of plenary control was for the purpose of later annexation, the attorneys pointed out, consistent with Chief Justice Marshall's description of territories being in a "state of infancy advancing to manhood, looking forward to complete equality so soon as that state of manhood shall be obtained." Coudert and Fuller quoted Justice Gray's opinion in *Shively v. Bowlby* (1894) that "territories acquired by Congress, whether by deed of cession from the original States, or by treaty with a foreign country, are held with the object, as soon as their population and condition justify it, of being admitted into the Union as States, upon an equal footing with the original States in all respects." It was "an inapt use of terms to speak of new peoples or new possessions coming under the Constitution," the attorneys argued. "The Constitution has no direct relation with new peoples or new possessions. It has a direct relation only with the agencies of government which it creates and which it regulates, on the one side, and with the people that ordained it on the other." The Constitution gave Congress its existence just as the Constitution granted Congress its authority over the territories.

Thus the Constitution's specification of uniform taxes and duties "cannot be read so as to include an exemption from this injunction of uniformity." As for the U.S. government's argument that Congress needed to make specific laws and construct dedicated customhouses in order to make the Puerto Rican ports domestic for the purposes of the tariff, Coudert and Fuller dismissed the argument out of hand. They responded that such an argument would be, in effect, to claim that Congress, through its *inaction* of *not* passing laws and *not* building new customhouses in Puerto Rico, could consequently impose unlawful duties and ignore the constitutional provision for the uniformity of imposts and duties throughout the United States.

The attorneys also addressed the U.S. government's contention that the tariff was needed on the grounds of expediency; that the government of Puerto Rico needed the funds raised from the tariff. Several of the government's briefs made this argument, as did the lawyers who filed the amicus brief in *Goetze v. United States* on behalf of "Industrial Interests in the States" — that is, the producers of "tobacco, sugar, rice, hemp, fruits," and other goods. Coudert and Fuller reasoned that it was not for the Supreme Court to change the scope of the uniformity clause. Rather, if the meaning of the clause were to be changed — such as to allow for the funding of territorial government from collected tariff duties — then there needed to be a constitutional amendment to that effect.

Neither could the two attorneys agree with Secretary Root's statement that the "people of Porto Rico have not the right to demand that duties should be uniform as between Porto Rico and the United States." Such a claim implied that the power of taxation could be exercised without restraint. But it had been precisely "the exercise of that power," Coudert and Fuller pointed out, that "fired the revolt of the American colonies."

The attorneys concluded by quoting former Supreme Court justice Stephen Field, who, in a speech he had given on the occasion of the centennial anniversary of the Supreme Court, remarked that "as the inequalities in the condition of men become more marked and disturbing, . . . *it becomes more and more the imperative duty of the court to enforce with a firm hand every guarantee of the Constitution*" (emphasis in original).

———

The Department of War's annual report for 1899 and the Division of Insular Affairs Report of February 12, 1900, anticipated the U.S. government's argument in *Downes v. Bidwell*. Puerto Ricans, the report stated, "are subject to the complete sovereignty of the [U.S. government], controlled by no legal limitations except those which may be found in the treaty of cession." Secretary Root further made the unexpected claim that "the people of the islands have *no right* to have them treated as States" (emphasis added) — as though Puerto Ricans' lack of legal guarantees and political participation was a condition preferable to that possessed by the citizens of the states. Puerto Ricans and other island inhabitants had no "legal rights whatsoever," in fact, "except for those found in the treaty" with Spain. They were not to be treated as were the inhabitants of the "territories previously held by the United States."

Root conceded that Puerto Ricans had "a moral right to be treated by the United States in accordance with the underlying principles of justice and freedom which we have declared in our Constitution," but he simultaneously insisted on the U.S. government's right to exercise full control over its island territories. "Nothing can be more preposterous [than] that [the Filipinos] were entitled to receive from us sovereignty over the entire country we were invading," Root told a *New York Times* reporter in a story of October 25, 1900. By the same logic, Root added, "the friendly Indians, who have helped us in our Indian wars, might have claimed the sovereignty of the West." The Division of Insular Affairs Report, drafted by the attorney Charles E. Magoon, based the government's plenary power on its control over unorganized territory. The Constitution applied to territories only when Congress, made up of the representatives of the several states, explicitly extended it.

U.S. attorney general John Griggs and U.S. solicitor general John K. Richards argued the U.S. government's case. Griggs, a former governor of New Jersey, filed the government's brief in *Goetze v. United States* and presented two separate oral arguments on behalf of the government. Griggs's arguments preceded Richards's and served as the foundation for Richards's own arguments in the U.S. government's brief in *Downes*. The two U.S. government attorneys made complementary arguments: both held to the constitutional arguments of those political and legal experts who took the minimal view of the United States — specifically, that the U.S. government possessed full authority over the territories.

Griggs based his lengthy brief in *Goetze v. United States* on an extensive reading of American history and judicial precedent, dating from the founding of the United States. Griggs made several points: the U.S. government had the power to dispose of its territories as it saw fit; the history of congressional and judicial action since the founding affirmed the fact that ports in countries acquired by the United States in war or through treaty are foreign until Congress extends the laws to include the new regions; the uniformity clause did not apply to the new possessions, since the United States was constituted by the states of the Union; the uniformity clause did not apply to "foreign" ports; and the Constitution did not extend of its own force over acquired territory. The doctrine of *ex proprio vigore*, Griggs commented, "was never heard of until it was invented and advocated by [Senator John C.] Calhoun as a means of fastening slavery upon California and New Mexico beyond the power of Congress to disturb or abolish it." Griggs noted, too, that the arguments of Chief Justice

Taney in *Dred Scott* quoted by Coudert and Fuller had already been overturned by Justice Bradley in the Court's opinion in the *Mormon Church Case*.

Solicitor General Richards's argument for *Downes* took up part of the U.S. government's extensive brief on the "Porto Rican Cases" (the brief addressed not only *Downes v. Bidwell* but also *De Lima v. Bidwell*, the two *Dooley v. United States* cases, and *Armstrong v. United States*). Richards essentially argued on practical grounds. He emphasized the constitutionality of the Foraker Act based on "the temporary character of the act," since it expired on March 1, 1902 — and possibly sooner if the Puerto Rican government acted to change the revenue laws. Richards also noted that Senator Joseph Foraker (R-Ohio), who had sponsored the legislation, had stated that the funds to be raised from the tariff on Puerto Rican trade were to be allocated for Puerto Rico's use only; the duties being collected were not for the general benefit of the U.S. Treasury. And the Puerto Rican government badly needed the funds because of the absence of systems of direct taxation and the "impossible burden" of even a small property tax of 3 or 4 percent.

Richards then addressed the scope of Congress's taxing powers. He noted that Congress had the grant of its taxing authority not from the revenue clause of Article I, Section 8, Clause 1, but from its authority under the territory clause. Richards argued, too, the tariffs on goods going to Puerto Rico from the states were not "exports from any State," since exports went to foreign countries. Yet because Puerto Rico was a territory of the United States according to the Treaty of Paris, the goods shipped into San Juan were "imports into Porto Rico." In short, the tariffs did not violate either the revenue clause or the constitutional prohibition on imposts, duties, or taxes imposed on exports from the states.

In his oral argument on January 9, 1901, Richards emphasized the minimal view of the United States. The solicitor general contrasted the "geographical" and "international" sense of the United States, which "includes necessarily all territory subject to the dominion of the United States," on the one hand, with the "constitutional sense" that "covers only the states, and was so intended by the framers of the Constitution." The next day Richards expanded his definition to include four meanings of the United States: (1) sovereignty, "that grand corporation," as Chief Justice Marshall termed it; (2) the "American confederacy" of the states and the electorate, or "the constitutional sense"; (3) the legislative and geographic sense of the states, federal district, and territories "which Congress has seen fit to treat as the United States" and to which U.S. laws are applicable; and (4) the "international sense" of all areas, "wherever situated, under the dominion of the United States, whether organized or not."

Richards made the contrast between the wording of the territory clause, which had "no safeguard or guarantee whatever" with respect to Congress's authority, and the phrasing of Articles I, II, and III of the Constitution as they directed the relationship between the federal government and the states. The founders had designed the congressional power over the territories to be plenary, Richards argued; the territories were to be "treated as property, as something distinct from the United States — something belonging to the United States, a subject to be ruled of Congress in its discretion as conditions may require, without being hampered by the restrictions which were framed for the States."

The arguments for the two sides could hardly have been more different.

———

On Monday, May 27, 1901, the Supreme Court — then housed in the U.S. Capitol — announced its decisions. The *New York Daily Tribune* described the setting:

> No such crowd either as to numbers or distinguished personnel has been seen in the Supreme Court room as that assembled there today. The hour for the Court to meet is noon, but long before that time arrived the little elliptical chamber was jammed with spectators representing every phase of life at the national capital, and long lines of eager people stretched in both directions from the doors down the gloomy corridors of the great Capitol Building. The colored bailiffs at the door had all they could do to hold the anxious throng on the outside in check, and thus protect the solemn dignity of the august tribunal from being rudely shocked. The bare rumor that the court would render its decision in the insular test suits was sufficient to create an interest among all sorts and conditions of people in Washington that sent them to the

Capitol in a frenzy of excitement. They realized that no such momentous issues affecting the growth and progress of the nation are likely again to come before the tribunal of last resort for arbitrament, and every man who was fortunate enough to gain access to the chamber during the delivery of the opinions appreciated that he was witnessing one of the most tremendous events in the nation's life.

The *Tribune* further noted that Secretary Root, Attorney General Philander Knox (who had replaced Griggs), Solicitor General Richards, Senators Lodge and William E. Mason (R-Ill.), two ex-senators, two U.S. representatives, James D. Richardson (R-Tenn.) and Charles Grosvenor (R-Ohio), and "many local lawyers and notables" were in attendance. In anticipation of the Supreme Court's decision the stock market on Wall Street experienced its lowest level of trading since the presidential election of 1900, the *Washington Post* reported; only tobacco stocks showed any movement of interest.

The justices entered the Supreme Court chamber "promptly at 12 o'clock." "Disappointment," though, "darkened every face in the chamber save the nine on the bench as Justice McKenna, in a treble voice, began to read a decision on some ordinary litigation by direction of Chief Justice Fuller," the *Tribune* reported. McKenna's "thin, reedy voice was followed by the drone of Justice Peckham," the next youngest member on the bench in terms of service, who read "out half audibly a decision in another case of no general interest," wrote the *Chicago Record-Herald*. "At last, Justice Brown lifted his voice from the dreary monotone it had hitherto followed, and the waiting listeners heard the magic words, 'Commonly known as the insular cases,'" the *Record-Herald* reported. "Instantly, there was a craning of necks and shuffling of feet in the vain desire to secure a better position. Impatience immediately turned to interest," the *Tribune* observed, "which was marked by a silence that was awe inspiring."

After Brown read his lead opinion in *De Lima v. Bidwell*, Justice McKenna read his dissenting opinion. Brown then proceeded to the short decisions in *Goetze v. United States* and *Crossman v. United States* (which, with *De Lima*, are discussed in the next chapter). Then he got to *Downes v. Bidwell*. Brown argued that the "United States" was constituted by its member states only, consistent with the first, narrow

86   { *Chapter 4* }

view of the United States and with the arguments of the U.S. government. Congress could thus impose taxes on Puerto Rico or any of the new territories.

Justice White, joined by Justices Shiras and McKenna, followed Justice Brown's opinion for the Court with a concurring opinion that argued that Puerto Rico was precisely one of those possessions of the United States that was acquired but not part of the United States, per Lowell's "third view" of the United States (to whom White credited his argument). Congress could levy taxes on goods shipped to New York from Puerto Rico.

Justice Gray concurred with White's opinion but also wrote a short opinion of his own.

The chief justice, joined by Justices Harlan, Brewer, and Peckham, then delivered his dissent. Fuller held that since the United States included its territories, consistent with the second view of the United States, and since the 1898 Treaty of Paris had ceded Puerto Rico to the United States, then Congress could not tax the oranges sent from San Juan and Mayaguez to New York. Harlan, while he "fully agreed" with the chief justice's dissenting opinion, also wrote a separate dissent in response to some of the points raised by Justices Brown and White in their separate opinions.

Thus the Court split five to four over Congress's authority to impose duties on products brought from Puerto Rico to the states and issued five separate opinions in the decision — an outcome "reached after one of the most spirited discussions ever held within the sacred circle of the Supreme Court bench," the Associated Press reported. Although a narrow majority supported the U.S. government's right to tax goods from Puerto Rico, no single opinion among the five opinions in *Downes* attracted a majority on the bench. The ruling in *Downes v. Bidwell*, with its three different majority opinions and its two dissenting opinions, was the longest and most complex of all the *Insular Cases*.

———

Henry Billings Brown, who wrote the lead opinion in *Downes v. Bidwell* and wrote the opinions for the Court in all seven of the *Insular Cases* of May 27, 1901, grew up in the small Massachusetts town of South Lee and was reared in a Puritan, upper-middle-class, Republican household.

Brown went to Yale for college and then studied law there before transferring to Harvard. After finishing law school, he went west, like so many other young men of the mid-nineteenth century — in Brown's case, to Detroit. He was soon made deputy U.S. marshal for Detroit, an appointment achieved through family connections. As deputy marshal and with the amount of commercial traffic on the Great Lakes, Brown quickly mastered admiralty law. A few years later, and after an unsuccessful run at Congress, Brown was appointed in 1875 to preside over the Eastern Michigan District Court. As district judge, a position he held for fourteen years, Brown obtained a national reputation for his command of admiralty law. Following the death of Justice Samuel Miller in late 1890, President Harrison appointed Brown to the Supreme Court in 1891.

Brown did not believe that the Constitution applied to Puerto Rico or any other territory in the absence of Congress's expressed extension of the Constitution. The United States was composed of the states only, he argued — consistent with the judgment of many of the best legal minds in the country and with the arguments of the U.S. solicitor general, the U.S. attorney general, and the War Department. Congress, as the representative body of the states, had plenary power over the territories, and because Congress had passed the Foraker Act, which imposed tariff duties on goods shipped from Puerto Rico to the states, the duties were necessarily constitutional.

Chief Justice Taney's opinion in *Dred Scott v. Sandford* did not apply, Brown argued; the idea that the Constitution applied throughout the territories was dictum — that is to say that Taney's argument in *Dred Scott* had no legal bearing on the case and was therefore irrelevant as precedent. For Brown and the U.S. government, Taney's interpretation of the Constitution had been overturned in 1865 at the Appomattox Court House, where General Robert E. Lee's surrender ended the Civil War. And the fact that the Constitution applied only when Congress explicitly extended it, Brown stated, was a reality apparent throughout the history of the United States.

Neither did Brown worry about the possible tyranny of unrestricted congressional power: "There are certain principles of natural justice inherent in the Anglo-Saxon character which need no expression in constitutions or statutes to give them effect or to secure dependencies against legislation manifestly hostile to their real interests." These "natural rights" Brown contrasted with

> artificial or remedial rights, which are peculiar to our own system of jurisprudence. Of the former class are the rights to one's own religious opinion and to public expression of them, . . . to worship God according to the dictates of one's own conscience; the right to personal liberty and individual property; to freedom of speech and of the press; to free access to courts of justice; to due process of law and to equal protection under the laws; to immunities from unreasonable searches and seizures, as well as cruel and unusual punishments; and to such other immunities as are indispensable to a free government.

These natural rights Brown contrasted with the "latter class" of "rights to citizenship, to suffrage, and to the particular methods of procedure pointed out in the Constitution, which are peculiar to Anglo-Saxon jurisprudence, and some of which have already been upheld by the States to be unnecessary to the proper protection of individuals." And Congress had to explicitly extend these latter rights to territorial inhabitants for them to inhere.

If Brown's opinion was based on a narrow conceptualization of the United States as constituted solely by the states, it was also based on the results that would follow from the Court's ruling — that is, it argued to the consequences of the decision. "We are also of opinion," Brown held, "that the power to acquire territory by treaty implies, not only the power to govern such territory, but to prescribe upon what terms the United States shall receive its inhabitants, and what their status shall be in what Chief Justice Marshall termed the 'American empire.'" Brown did not see any "middle ground" between his position and the contrary doctrine that territorial inhabitants, immediately upon annexation, become "citizens of the United States, their children thereafter born, whether savages or civilized, are such, and entitled to all the rights, privileges, and immunities of citizens."

The consequences, if this were to be their status, would "be extremely serious." "Indeed," Brown concluded, "it is doubtful if Congress would ever assent to the annexation of territory upon the condition that its inhabitants, however foreign they may be to our habits, traditions, and modes of life, shall become at once citizens of the United States." Indeed, "a false step" at this time would be "fatal" to the American empire. What would make the step "fatal," as Brown saw it, would be to insist on the annexation of areas with "alien races, differing from us in religion, customs, laws, methods of taxation and modes of thought" and then to bestow the full "blessings of a free government under the Constitution" on these alien races. Nothing in the Constitution forbade such exclusion, for Brown: "*We are therefore of the opinion that the Island of Porto Rico is a territory appurtenant and belonging to the United States, but not a part of the United States* within the revenue clauses of the Constitution" (emphasis added). The Foraker Act was constitutional, "so far as it imposes duties upon imports from such island." Accordingly, the plaintiff, S. B. Downes & Co., "cannot recover back the duties exacted in this case."

Although Brown's argument paralleled the arguments of the U.S. government's attorneys, as well as that of those legal and political experts who held the first, minimal view of the United States, no other justice joined his opinion.

———

Justice White then presented his concurring opinion, joined by Justices Shiras and McKenna.

Edward Douglass White was born in 1845 in Thibodaux, Louisiana. His father was a former Louisiana governor and the owner of a sugar plantation. White went away to Jesuit prep schools in New Orleans and Maryland, then studied at Georgetown. He left college at the age of sixteen, however, to serve in the Confederate army. After the Civil War, White returned to New Orleans to work with a well-known Louisiana lawyer and, at the same time, to study law at what is now Tulane University. White soon became a leading lawyer and Democratic politician in New Orleans and Louisiana. In 1891, Governor Nichols appointed White to the U.S. Senate after White had successfully managed Nichols's election campaign for governor. White served for three years in the Senate, where he supported the gold standard and other policies of the Cleveland administration. White also sought to protect states' interests — especially those of Louisiana and other former Confederate states — by rejecting the efforts to annex Hawai'i in 1893 and by retaining high tariff rates on sugar imported from Hawai'i and elsewhere. Cleveland chose White given his credentials as a conservative Democrat, and on February 16, 1894, the Senate confirmed White's appointment to the Supreme Court to replace Justice Blatchford, who died in July 1893. (The Senate had previously rejected President Cleveland's first two nominees, William Hornblower and Wheeler Peckham, the brother of later Supreme Court Justice Rufus Peckham.) But White did not resign from the Senate until he was sure of the final draft of the Wilson-Gorman Act, which secured a 40 percent duty on imported raw sugar for the benefit of domestic sugar growers — in marked contrast to the provisions under the McKinley Tariff. Once on the Court, White served from 1894 to 1910 and was then appointed chief justice, a position he held from 1910 to 1921 — the first associate justice ever to be appointed chief justice.

White "read his opinion" in *Downes* "with some feeling and with a good deal of effectiveness," one reporter commented, "and he again made it quite apparent that the court in discussing these great cases among themselves, had some rather lively times."

White followed Lowell's argument: that territories could be one of two kinds, those that came fully under the Constitution, and those that were subject to limited provisions of the Constitution, depending on treaty conditions and congressional legislation. White established that Congress had plenary power over the territories, since it had already been accepted in *National Bank v. County of Yankton* (1879) that Congress's power over the territories was like that of states' power over municipalities. As to Puerto Rico's status and that of the new territories, White cited *American Insurance Company v. Canter*, in which Marshall held that "if conquered territory be ceded by treaty, the acquisition is confirmed, and the ceded territory becomes a part of the union to which it is annexed, either on the terms stipulated in the treaty of cession *or on such as its new master shall impose*" (emphasis added).

White, in contrast to Justice Brown, thought it "self-evident" that the Constitution applied to U.S. territories. The question was, White wrote, which particular provisions were operative in the United States' "appurtenant" possessions (i.e., "annexed to a more important thing"). The answer depended "on the situation of the territory and its relation to the United States." The United States encompassed the states and the territories that had been incorporated; Congress could also exert plenary control over the appurtenant territories through the Constitution's territory clause.

With Lowell, White stressed the power of the treaty clause. The principles of the law of nations, White argued, "indubitably" settled the point that "the treaty-making power cannot incorporate territory into the United States" without Congress's express or implied assent; that the U.S. government may insert "conditions against immediate incorporation" in a treaty; and that if the text of a treaty recognizes certain "conditions favorable to incorporation, Congress won't repudiate the treaty and it shall have the force of law." To take the position that the U.S. government could acquire other areas only if they were fully incorporated into the United States was, for White, "to admit the power to acquire [new territory] and immediately to deny its beneficial existence."

This did not mean a license for despotism, White was careful to point out. White agreed that congressional authority was limited, and he recognized that there were "inherent, although unexpressed, principles which are the basis of all free government" and which the government could not violate. White further agreed with Justice Brown that "there are certain principles of natural justice inherent in the Anglo-Saxon character, which need no expression in constitutions or statutes to give them effect or to secure dependencies against legislations manifestly hostile to their real interests." The inhabitants of the new territories could not be subject "to the merely arbitrary control of Congress" and were not wholly "unprotected by the provisions of our Constitution."

As for the tariff, White argued that when the duties were collected from Downes & Co., Puerto Rico was not a foreign country in the international sense, "since it was subject to the sovereignty of and was owned by the United States." Rather, Puerto Rico "was foreign to the United States in a domestic sense," since it "had not been incorporated into the United States, but was merely appurtenant thereto as a possession." As a result, the tariff imposed "on merchandise coming from Porto Rico into the United States after the cession was within the power of Congress," and therefore not controlled by the uniformity clause. Whereas Brown had based the constitutional authority of the Foraker Act on the fact that the new island territories were not part of the United States, White merely argued that the treaty-making power did not, by itself, incorporate Puerto Rico. Congress was therefore free to tax trade with the island.

Like Brown, though, White also argued from the results: White thought the idea that were the United States to have the right to acquire new territory but then, at the same time, be stripped of the authority "to protect the birthright of citizens" and rule the territory in a way that "in view of its condition be essential," made no sense whatsoever. It would be "to say that the United States is helpless in the family of nations, and does not possess that authority which has at all times been treated as an incident of the right to acquire." For White, the United States had now joined the family of great national powers, and it needed the governmental authority to act its part. White "ridiculed the minority without reserve," one reporter remarked, and pointed out "what a misshapen, bungling nation ours would be were its powers circumscribed as they had proposed."

———

Justice Gray, who agreed in "substance" with White's opinion, submitted a short opinion of his own.

Horace Gray came from a prominent upper-class Boston family, attended Harvard, and then, after his father's businesses failed, entered Harvard Law School in 1848. Three years later he started his own practice in Boston. Shortly thereafter, he was appointed reporter for the Massachusetts Supreme Judicial Court and thereby became acquainted with many of the leading local lawyers. Gray strongly opposed slavery, joined the Free Soil Party (which opposed the extension of slavery in the new western states), and became a Republican as soon as the party came into existence. In 1864, Gray was appointed to the Massachusetts Supreme Judicial Court — at age thirty-six, the youngest appointee in history — and he became chief justice of the state supreme court in 1873. Eight years later, Senator George F. Hoar (R-Mass.) recommended Gray to President Chester Arthur for an appointment to the U.S. Supreme Court. Gray took his seat on the bench in December 1881.

In his concurring opinion Justice Gray wrote that a president's and the military's temporary powers over territorial affairs persisted until Congress acted otherwise. Since Congress had passed the Foraker Act, the tariff on trade with Puerto Rico was necessarily legitimate. Imposing the tariff was the prerogative of the U.S. president, Gray argued, and Congress had not acted to alter the tariff.

———

Chief Justice Fuller presented the first dissenting opinion, joined by Justices Harlan, Brewer, and Peckham.

Melville Weston Fuller grew up in Augusta, Maine, in an upper-class family, the son of a lawyer and Maine politician. He attended Bowdoin College and studied law at Harvard. But Fuller was at Harvard for only one year before moving to Bangor, Maine, to work in his uncle's private law practice. Fuller then left that practice to edit a Democratic newspaper and serve in Augusta city politics. In May 1856, at the age of twenty-three, however, he left for Chicago. In Chicago, a rapidly growing city at the time, Fuller became a moderately successful lawyer and, more significantly, a very successful young Democratic politician. In 1863 he was elected to the state legislature, and he quickly became one of the leaders of the Illinois House Democrats. After the Civil War, Fuller became an extremely successful corporate lawyer and real estate investor — success due in part to his marriage to the daughter of the president of Chicago's largest bank. With the death of Chief Justice Morrison Waite in 1888, President Cleveland turned to Fuller for the position of chief justice, given Fuller's prominence in Chicago and Illinois politics and the fact that there was then no one from the Seventh Circuit Court of Appeals serving on the Supreme Court. Fuller's record as a Copperhead — an antiwar Democrat — and his lack of legal scholarship made his Senate confirmation a difficult one, however.

Fuller read his dissent in a calm, smooth voice. He argued that the Constitution applied throughout the states and territories, and he quoted Chief Justice Marshall in *Loughborough v. Blake* on the point that the United States "is the name given to our great republic, which is composed of the States and territories," the District of Columbia, and "the territory west of Missouri," just as it encompassed "Maryland or Pennsylvania." And "the uniformity in the imposition of imposts, duties, and excises" had to be observed in one, just as in the other.

The chief justice emphasized that the Constitution does not change over time. On the contrary, it stands as "a law for rulers and people, equally in war and in peace, and covers with the shield of its protection all classes of men, at all times and under all circumstances." The Constitution could change only if it were amended.

The chief justice scorned Justice White's concurring opinion: "Great stress is thrown upon the word 'incorporation' as if possessed of some occult meaning, but I take it that the [Foraker Act] made Porto Rico . . . an organized territory of the United States." Assuming this to be the case and given the presence of the uniformity clause, Fuller asked how it was then possible for Congress to exercise extraordinary powers "in respect of commerce with that territory." For Fuller, who accepted the second, full view of the United States, Congress could exercise only those powers that the Constitution had prescribed. And since the Treaty of Paris clearly made Puerto Rico a part of the United States, the tax on Puerto Rican trade stood in clear violation of the uniformity clause:

> The contention seems to be that, if an organized and settled province of another sovereignty is acquired by the United States, *Congress has the power to keep it, like a disembodied shade, in an intermediate state of ambiguous existence for an indefinite period;* and, more than that, that after it has been called from that limbo, commerce with it is absolutely subject to the will of Congress, irrespective of constitutional provisions. . . .
>
> That theory assumes that the Constitution created a government empowered to acquire countries throughout the world, to be governed by different rules than those obtaining in the original states and territories, and substitutes for the present system of republican government a system a domination over distant provinces in the exercise of unrestricted power. (emphasis added)

Although the Constitution may not have necessarily granted "the subjects of the former sovereign . . . the full status of citizens," Fuller recognized, that was not the issue before the Court.

———

Justice Harlan also delivered a dissenting opinion, even though he had not originally planned on doing so, as he confided to Taft:

> I had intended to stand upon the opinion prepared by the Chief Justice for himself, Brewer, Peckham, and myself in the Downes

case. But Friday night before . . . Downes was decided, I concluded to say something on my own responsibility which was suggested by certain parts of Brown's and White's opinions. My friend Brown particularly had said some things which I was unwilling to pass without explicitly referring to them. Hence my dissent which you have perhaps seen and read. It expresses views about which I feel strongly.

John Marshall Harlan was born in Boyle County, Kentucky, to a wealthy family, and grew up as a Presbyterian and a Whig — a follower of Henry Clay who at once supported slavery and sought to keep the Union intact. Harlan attended Centre College and studied law at Transylvania University. He practiced law first in his father's office, and then with others in Frankfort, the state capital. A Whig from a border state, Harlan decided to oppose the secession of the South although his family owned slaves and he himself had owned them as an adult. Harlan proceeded to form the Tenth Kentucky Volunteers and then lead it as a colonel. He was subsequently elected Republican attorney general of Kentucky in 1864 and came out in support of Ulysses S. Grant for president in 1868. It was during the difficult years of Reconstruction that Harlan reevaluated his earlier beliefs that the Emancipation Proclamation was unconstitutional, that the Thirteenth, Fourteenth, and Fifteenth Amendments were wrongheaded, and that slavery was legitimate.

When Harlan with his changed views ran for governor of Kentucky on the Republican ticket in 1871, he was, not surprisingly, roundly defeated. But his candidacy attracted the interest of Republicans from around the country, and he became a power in Republican Party politics. As a party leader in Kentucky, Harlan was able to maneuver the state delegation to the side of Rutherford B. Hayes for the Republican presidential nomination in 1876. He then proceeded to use his political influence to enforce the Compromise of 1877 by installing a Democrat as Kentucky governor — even though a Republican appeared to have won the race. After Justice Davis resigned from the U.S. Supreme Court in the spring of 1877, Hayes sought to have another southerner on the court and proposed Harlan. The Senate confirmed him in October 1877, over the opposition of northerners and southerners both. By 1901, John Marshall Harlan had served on the bench longer than any other justice. (He is also the grandfather of the Supreme Court Justice of the same name.)

Harlan did dissent strongly. He "wanted to speak his mind, and he spoke it freely," reported the *Chicago Record-Herald*. "With his voice lifted, his right hand occasionally pounding the bench, he denounced the imperialism of the majority decision in most vigorous fashion." He "threw his words out as if he was shying bricks at an enemy," wrote another reporter. Neither was Harlan dissuaded by the fact that President McKinley had appointed his son, James Harlan, attorney general of Puerto Rico.

On the contrary, Harlan could hardly have opposed the government's position more fundamentally and forcefully. Harlan argued that the U.S. Constitution, not congressional legislation and not political expedience, was the ultimate law of the land: "Congress has no existence and can exercise no authority outside the Constitution. Still less is it true that Congress can deal with new territories just as other nations have done or may do with their new territories. This nation is under the control of a written constitution, the supreme law of the land and the only source of the powers which our government, or any branch or officer of it, may exert at any time or at any place." The Constitution applied *ex proprio vigore:* "To say otherwise is to concede that Congress may, by action taken outside of the Constitution, engraft upon our republican institutions a colonial system such as it exists under monarchical governments."

Harlan disagreed with Justice Brown, the attorney general, and the solicitor general that the United States consisted only of the states. Harlan pointed to the phrase "We the People" in the Preamble of the Constitution, and to Chief Justice Marshall's opinions in *Martin v. Hunter's Lessee* (1816) and *McCulloch v. Maryland* (1819), where Marshall had in each emphasized that the United States was composed of the American *people* and not of the states.

Harlan dismissed, too, the idea that the United States now was an imperial power, like the European states it appeared to be imitating. "The idea that this country may acquire territories anywhere on earth, by conquest or treaty, and hold them as mere colonies or provinces, — people inhabiting them to enjoy only such rights as Congress chooses to accord them — is wholly inconsistent with the spirit and genius as well as the words of the Constitution." If the United States were to follow the path suggested by the *Downes* majority, "We will . . . pass from the era of constitutional liberty guarded and protected by a written constitution into an era of legislative absolutism." If governments could exercise despotic authority over their territories, "unrestrained by written constitutions," then there was no fundamental law.

Harlan agreed with the chief justice and the justices of the majority that territorial claims hinge on "whether a particular race will or will not assimilate with our people, and whether they can or cannot with safety to our institutions be brought within the operation of the Constitution." But such considerations had to take place at the time of acquisition. "A mistake" on the part of the U.S. government in the acquisition of territories "cannot be made the ground for violating the Constitution or giving full effect to its provisions. The Constitution is not to be obeyed or disobeyed as the circumstances of a particular crisis in our history may suggest the one or the other course to be pursued. The People have decreed that it shall be the supreme law of the land at all times." Furthermore, "If our government needs more power than is conferred upon it by the Constitution, that instrument provides the mode in which it may be amended and additional power thereby sustained. The People of the United States who ordained the Constitution never supposed that a change could be made in our system of government by mere judicial interpretation."

Neither did Harlan have much patience for the notion that the Anglo-Saxon or Teutonic races were more virtuous or worthy of political trust. "The wise men of the Constitution . . . well remembered that Anglo-Saxons across the ocean had attempted, in defiance of law and justice, to trample upon the rights of Anglo-Saxons on this continent." Common ancestry was no guarantee of political liberty or personal security.

Notwithstanding Fuller's and Harlan's dissenting opinions, a five-person majority affirmed Congress's authority over the new territories with respect to the tariff. Although the justices did not agree on which clauses gave Congress its authority or on the extent to which the Constitution limited Congress's power, five of the justices refused to overturn the Foraker Act and challenge Congress's territorial policy.

Frederic Coudert later called the justices in the majority "modernists," when he wrote of the development of the Incorporation Doctrine, those "who took a relative view of the Constitution as a document of great, but limited, social value, whose doctrines were not immutable and everywhere and at all times applicable." Coudert labeled the four dissenting justices — and those whose side he argued for as counsel to S. B. Downes & Co. — "strict constructionists, of the Constitution . . . men who reverenced not only the spirit but the letter of that document." For these latter justices, the Constitution contained "fundamental and absolute principles of justice from which there could be no deviation if the United States were to remain in the path traced by the founders."

Reaction to the decision in *Downes* was fast and divided. "The Constitution Follows the Flag," read the headlines of some newspapers around the country. Other headlines read, "The Constitution Does Not Follow the Flag." And still other newspapers made hay of the fact that their competitors were running contradictory headlines. "There seems to be some confusion in the newspaper reports of the decisions rendered by the Supreme Court in the insular cases," Senator Foraker remarked the next day — and Foraker himself was being mentioned as a possible presidential candidate for the Republican nomination in 1904.

The reason for the confusion was that the first reports of the Supreme Court's decisions got it wrong — not surprisingly, perhaps, given the length of the justices' opinions and "the conflict and confusion of so many opinions," as the *New York Herald* put it. The first news reports were that the U.S. government had been defeated by the Supreme Court. Although later newspaper editions and most newspapers got it right, the mistaken reports sowed even further confusion: "Brown had read scarcely a third of the opinion before it became evident that the decision was against the government. It was not known for some time afterward that the suit of De Lima did not involve the vital point at issue — the right and power of Congress to apply to the territories just so much of the revenue and tariff laws of the nations as Congress might elect to apply," the *New York Daily Tribune* reported. "And so it happened that bulletins were scattered broadcast over the country, and perhaps over the world, that the Supreme Court had decided against the government. For fully an hour this belief weighed heavily on scores of men in the courtroom."

"A false report as to the nature of the Supreme Court's decision gave us a very unhappy night," the Puerto Rican treasurer, John Hollander, telegraphed Root, "but this morning's dispatches . . . indicate that everything is right as far as Porto Rico is concerned and that we shall be permitted to work out undisturbed our own financial salvation." Governor Charles Allen of Puerto Rico similarly wrote Root, "We were very much shocked yesterday by cables announcing the complete overthrow of the whole tariff system of the Island by decision of the Supreme Court, and I confess we had a very, very unhappy night of it. But the dispatches in the papers this morning give us the true decision, which leaves us a perfectly free hand to carry out our scheme as we had planned it, and the sun is shining brightly again."

No matter how newspapers reported the story, the decision(s) made headlines and prominent news. Some headlines spanned the entire front page; some newspapers featured pictures of all or some of the nine justices on the Supreme Court on the front page or on their inside pages; and in almost every instance the decisions were the subject of editorials and one or more lengthy stories, often for several days on end.

Many newspapers applauded the decisions in their news articles and editorials (the *New York World, Chicago Record-Herald, San Francisco Examiner, Philadelphia Inquirer, Buffalo Evening News and Telegraph*, and *Santa Fe New Mexican*); many criticized the decisions (the *New York Herald, Philadelphia Record, Denver Post*, and *Seattle Daily Times*); and others expressed caution or voiced only mild agreement or disagreement (the *New York Daily Tribune, New York Times, Washington Post*, and *St. Louis Post-Dispatch*). But all the papers acknowledged *Downes v. Bidwell* to be the seminal case, "the most far-reaching" of the decisions given that it affected "our future relations," as the Associated Press reported in a widely published story.

The *Chicago Record-Herald*, a Republican paper, celebrated the Supreme Court's decision. The "broad and sweeping judgment" in *Downes* marked an "emphatic" victory for the U.S. government:

Men saw at once that under this decision the nation had taken a new place in the world. It had thrown off its swaddling clothes. It had come forth full-powered, full-statured among the sovereign nations of the earth. It could make war without being compelled to take conquered territory within its borders. It could hold conquered or purchased territory according as its own interests as master and the interest of the conquered, humanely considered, might dictate. It could even hold such territories indefinitely, as colonies, if that were deemed best by public opinion operating through Congress, which is declared the governing body.

The *Philadelphia Inquirer*, another Republican paper, also approved. "It is a victory for the administration" over "the contention of Mr. [William Jennings] Bryan and his followers that the Constitution followed the flag in the broadest possible sense," read one editorial. "The decision concerning Porto Rico cuts the ground from under the feet of those persons who have opposed the annexation of Cuba on the ground that free sugar and free tobacco would ruin the home industries. There need not be free sugar and free tobacco." The decisions represented "expansion without imperialism" and put the Philippines and Puerto Rico "on the same footing as with other territories," the *Inquirer* wrote. With the Court's ruling, "the ogre-teeth of the Foraker act have been drawn. It is no longer an exhibition of lawless tyranny, paving the way for worse things to come, but merely a revenue measure." Now Congress "can frame one tariff for one island and another for another," in the view of the *Inquirer*. "It can do the same for Arizona or the District of Columbia."

The *Herald-Record*, the *Inquirer*, and other newspapers sympathetic to expansionism also approvingly quoted members of the McKinley administration. "It is a splendid victory for the administration on the vital principle of expansion, the only really important point involved," said Griggs, the former U.S. attorney general who had argued the cases. "The court decides that the Foraker act is constitutional, that this country has a legal right to govern its new possessions as territories, make special laws for them and tax their products. This has been the contention of the administration from the very start." The papers quoted Secretary Root on the same point: "Unquestionably the decision of the court sustains the contentions, theories and the policy adopted by the administration in conducting the affairs of the Spanish islands since the ratification of the Paris Treaty." On a lighter note, the papers quoted Root's reply to the question of whether the Constitution now followed the flag. "Ye-es," Root quipped, "as near as I can make out the Constitution follows the flag — but doesn't quite catch up with it."

Other newspapers were more skeptical. The *New York Herald*'s full-page headline on Tuesday read, "Congress Unhampered in Its Control of the Colonies" (quoting Solicitor General Richards in a statement he had made to Griggs). A *Herald* editorial noted the "broad sweep" of "the most important of the insular cases decided yesterday" — the ruling in *Downes*. A "bare majority of one holds that the constitution is supreme only in the States, and that a million square miles, or one-fourth of the national domain, and ten million people [i.e., roughly the combined populations of the island territories] are subject to no law but the will of Congress." Added the *Herald*, "It can hardly be said that either the Court or the country is to be congratulated on a decision which four of its members say 'overthrows the basis of our constitutional law and asserts that the States, and not the people, created the government.'"

The *Herald* also quoted Griggs, but to a different end: "Congress was free not only to set up a dictatorship or a despotism in the national domain beyond the States," as a result of *Downes*, Griggs said, "but also to deny the personal rights guaranteed by the constitution." The *Herald* wondered, "Where is the line to be drawn between the unlimited power of Congress to govern and its limited authority over personal rights? For example, the right of Congress to levy taxes is affirmed. Yet power to tax is power to destroy."

In another editorial, the *Herald* noted, "The more the majority decision in the leading insular case, with the ambiguous and conflicting opinions of its supporters, is examined, the more absurd and mischievous it appears. Going as it does to the very heart of our form of government, it is difficult to speak of it with patience or moderation. It is well calculated to lessen respect for the Court, since it is more deplorable than the Dred Scott decision, with the legal tender and income tax reversals all put together." It was a "judicial hodge podge," so no wonder "that neither lawyers nor laymen have been able to agree as to its meaning or scope." The *Herald* asked: "Can such an amazing exhibit of judicial conflict and absurdity either command respect for the highest court of the nation or prove acceptable to the country?"

The *Philadelphia Record*, also a Democratic newspaper, called the new territories "colonies as distinguished from territories" in its next-day editorial. "For tariff purposes they are held, though domestic territory, to be without the pale of the Constitution, which establishes free trade between the States and forbids the levy of export duties." The *Record* commented on the significance of *Downes:*

> The decision, as we now understand it, is a most momentous one, involving a grave change in the character of our government. Congress, itself the creature of the Constitution, is apparently invested with imperial powers which find no warrant in the Constitution. The Court has taken a long time to arrive at any conclusion, and has been unable to reach a decision satisfactory to more than a bare majority of its membership. . . . [B]ut instead of clearing away difficulty, new difficulties have seemingly been created. Henceforth we are to have two kinds of a country.

An editorial in the Thursday *Record* read: "The Supreme Court of the United States has sustained President McKinley and reversed Chief Justice Marshall. It has reasserted the right of taxation without representation that the colonies fought to overturn. It would have been better to abandon our islands than our Constitution."

The *Denver Post,* another Democratic paper, simply feared imperialism. "The decision of the supreme court is therefore epoch making in the history of our country; it is an advance along a new line . . . bringing us at one fell swoop into the ownership of colonies and putting us into the rank of the land-grabbing nations of Europe," read its Wednesday editorial. "We are now following in the footsteps of England . . . in conquering and ruling unwilling alien races as it did in India, and incidentally exploiting them." The *Post* commented, "No pronouncement of the supreme court since Chief Justice Taney's decision in the Dred Scott case is likely to provoke more widespread discussion, and none which has been rendered since the days of Marshall is likely to have a tithe of its wide reaching consequences. . . . Therefore the question no longer is whether or not the constitution follows the flag, whether we shall have colonies, but what methods congress shall adopt to govern them — only this and nothing more."

The *Seattle Daily Times* was harsher still. It concluded a long editorial in Wednesday's paper by making the point that the Supreme Court majority had effectively made Congress, which was the creation of the U.S. Constitution, "greater than its creator." That is to say that the Supreme Court's ruling gave Congress authority under the territory clause to violate the rest of the Constitution, including the restrictions on Congress's own authority.

Neither did the British press share a common view of the decision. "The *Standard* considers that America can now govern her conquests as wholly separate territory," the *London Tribune* reported, "while the *Daily Graphic* takes the view that the Supreme Court has given its sanction to 'the imperialist policy of the McKinley administration.' *The Post*'s dispatch from Washington, on the other hand, holds that the court has decided that 'imperialism' is contrary to the constitution." The *London Daily News*, for its part, was scathing of "perhaps the most momentous" decision that the Supreme Court "was ever called upon to make." According to the *News*, "It is not progress but retrogression; not the advancement of humanity, but that disheartening product of our times, the militarism of democracy. We venture to think the framers of the United States constitution would have laughed at the possibility of such a development as incredible." The *News* concluded: "The decisions have extricated President McKinley from an uncommonly awkward position, but it is a lamentable, headlong fall in the moral scale and a turning of the back on all that had been the special glory and distinction of the United States in order to join in the barbaric scramble for the waste places of the earth."

In Puerto Rico, the reaction was "a general feeling of disappointment," the Associated Press reported. Puerto Ricans "generally expected that the courts' decisions would grant Porto Rico free trade and her citizens full citizenship and constitutional privileges." They were therefore "disappointed" with the Court's decisions. As a spokesman for the Fritze Lundt Company stated — and the Associated Press identified the company as "the largest shippers of sugar in Porto Rico" — "The constitution of the United States applies when against us, but not when in our favor. This has always been so since the beginning. If the tariff had been removed at first Porto Rico would now have double crops. The American system of taxation cannot be applied here; there should be some sensible tax on flour and rice, but sugar should be free. This legislation appears to be for Americans and against Porto Ricans." Meanwhile, other island residents, merchants included, believed that the Court's decision would spur the Puerto Rican government into action so as to make the island's finances self-sufficient. Governor Allen, for instance, was "giving earnest consideration of securing, at an early date, free trade relations between Porto Rico and Germany," the Associated Press reported. Puerto Ricans expected their legislature to pass a resolution for free trade with the American states.

The business community weighed in as well. "Great interest was shown in lower Wall Street in the Supreme Court's decision in the De Lima case, especially in sugar and coffee brokers' offices," reported the *New York Herald* on May 28, 1901. "Numerous importing houses in the sugar district had more than a general interest in the decision, for practically all of the raw sugar brokers had at one time or another imported Puerto Rican sugar, which they were compelled to pay fifteen per cent of the tariff on sugar from other points." Another story in the *Herald* quoted Henry O. Havemeyer, the president of the American Sugar Refining Company, who "seemed much pleased by the [*De Lima*] decision. 'I do not see how the Court could have reached any other conclusion'" than that trade between Puerto Rico and the mainland United States could not be taxed under the uniformity clause once Puerto Rico became part of the United States with the peace treaty with Spain. But the *Herald* did not report Havemeyer's reaction to the decision in *Downes* — where the Sugar Trust lost out — since the five-to-four majority ruled that Congress *could* tax trade between Puerto Rico and the American states, of course, according to the terms of the Foraker Act of 1900.

Not surprisingly, political and legal experts were no less divided and confused than were reporters and editors.

As Charles E. Littlefield, a former Republican congressman from Maine, wrote in the *Harvard Law Review:* "The Insular Cases, in the manner in which the results were reached, the incongruity of the results, and the variety of inconsistent views expressed by the different members of the court, are, I believe, without parallel in our judicial history." The historian Samuel Eliot Morison commented, too, that as a result of the decision, "the Republican party was able to eat its cake and have it: to indulge in territorial expansion, yet maintain the tariff wall against such insular products as sugar and tobacco, as foreign."

But most political experts had strong views of the case, favoring one side or the other. Some supported Justice Brown, others Justice White, and still others the dissenting justices. Eugene Stevenson, the departing president of the New Jersey Bar Association, endorsed Justice Brown's opinion for the Court. "The Constitution of the United States expresses the will and is maintained by the force of the inhabitants of the forty-five States of the Union," Stevenson argued, and "it neither expresses the will nor is it maintained by the force of the inhabitants of the District of Columbia or of the territories of New Mexico and Arizona, or of Alaska, Porto Rico, the Sandwich Islands or the Philippine Islands." Stevenson claimed that "all the territories of the United States, including the District of Columbia, occupy a position of *absolute political servitude to the inhabitants of the forty-five States* who compose the great body politic and who of themselves have the power to enact and re-enact and alter and amend from time to time the supreme law of the land which governs so much of the land as the lawgiver sees fit to include within the operation of his law" (emphasis in original).

Stevenson concluded with a warning. "If the minority of these learned Justices are right and no distinction can be drawn between Porto Rico on the one hand and the Philippine Islands and possible slices of China and Africa on the other, this would be the result: The treaty-making power composed of the President and Senate, could secretly effect the addition of fifty millions of Chinamen to the citizenship of the United States, all of whom would become voters upon establishing a residence in any State."

Beckles Willson, a prominent political writer from Canada, also held Brown's view to be "sounder, and, in the long run, a safer doctrine." Willson thought that Brown's views "have obtained very wide acceptance, and that he ha[d] made converts of his own colleagues." Gus Willson (no relation), a friend and former law partner of Justice Harlan, also agreed with Brown. He wrote Harlan that he "was always sorry when any opinion or any influence in this country hinders, hampers, or drags on the full and complete power of this country to own any property or territory that any other country in the world can own." Willson commented, "I should not be willing to belong to a country that could not . . . exercise all the National powers, authority and rights that any other country can exercise, and I believe not merely in the legality, but in the desirability of holding Porto Rico, the Hawaiian Islands and [the Philippines,] and in exercising all the necessary powers to regulate the people who happen to be tenants of these possessions."

Other commentators thought less of Brown's opinion. They noted that Brown stood alone in *Downes*, that he took the most extreme and most imperialist position, and that he was the only justice who held that the Constitution did not apply to the new territories. One widely circulated comment was "that four of the judges said the constitution did follow the flag, that four of them said it did not follow the flag, and one said, 'It sometimes follows the flag and sometimes does not, and I will tell you when it does and when it does not.'" An editorial in the *New York Times* predicted that Brown's opinion in *Downes* "will share the fate of the Dred Scott decision" — that is, to be widely condemned and later overruled.

Judge L. S. Rowe, a future president of the American Academy of Political and Social Science, favored Justice White's position. "His views give evidence of a desire to formulate a principle at once simple and readily intelligible. Whether we agree or disagree with his conclusions they furnish a clear and definite rule by which the political organs of the government may guide their conduct in dealing with newly acquired territory," Rowe wrote in the *Annals of the American Academy*. "The principle of interpretation as laid down gives to them complete power over such territory until, by express legislative enactment or by acquiescence in a rule contained in a treaty of cession, such acquired territory is made a part of the United States. Until such action is taken by Congress," he added, "the territory remains subject to the jurisdiction of the United States, but does not become a part thereof, and the only limitations upon the power of Congress are those prohibitions of the Constitution which go to the very root of the power of Congress." The *New York Times* agreed: "Justice White's majority opinion is historically and, we think, legally, much sounder than that of Justice Brown," it wrote. White expressed "a clearly reasoned opinion," the *Times* added in an editorial the following day.

Others, however, found the majority's opinions wanting. "The judgment in the Downes case is . . . nothing but an arbitrary bit of patchwork," wrote the political scientist John W. Burgess. "Its purpose is to satisfy a certain demand of fancied political expediency in the work of imperial expansion. It is based upon the narrowest possible view of that expediency." A prominent New York attorney wrote Harlan that he hoped that *Downes* would be "the Dred Scott of Imperialism!" And Senator John Tyler Morgan (D-Ala.) applauded Harlan's "mental and moral honesty." (In fact, William Jennings Bryan and others recommended Harlan, though a Republican, as the Democrats' 1904 presidential candidate.)

Surely the most famous response to *Downes v. Bidwell*, however, was that of Finley Peter Dunne's fictitious Irishman, Mr. Martin Dooley, who stated, "No matther whether th' Constitution follows th' flag or not, th' Supreme Coort follows th' iliction returns" (a passage that immediately follows this chapter's epigraph). So did the five-justice majority concede to electoral politics?

No. For one, the Court was deeply divided on *Downes* in terms of both numbers and judicial doctrine — divisions that typified the other decisions of 1901 (see chapter 5). The several opinions of the Court suggest the complexity of the justices' arguments and the delicate politics on the Court. Any five-to-four ruling makes it hard to think of the Supreme Court as a single institution. The notion of the Court as being a single institution is even harder to maintain when no one opinion receives the support of a majority of justices, when a case attracts five separate opinions, and when the Court decides *six* five-to-four opinions on the same general question *in one day*.

In addition, the election of 1900 was by no means a straightforward referendum on imperialism. The principal issue in the campaign was the money issue. Bryan insisted on the free coinage of silver, which would mean more money in circulation, the support of the western states that mined silver, and a policy of easier money (and very possibly inflation, since free silver would increase the money supply and help debtors at the expense of creditors). But it also meant that the Democrats would effectively be conceding New York State, dominated by conservative financial interests, to the Republicans. Such a move not only made the odds of winning the presidential election that much worse but also meant that Bryan and the Democratic Party would lose the support of gold Democrats such as former president Cleveland and former House Speaker Thomas Reed (both of whom abstained from the election) and that of anti-imperialist Republicans (such as Senator Hoar and former president Harrison). Although the Democratic platform conspicuously featured an anti-imperialist plank

("We hold that the Constitution follows the flag, . . . and we warn the American people that imperialism abroad will lead quickly and inevitably to despotism at home"), and although Bryan attacked imperialism during his campaign, the McKinley campaign avoided any mention of the issue and the Republican platform nowhere mentioned Puerto Rico or the Foraker Act. After the election, expert analysis directly attributed Bryan's defeat to the money issue.

A third reason for doubting that the Court followed the election returns is the political climate in 1900. Whereas the United States was just coming out of the depression of 1893 when McKinley was first elected in 1896, the year 1900 was one of prosperity. Gold discoveries in the Klondike and in South Africa had already boosted the economy by increasing the money supply, thereby further undermining Bryan's appeal on the money issue. With the improved economy, too, fewer voters were as motivated as they had been four years earlier to support Bryan's attacks on the trusts and there was less reason to abandon the incumbent.

Fourth, there was Bryan himself. Gold Democrats, most Republicans, and many Mugwumps — political independents — disliked Bryan for what they viewed as his demagoguery and his radicalism. Bryan damaged his credibility, too, by supporting the ratification of the Treaty of Paris of 1899 when it came up before the U.S. Senate (where it passed by a narrow margin, as noted in chapter 2) and by then using imperialism as a major issue of his 1900 presidential campaign. Bryan and his supporters argued that the peace treaty "was necessary to end the war." "The Democrats could not afford the burden of having continued the conflict," Bryan said, and "it would be easier to secure the independence for the Philippine Islands through the United States than to force it about Spain." Less charitable persons thought that Bryan was simply being opportunistic and manipulative.

Fifth, imperialism cut across party lines. Not only did some Democrats support U.S. expansion, particularly Democratic newspapers such as the *Washington Times*, the *Atlanta Constitution*, and the *Louisville Courier-Journal*, but the Democratic Party had historically been the party of geographic expansion. Likewise, many conservative Republicans opposed expansion, as had their Whig predecessors. The Court's split in *Downes* suggests as much. Justice White, a Democrat, provided crucial support for the Republican administration, while Justices

Brewer and Harlan, both Republicans, opposed the government's expansionist policies and dissented, along with the Democrats Fuller and Justice Peckham.

Still, Mr. Dooley has a point: the justices on the bench were clearly aware of the serious and wide-ranging implications of *Downes* and the other cases of 1901, as their "spirited debate" in conference suggests. The justices' own correspondence and the news reports likewise suggest such an awareness. A majority on the Court *did* agree to a decision that avoided a confrontation with Congress and happened to be consistent with the United States' new imperial policy. And no doubt but that for many, McKinley's landslide election in 1900 appeared to be an endorsement of existing White House policies. Revealingly, U.S. attorney general Griggs, solicitor general Richards, and Justices Brown, White, and McKenna (in his dissenting opinion in *De Lima v. Bidwell;* see chapter 5), all saw the *Insular Cases* as deciding *political* questions — "political" referring to the domain of the legislative and executive branches rather than the "judicial" domain of the courts. At the end of the day, a deeply divided Supreme Court avoided declaring the Foraker Act unconstitutional and denying Congress plenary power over the new territories, in contrast to the Taney Court's willingness in *Dred Scott* to tackle the constitutionality of the Missouri Compromise and to directly address the question of the extension of slavery in the western territories and states.

CHAPTER 5

A Court Torn

The *Insular Cases* of 1901

If they become states on an equal footing with the other states . . . they will take
part in governing the whole republic, in governing us, *by sending senators
and representatives into our Congress to help make our laws, and by voting for
president and vice-president to give our national government its executive.*
The prospect of the consequences which would follow the admission of
Spanish creoles and the negroes *of the West India islands and of the* Malays
and Tagals *of the Philippines to* participation in the conduct of
our government is so alarming *that you instinctively pause.*
CARL SCHURZ, "American Imperialism," 1899

Eight of the ten *Insular Cases* of 1901 were decided on the basis of timing: when the tariff was being collected. U.S. policies with respect to
the new territories could be divided into three periods, as a number
of lawyers, legal scholars, congressmen, and reporters pointed out: (1)
the period of U.S. military occupation, beginning on different dates
for the different islands, and lasting until the Treaty of Paris went into
effect, on April 11, 1899; (2) the one-year period between the date of
the treaty of peace and May 1, 1900, when the Foraker Act took effect
(the Foraker Act passed on April 12, 1900); and (3) the period after
the Foraker Act, in which commerce between Puerto Rico and the
states was "to be dutiable at fifteen percent of the rates fixed by the
Dingley Act," and "foreign imports into Porto Rico shall pay the same
duties as foreign imports into 'the United States.'" No duties were to
be collected after March 1, 1902, however, and all revenues were to
be for the use and benefit of the Puerto Rican government.

The decision in *Downes v. Bidwell* addressed the status of duties imposed on Puerto Rico in the third period only — that is, the present
for the purposes of the McKinley administration, Congress, and the
Supreme Court. But *De Lima v. Bidwell, Goetze v. United States, Crossman v. United States, Dooley v. United States I, Armstrong v. United*

States, and *Fourteen Diamond Rings v. United States* — the only Philippine case — involved the tariffs collected by the U.S. government from various persons and businesses in one or both periods *before* the Foraker Act.

With Justice Brown in the majority in all the *Insular Cases* of 1901 and an expert in the related field, admiralty law, Chief Justice Fuller assigned Brown to write the opinion for the Court in eight of the cases. Fuller himself wrote the lead opinion in *Fourteen Diamond Rings v. United States*, and Justice Harlan wrote the Court's unanimous opinion in *Neely v. Henkel*.

———

In *De Lima v. Bidwell*, the first case decided on May 27, 1901, the Supreme Court had to rule whether "territory acquired by the United States by cession from a foreign power remains a 'foreign country' within the meaning of the tariff laws." Three attorneys for Coudert Brothers — Coudert, Fuller, and Charles Frederick Adams — argued for De Lima & Co. that treaties were the supreme law of the land, per Article VI (that "all treaties made, or which shall be made, under the authority of the United States, shall be the supreme law of the land"). A treaty, Chief Justice Marshall wrote, is the "equivalent to an act of the legislature wherever it appears." So with the Treaty of Paris, Puerto Rico became part of the United States.

Neither was *Fleming v. Page* (1850) — the case that the U.S. government's lawyers cited in support of their position — actually relevant, attorneys for Coudert Brothers argued, since Mexico was under U.S. army *occupation* and was not *acquired* territory. The attorneys made the further point, consistent with Chief Justice Taney's arguments and the second, fuller view of the United States, that to speak of "extending" the Constitution was "fallacious." The U.S. Constitution was itself a system of government and therefore sovereign. It represented a grant of power from the people of the United States that extended everywhere that the U.S. government and its officials exercised dominion. The United States had always had "colonies or dependencies," the attorneys pointed out, and the U.S. government had no choice but to govern them according to constitutional rule.

John K. Richards, the solicitor general, argued on behalf of the U.S. government. If Chief Justice Taney could contend in *Fleming v.*

Page that the United States could demand territory in order to compensate citizens or the U.S. government for damages or expenses, Richards contended, then territory "certainly may be taken and held upon such terms and conditions as may be proper and necessary to carry the purpose into effect." Such terms included the imposition of tariffs levied on trade between a territory and the several states.

As for the claim that a treaty was the supreme law of the land, the solicitor general quoted from Article IX of the Treaty of Paris: "The civil rights and political status of the native inhabitants hereby ceded to the United States shall be determined by Congress." Richards pointed out that the peace treaty made other exceptional provisions, namely, that ships and merchandise of Spain were for a four-year period to be admitted to the Philippines on the same terms as those of the United States, and that Spanish scientific, literary, and artistic works were for a ten-year period to be admitted free of duty. Neither of these other provisions could go into effect, Richards observed, "if the Constitution requires our customs regulations to apply there as here." He emphasized that the "treaty never intended to make these tropical islands part of the United States in the constitutional sense, and just as certainly did make them part of the United States in the international sense." The solicitor general then reviewed at length the legal and historical precedents for the U.S. government's position.

The Supreme Court decided five to four in favor of De Lima & Co. Justice Brown, writing the opinion of the Court, ruled that at the time the duties were levied in the fall of 1899 — after the ratification of the Treaty of Paris and before the Foraker Act, the second period in question — Puerto Rico was *not* a foreign country within the meaning of the Dingley Tariff (Brown defined "foreign country" as "one exclusively within the sovereignty of a foreign nation and without the sovereignty of the United States"). Brown then cited three cases in particular in support of the majority opinion.

United States v. Rice (1819) concerned the question of whether goods imported into Castine (Maine) during the British occupation in the War of 1812, from September 1, 1814, to when the peace treaty was ratified, February 1815, could be taxed under the revenue laws subjecting goods imported into the United States. The goods were imported into Castine by the terms set by the British. When the United States reoccupied Castine, the customs collector demanded the payment of U.S.

duties. Justice Story decided for the Supreme Court that Castine, while under British occupation, was "a foreign port and that goods imported into it by the inhabitants were subject to such duties only as the British government chose to require. Such goods were in no correct sense imported into the United States."

Fleming et al. v. Page (1850) involved the payment of tariff duties in Philadelphia on goods imported from the port of Tampico during the Mexican War, when it was under the control of U.S. troops. Chief Justice Taney denied that the U.S. president had any power to enlarge the territory of the United States by virtue of a declaration of war. Rather, any such enlargement had to be done by treaty or congressional legislation.

In *Cross v. Harrison* (1853), the Court came to a different conclusion. The plaintiffs sought to recover from Harrison, the acting collector of customs, the duties paid on foreign goods imported into California in the period between February 2, 1848 (the date of the treaty between Mexico and the United States), and November 13, 1849 (when the newly appointed collector of customs took office). From August 1847 until September 3, 1848, the military had imposed a war tariff under the president's authority. The Court ruled that the United States, acting under its sovereign power over a conquered territory, was entitled to levy tariffs and that "by the ratification of the treaty [of peace with Spain] California became part of the United States" and was therefore subject to U.S. revenue laws.

Brown argued that the Supreme Court's decision in *Cross v. Harrison* effectively superseded its ruling in *Fleming v. Page*; territories ceded to the United States by treaty were a part of the United States and therefore subject to all its laws. This was consistent, he held, with the history of U.S. expansion and with the applicability of U.S. tariff laws in the area of the Louisiana Purchase and in the acquisitions of East and West Florida, Texas, California, and Alaska. Congress "has full and complete legislative authority over the people of the territories and all the departments of the territorial governments," Brown quoted from *National Bank v. County of Yankton*. "It may do for the territories what the people, under the Constitution of the United States, may do for the states."

Brown was therefore "unable to acquiesce in the assumption that a territory may be at the same time both foreign and domestic." And the United States had already acted, by the Senate's ratification of the peace treaty, to change the status of Puerto Rico from foreign to domestic for revenue purposes. Brown therefore concluded that "Porto Rico was not a foreign country within the meaning of the tariff laws," at the time that duties were collected, "but a territory of the United States." De Lima & Co., like other firms in the same situation, was therefore entitled to recover the "illegally exacted" duties.

The chief justice and Justices Harlan, Brewer, and Peckham joined Brown's opinion.

Justice McKenna dissented, joined by Justices Gray, Shiras, and White.

Joseph McKenna was an Irish Catholic whose father, a baker, moved out to California in the mid-1850s (along with so many others). McKenna, who was self-taught, passed the California bar exam in 1865 and was elected district attorney for Salano County at the age of twenty-two. McKenna, who switched to the Republican Party, practiced law after serving two terms as district attorney and was then elected to the state assembly. He twice ran for U.S. Congress, unsuccessfully both times, but on the third try in 1884 he narrowly won the election in a new, redrawn district. In the House of Representatives McKenna represented the railroads, legislated against Chinese immigrants, and worked on behalf of local projects — such as harbor improvements. McKenna served on the Ways and Means Committee, where William McKinley befriended him. McKenna kept his seat in Congress until President Harrison in 1890 appointed him to the Ninth Circuit Court of Appeals. Once McKinley was elected U.S. president in 1896, he appointed McKenna as U.S. attorney general. And when Justice Stephen Field resigned from the Supreme Court in 1898, McKinley nominated his attorney general for the vacant seat. The Senate approved McKenna's appointment, although McKenna was criticized for his lack of experience in constitutional law.

In his dissenting opinion in *De Lima v. Bidwell*, McKenna argued that Puerto Rico occupied an in-between status; it was neither a domestic territory nor a foreign country — consistent with White's concurring opinion in *Downes* and with Lowell's "Third View." In the absence of Congress's explicit incorporation of the islands, the United States could collect the duties on exports from Puerto Rico. Nothing in the Treaty of Paris, McKenna pointed out, mentioned "incorporation."

McKenna emphasized the distinction between the military occupation of a territory and its cession at a treaty of peace. American history and constitutional law were full of examples of U.S. territory being treated as foreign for some purposes and as domestic for others. In fact, even the terms "foreign" and "domestic" meant "nothing," McKenna wrote, since everything hinged "on whether a particular tariff law applies."

And whether a tariff law applied or not depended on the text of a treaty or congressional statute. In *Cross v. Harrison*, for instance, California did not automatically become part of the United States, McKenna wrote; instead, the wartime tariff had to be withdrawn by an act of the U.S. president. Whereas the cession of California marked a permanent expansion of U.S. national boundaries, Puerto Rico represented only the transfer of territory.

McKenna also used results-oriented language. The denial of plenary power to Congress "takes this great country out of the world and shuts it up within itself," McKenna wrote. For McKenna and the other dissenting justices "an empire had to be constitutionally possible," as Linda Przybyszewski, a biographer of Justice Harlan, puts it. Otherwise, the Supreme Court was tying the hands of the nation's representatives and limiting their options.

Justice Gray wrote a two-sentence dissent. He merely stated that the decision in *De Lima* was inconsistent with the Court's unanimous decision in *Fleming v. Page* and with the majority ruling in *Downes*.

The significance of *De Lima v. Bidwell* in conjunction with *Downes v. Bidwell* was that treaties were fully operative and that the executive branch could not itself impose a tariff once hostilities had ceased in the absence of expressed congressional policy otherwise (e.g., the Foraker Act of 1900). The decision affirmed the treaty power and denied the McKinley administration the discretion to impose tariffs on annexed territories; such imposts were contrary to the uniformity clause.

The Court jointly issued its decisions in *Goetze v. United States* and *Crossman v. United States*.

John H. Goetze & Co. imported a shipment of leaf or filler tobacco and other goods into New York from the port of Arecibo in Puerto Rico, and paid customs duties on the shipment, assessed at thirty-five cents per pound according to the rates set in the Dingley Tariff. The attorneys for Goetze & Co., Edward D. Perkins, Albert Comstock, and Everit Brown of Comstock and Brown, filed suit against the U.S. government to claim a return of the collected payment on the basis that (1) Puerto Rico was not foreign, hence the goods did not come under the purview of the Dingley Act, and (2) since Puerto Rico was within the United States, the collection of duties violated the uniformity clause. *Goetze v. United States* therefore tested the validity of import duties imposed on tobacco shipped from Puerto Rico in the period *after* the ratification of the treaty and *before* the passage of the Foraker Act. The U.S. attorney general, John Griggs, filed the brief for the U.S. government.

In *Crossman v. United States*, George W. Crossman and his partners, who were with the trading firm of W. H. Crossman & Brothers, challenged the U.S. government's collection of duties on whiskey, brandy, and jam imported into New York from Honolulu in April 1900— after the passage of the Newlands Resolution annexing Hawai'i, but before the passage of the Hawai'ian organic act. There was little new in the arguments made by Charles Curie and W. Wickham Smith, the plaintiff's attorneys, except that they were making an argument for the free trade of goods shipped from Hawai'i, rather than those shipped from Puerto Rico or the Philippines. (During oral argument, Chief Justice Fuller and other justices took note of the fact that Hawai'i was annexed by resolution, rather than by treaty— as was Texas— but this fact had no bearing on the Court's decision.)

Instead, the "sole question" in *Goetze v. United States* and *Crossman v. United States*, Brown wrote, "was whether Porto Rico and the Hawaiian Islands were foreign countries within the meaning of the tariff laws." And this question the Court had addressed in *De Lima v. Bidwell*, "just decided." So the imposition of duties on Hawai'ian trade, just like that on Puerto Rican trade for the period in question, was "a clear breach" of the uniformity clause.

———

The Court effectively treated *Dooley v. United States I* and *Armstrong v. United States* as a single case as well. *Dooley v. United States I* involved the question of whether Dooley, Smith, & Co. could be reimbursed for the $5,374.68 in taxes the company had paid on shipments into

Puerto Rico from the states; the tariffs had been collected under a U.S. military directive in the periods both *before* and *after* the treaty's ratification, but before the Foraker Act went into effect.

Armstrong v. United States was brought forward by Carlos Armstrong, a British citizen, who sought to recover from the U.S. government customs duties totaling $31,530.65. The duties had been collected in Ponce, Puerto Rico, on "goods, wares, and merchandise" brought in from New York, Baltimore, and Philadelphia between August 12, 1898, and December 5, 1899—that is, during the first and second periods.

John C. Chaney, Alphonso Hart, John G. Carlisle, and Charles C. Leeds, all attorneys with Curtis Mallet, filed a long brief for the two *Dooley v. United States* cases, as well as a lengthy brief for *Armstrong v. United States*. The brief on behalf of Armstrong repeated several of the arguments made in *De Lima* and *Downes*. John G. Carlisle, U.S. Treasury secretary under President Cleveland, a former member of Congress, and at the time also an attorney with Curtis Mallet, presented a separate oral argument on behalf of both Dooley, Smith, & Co. and Carlos Armstrong.

Carlisle's argument stood out for its explicit mention of the "commerce" of the United States and, by implication, the commerce clause — that is, Congress's power "to regulate Commerce with foreign Nations, and among the several States, and with the Indian Tribes" (Art. 1, Sec. 8, Cl. 3). "If Congress possesses the exclusive power to govern the Territories, it can, of course regulate the commerce between them," Carlisle noted, "but by what authority, except the authority derived from that part of the Constitution referred to, can it regulate and control the commerce between a Territory and a State?" The Supreme Court had already established in *Stoutenburgh v. Hennick* (1889) that trade between states and territories — between Maryland and the District of Columbia in *Stoutenburgh* — "was interstate commerce within the meaning of the Constitution." Carlisle pointed out, "The exclusive power of Congress to *regulate commerce* extends under the Constitution all over the United States and includes commerce between the States and Territories, because the Territories are within the United States and parts of the United States" (emphasis added). The power to regulate commerce "is of a national character and is a unit, the proper control of which requires the enactment of uniform and harmonious laws and regulations."

Carlisle also rejected the idea proposed by the U.S. government attorneys that because the revenues from the duties under the Foraker Act would be applied to Puerto Rican government rather than go into the U.S. Treasury, the Foraker Act came under the territory clause rather than the revenue clause (Art. 1, Sec. 8, Cl. 1). He noted that just because the revenue collected was from goods in transit from the states, the duties could not be considered as a provision for Puerto Rican government: "It is palpably an abuse of terms to say that such a tax is local and that it is imposed in the exercise of the power to govern the Territories." Carlisle commented that "it would be very strange if the framers of the Constitution . . . put a clause into the Constitution under which Congress could lay destructive taxes upon the trade and commerce of the States, and not require them to be uniform anywhere, or in any respect. This clause, this absolute prohibition, must be construed as applying to every export from a State, whether it goes to a foreign country or not."

Solicitor General Richards, for his part, did not make a separate argument in *Dooley I* but rather argued the U.S. government's case in *Dooley* in his comprehensive brief for the six "Porto Rican Cases" and in his oral testimony for the same six cases.

The Court aligned in *Dooley I* as it had in *De Lima*. Justice Brown again wrote the lead opinion, joined by Fuller, Harlan, Brewer, and Peckham; White, Gray, Shiras, and McKenna opposed. White wrote the opinion in dissent.

Brown built his argument around three principal points. The first point settled a technical question: whether the court of claims and the circuit courts had jurisdiction over the recovery of duties illegally exacted on imports from Puerto Rico to New York. Although the U.S. government contended they did not, Brown and a majority of justices on the Court found that they did.

Brown's second point addressed the issue of the different times in which the taxes had been collected. Here, Brown upheld the powers of the military and executive branch to collect the duties prescribed under the military order of July 26, 1898, and by orders of President McKinley as commander in chief on August 19, 1898, and February

1, 1899. The military, Brown wrote, "may do anything necessary to strengthen itself and weaken the enemy" in times of war and up to the time of a peace settlement. The fact that the goods were levied in the port of a conquered country on goods coming from New York, rather than on goods coming from foreign countries into a U.S. territory (California, in *Cross v. Harrison*) was "quite immaterial."

Brown's third point concerned the duties levied after the ratification of the peace treaty, at which time "Porto Rico ceased to be a foreign country," thus the military and presidential orders for tariff collection no longer held. And "until Congress otherwise constitutionally directed, such merchandise was entitled to free entry. . . . In our opinion the authority of the President as Commander–in-Chief to exact duties upon imports from the United States ceased with the ratification of the treaty of peace." To act otherwise would have been to put Puerto Rico in an untenable situation: it would have made Puerto Rican exports subject both to U.S. duties and (the newly imposed) Spanish tariff barriers. The U.S. government thus owed Dooley, Smith, & Co. the duties collected during the second period of occupation, but not those collected during the first period.

Justice White dissented on the grounds that Puerto Rico was still a foreign country for the purposes of the tariff. As long as Congress could levy a duty on merchandise from a country coming into the United States, then "such a country must be a foreign country within the meaning of the tariff laws." Furthermore, White pointed out that the Court had just decided in *Downes v. Bidwell* that Congress *could* tax goods being shipped from Puerto Rico to the states. How, then, White asked, could the island be considered as "no longer a foreign country within the meaning of tariff laws?" Congress had legislated that Puerto Rico was a foreign country for tariff purposes, and Congress could exercise such authority under the power of the territory clause.

As for the difficult situation Puerto Rico would have were it to face U.S. tariff barriers as well as Spanish import duties, White noted that Congress had both the constitutional authority and "the opportunity to adjust the revenue laws of the United States to meet the new situation."

The Court ruled in *Armstrong v. United States* as it had in *Dooley I*. Justice Brown presented the Court's opinion: "The case is controlled by the case of *Dooley v. United States*, No. 501, just decided. So far as the duties were exacted upon goods prior to the ratification of the

Treaty . . . they were properly exacted. So far as they were imposed upon importations after that date and prior to December 5, 1899, plaintiff is entitled to recover them back."

———

In the last case decided on Monday, May 27, 1901, *Huus v. New York and Porto Rico Steamship Co.*, the issue before the justices was whether Puerto Rican ports were foreign ports for the purposes of New York laws regulating harbor pilots (where licensed pilots familiar with particular harbors assumed piloting duties in place of the ship's master). Christian Huus had been denied his services and filed suit to recover his piloting fees. He was represented by former U.S. senator William Lindsay. F. Kingsbury Curtis and Edmond W. Curtis — son and father and both with Curtis Mallet — represented the New York and Porto Rico Steamship Company. Was, then, the steamship *Ponce* engaged in "coasting trade" as the term was used in the state of New York statutes ("coasting trade" stood in opposition to the shipping trade in the interior of the United States)? And were steamships trafficking between Puerto Rican and stateside ports engaged in coasting trade, for the purposes of U.S. laws?

Justice Brown wrote the unanimous opinion for the Court. New York laws and Section 9 of the Foraker Act both specified that vessels engaged in the coasting trade were not required to employ licensed pilots when entering New York or other U.S. ports, Brown noted. And trade with Alaska and Hawai'i was already covered under coastwise trade. In other words, coastwise trading could include trade with offshore territories; it did not just have to be along contiguous coasts. Thus the New York pilotage laws did not apply to the *Ponce*, and Huus had no case — just as the district court had previously decided.

The *Santa Fe New Mexican*, alone among the newspapers I surveyed, focused on the decision in *Huus v. New York* in a single, brief story on the May 27 decisions — instead of on *Downes* or any other of the nine decisions. But in general, newspapers had only very short paragraphs on *Huus v. New York*, if they covered the decision at all.

———

In a single day, the U.S. Supreme Court had decided that Puerto Rico and Hawai'i *were* part of the United States for the purpose of merchant marine laws and that Puerto Rico *was* domestic for the purpose of tariffs on trade in the period between the ratification of the Treaty of Paris and the date the Foraker Act went into effect. But Puerto Rico was *not* part of the United States for the purpose of the tariff and the uniformity clause in the periods both *before* the treaty of peace and *after* the Foraker Act went into effect.

Justice Brown made the difference. The other eight justices on the bench held positions that did not depend on timing. They either argued that Congress or the executive had the authority to impose tariffs on trade with the territories (White, Gray, Shiras, McKenna), or that the Constitution fully applied to the territories of the United States, and that Congress could thus not legislate otherwise (Fuller, Harlan, Brewer, Peckham).

The Court delayed decisions in two of the *Insular Cases* heard in late 1900 and early 1901, however, even though many observers thought the Court would issue the decisions the next day, on Tuesday, May 28. Justice Brown had requested that *Fourteen Diamond Rings v. United States* (the "Philippine case") and *Dooley v. United States II* be postponed until the next term, and Chief Justice Fuller agreed to do so.

Both cases posed distinct challenges to the Court. *Fourteen Diamond Rings* was the first case concerning the Philippines, where U.S. forces were fighting a rebellion and where there was no equivalent to the Foraker Act. *Dooley II* involved imports *into* Puerto Rico from New York (as did *Dooley I*), but in the period *after* the Foraker Act went into effect. Further distinguishing *Dooley II* from *Dooley I, Armstrong, Goetze,* and *De Lima* was the fact that the case not only raised the issue of the applicability of the uniformity clause but also the constitutional prohibitions on export taxes, the export clause ("No tax or Duty shall be laid on Articles exported from any State" [Art. 1, Sec. 9, Cl. 5]), and on the granting of preferences among U.S. ports, the preference clause ("No Preference shall be given by any Regulation of Commerce or Revenue to the Ports of one State over those of another; nor shall Vessels bound to, or from, one State, be obliged to enter, clear, or pay Duties in another" [Art. 1, Sec. 9, Cl. 6]). Edward Whitney had earlier raised exactly these points (see chapter 2), as also had John Carlisle in his arguments on behalf of Dooley, Smith, & Co.

and Armstrong. But these issues had not yet attracted direct attention from the Court.

Court observers, lawyers, politicians, and editors guessed how the "Philippine case" and *Dooley II* would be decided. Most believed that *Fourteen Diamond Rings* would be decided on the basis of *De Lima*, since it concerned duties collected from goods imported from the Philippines after the ratification of the Treaty of Paris but before the Foraker Act, and that *Dooley II* would be decided on the basis of *Downes*, since it applied to duties collected in Puerto Rico from goods imported from the mainland after the passage of the Foraker Act. Yet if the decisions in *De Lima* and *Downes* were to simply map onto the two undecided cases, then, as the former U.S. attorney general Griggs pointed out, there would have been no reason for delaying the decisions.

"There are important legal points involved in the Philippine controversy that did not appear in the Porto Rican cases," an editorial in the *Philadelphia Inquirer* anonymously quoted one of the Supreme Court justices as saying. Or, as the *Philadelphia Record* asked, would the Supreme Court regard the Spooner Amendment of March 2, 1901, as being sufficient to validate the government's action? (The Spooner Amendment, which Congress attached to an army spending bill, gave the executive branch the power to impose temporary tariffs on Philippine goods.) It was by no means clear that the Court's decisions of May 27 would be dispositive.

Senator Lodge, chairman of the Philippine Committee, thought that "in the fourteen rings case" the Court was "likely to say that cession and possession were never combined" because of "the existence of war in those islands after the ratification of the treaty with Spain." Once the United States recognized "that war is at an end," whether "by proclamation or by the establishment of civil government," however, "then the possession would be complete and the doctrine of the De Lima case would apply," he wrote Taft on June 17, 1901.

Lodge and other members of Congress therefore asked for Congress to be allowed to settle matters, given the closeness of the Court's decisions of May 27 and the many constitutional and political issues remaining to be resolved. As Lodge put it in the same letter to Taft, however the Supreme Court decides "the diamond rings case there must be extensive general legislation for the Philippines, because, while they have asserted the omnipotence of Congress in legislating for our new possessions, they have also, in the De Lima case, held that after cession and possession all existing laws applicable to the new possessions apply until otherwise ordered by Congress." Lodge wanted Congress to pass "an organic act for the government of the Philippine Islands . . . at the earliest possible moment." He therefore asked Taft to "make a draft of an act which, like the Porto Rican act, will cover not only the franchise and the mining and timber rights, but also the frame of government and the application for exclusion of the laws of the United States; that is our navigation laws must be excluded, and those for the collection of internal revenue."

Two days later, Lodge sent Secretary Root the same message: the Philippines needed a "general organic act" that "ought to have a clause stating that the Constitution and the laws of the U.S. do not apply except as specifically extended to them by Congress." Senator Morgan (D-Ala.), too, wrote Secretary Root to express his "sincere apprehension of the difficulties and dangers that arise from the recent decisions of the Supreme Court," and to suggest that "such difficulties and dangers can only be increased by delay and exaggerated by discussions to which they will provoke among our people." "Let the discussion take place in Congress, *where it can result in action*" (emphasis in original), Morgan encouraged Root in his letter of May 29, 1901. If not, "Our military success in the Philippines may be retarded and our influence in 'the pacification of Cuba' will be lessened by the doubts that exist as to the powers of the President in controlling tariff legislation in places subject to our jurisdiction."

Root replied to Morgan almost immediately, writing him on June 1, 1901, that the question with respect to "the power to impose duties in the Spanish islands, on goods coming from the United States," would "better be settled by the Court than discussed in Congress, where, after months of heated debate, it might result in conclusions only to be overruled by the Court."

Yet the justices on the bench themselves did not even know what the outcome of the cases would be. "I do not feel sure that we will hold the judgment in [the *Fourteen Diamond Rings*] case," Harlan wrote Fuller on July 8. "I think it would be well for you to prepare something on the Fourteen Diamond case to be used as a concurring or dissenting opinion as the situation may require." On August 6, four weeks later, Harlan again wrote Fuller of his concern: "My fear that Brown might change his vote on the Diamond case arose from what he said, this summer when he asked that the Diamond case go over to the next term." Given the unpredictability of how Brown would decide, Fuller took Harlan's suggestion and prepared opinions for both *Fourteen Diamond Rings* and *Dooley II;* one became the Court's lead opinion, the other the dissent.

Justice Brown was the swing judge on the Court, just as the *New York Herald* figured out. "Brown held the balance of power in the Supreme Court, during the weeks that the insular cases were under consideration," the *Herald* wrote in its editorial of May 29, 1901.

> On one side were the Chief Justice and Justices Harlan, Brewer and Peckham, who held that the power of Congress to legislate for the territorial possessions of the United States was limited by the Constitution. On the other side were Justices Gray, Shiras, White and McKenna, holding firmly to the opposite view. Justice Brown was in doubt. Both sides labored with him week after week each trying to convince him that it was right. He wavered, but at last took a middle course, which was not entirely satisfactory to either side and which resulted in dissenting opinions from every decision which he rendered. He sided with the Chief Justice and those agreeing with him on the De Lima case, but on the still more important Downes case he went over to the other group.

In the case of *Fourteen Diamond Rings v. United States,* Emil J. Pepke, a soldier who had served on Luzon (the largest and northernmost island in the Philippines, which includes Manila), brought fourteen rings back to the states at the end of his tour of duty. But U.S. customs officials in Chicago seized the rings for the import duties that Pepke owed on them, according to the terms of the Dingley Tariff. Pepke filed suit on the grounds that the U.S. government's imposition of duties on the rings was contrary to the Constitution and in violation of his rights as a U.S. citizen.

The chief justice's lead opinion was joined by Justices Harlan, Brewer, and Peckham. Fuller held that the ruling in *De Lima v. Bidwell* stood: there was no appreciable difference between Puerto Rico and the Philippines with respect to the U.S. Constitution and the terms of the Treaty of Paris. The Philippines were a part of the United States with respect to the tariff and the uniformity clause, just as the Court had decided in *De Lima*.

In response to the argument that the Philippine situation was different because of the U.S. Senate's resolution of February 14, 1899 (which endorsed the tariff levied by the McKinley administration, and which passed by a majority vote rather than by a two-thirds majority), Fuller held that the resolution was "absolutely without legal significance on the question before us. The meaning of the treaty cannot be controlled by subsequent explanations of some of those who may have voted to ratify it." The chief justice added, "No reason is perceived for any different ruling as to the Philippines. . . . The treaty was ratified; congress appropriated the money; the ratification was proclaimed. The treaty making power, the executive power, the legislative power, concurred in the completion of the transaction."

Fuller also dismissed the idea that the rebellion in the Philippines — in contrast to the peaceful occupation of Puerto Rico — prevented the United States from taking full possession of the islands: "We must decline to assume that the government wishes thus to disparage the title of the United States, or to place itself in the position of waging a war of conquest." The decision in *De Lima* stood.

Justice Brown wrote a separate concurring opinion in which he emphasized that the Senate resolution of February 14, 1899, could not be considered a part of the peace treaty with Spain, since a treaty was the equivalent of a contract between foreign states. The Senate resolution, which did not even receive a vote in the House of Representatives, had no such standing.

Justices Gray, White, Shiras, and McKenna simply noted that they dissented on the grounds of their opinions previously expressed in *De Lima v. Bidwell*, *Dooley v. United States I*, and *Downes v. Bidwell*.

———

The circumstances of *Dooley II* were essentially the reverse of those of *Downes v. Bidwell*. Dooley, Smith, & Co. filed suit for the return of $1,433.11 in tariff duties collected from May 1, 1900, to October 23, 1900 — in the period after the Foraker Act went into effect — on goods and merchandise shipped from New York to San Juan, Puerto Rico. The question in *Dooley II* was whether the duties paid under the

Foraker Act on exports to Puerto Rico violated the constitutional prohibition on export taxes. The arguments for the two sides were the same as those for *Dooley I* and were filed by the same attorneys.

Brown again was the pivotal vote in the Court's five-to-four decision. Brown held in his lead opinion that the tax on imports into Puerto Rico did not violate the Constitution's prohibition on state exports, since it had already been established in *Woodruff v. Parham* (1869) that the export clause applied only in conjunction with "articles imported from foreign countries into the United States." Brown cited Justice Miller in *Woodruff v. Parham* on the point that exports should be "applied only to goods exported to a foreign country." The duties levied under the Foraker Act and the duties that Dooley, Smith, & Co. sought to recover were "neither exports nor imports." The duties *were*, then, liable to Congress's taxing authority.

Furthermore, Brown argued that the tax was a "temporary expedient" for raising revenues for "a separate fund for the government and benefit of Porto Rico," consistent with the argument made by the U.S. solicitor general. The Court's decision in *Downes*, moreover, had already established that Congress "could lawfully impose a duty upon imports from Porto Rico," the uniformity clause notwithstanding.

Justice White wrote a concurring opinion joined by Justices Gray, Shiras, and McKenna, in which he also argued that goods traded with Puerto Rico were neither imports nor exports for the purposes of the prohibition on the imposition of duties on exports from the states. He, too, cited *Woodruff v. Parham* in support of his claim. White added, though, that the interpretation of "the words export and import" as established in *Woodruff* and later cases still preserved "the necessary powers of taxation of the several States." The words "export" and "import" as used in the Constitution were for the prohibition of direct and indirect burdens alike on the movement of goods between the states. Puerto Rico was within the sovereignty of the United States consistent with the previous rulings in the *Insular Cases* — for all the justices on the bench save one, Brown — but "it had not been so made a part of the United States as to cause Congress to be subject . . . to the uniformity clause." Thus the duties levied under the authority of the Foraker Act on goods shipped to Puerto Rico from New York were within Congress's powers under its authority to raise revenue and regulate commerce.

Fuller's dissent, joined by Harlan, Brewer, and Peckham, reiterated the claims that Puerto Rico was domestic territory and that it could not levy duties on goods imported from the states. The fact that the net proceeds from the act were to be used by Puerto Rico "did not affect their character," since taxation was "national and not local, even though the revenue derived therefrom is devoted to local purposes." Fuller stressed that this was *commerce* Congress was taxing, consistent with Carlisle's argument and contrary to the opinions of Justices Brown and White. "The power to tax and the power to regulate commerce are distinct powers," Fuller pointed out, "yet the power of taxation may be so exercised as to operate in regulation of commerce." The commerce clause, the uniformity clause, the export clause, and the preference clause were all included in the Constitution, the chief justice pointed out, to prevent laws that discriminated "between one part of the country and another." Yet the majority opinions upholding the Foraker Act legitimated exactly such discrimination.

If Puerto Rico were foreign, Fuller argued, then "the prohibition of clause 5" — the export clause — "would be fatal to these duties." And if Puerto Rico were domestic, then the customs duties could not be sustained under the uniformity clause. But if the export clause pertained only to *foreign* trade, then the power of Congress to impose duties on trade with Puerto Rico must come from the "broad power" of Congress "to lay and collect taxes" under the authority of the revenue clause (Art. I, Sec. 8, Cl. 1).

Fuller recognized that Congress could regulate trade between states and that it could tax duties and imposts on foreign trade. But the prohibition on exports from the states applied to international trade and not to interstate trade, Fuller argued (consistent with Justice Miller's ruling in *Woodruff v. Parham*). The Court had "repeatedly answered" the point that "no State has the right to lay a tax on interstate commerce in any form," whether on the shipper, on the mode of transportation, on trade receipts, or on the occupation conducting the trade. Any "such taxation is a burden on that commerce, and amounts to a regulation of it"; only Congress, and not the states, had the power to regulate trade. Fuller emphasized that "if that power of regulation is absolutely unrestricted as respects interstate commerce," then this would allow Congress, the creation of the Constitution, to overthrow the national unity that "the Constitution was framed to secure."

The chief justice distinguished between the prohibition against duties on state exports and Congress's "general power to regulate commerce, whether interstate or foreign." The two provisions operated, and were "intended to operate," in exclusion of each other. This same principle was "equally true with respect of commerce with the territories." Congress's power to regulate such trade involved its power to regulate trade "between foreign countries and the territories," on the one hand, and "also by necessary implication as between the States and Territories," on the other hand. It was not the role of the Court to make a "blank paper" of the Constitution by confusing the issue of whether the imposts were foreign tariff duties on state exports or taxes imposed by Congress on state exports.

The fact that the duties were being collected in Puerto Rico, rather than in the states, was immaterial to the ruling, Fuller added (just as Carlisle had argued). While Fuller agreed that Congress could lay local taxes in the territories, Congress had no authority to tax state exports to other states, to tax exports from states to the territories, or to tax exports from states to foreign countries. There was still a penalty being paid on goods shipped from New York into Puerto Rico, whether a tax on "exports" from the states or on "imports" into the island. Either way, Congress and the Court majority were sanctioning an abuse of constitutional power and endangering commerce by supporting "the principle that Congress could tax exports from one state to another." The chief justice concluded by commenting, "Congress might crucify any state or section of the country by laying a prohibitive tax upon its exports to other states."

In fact, Fuller's fear of congressional interference in the economy was a telltale of his judicial career, as evidenced in his earlier rulings in the *Income Tax Case* and the *Sugar Trust Case*. Fuller's dissent in the *Lottery Case* (*Champion v. Ames*) of 1903 just two years later fully supports this view. (In the *Lottery Case*, Fuller argued that lottery tickets were not articles of commerce; they were therefore not subject to Congress's authority under the commerce clause.) Fuller was very much a Jacksonian Democrat in this respect, seeking to protect entrepreneurialism and economic liberty as fully as possible — even in an era of corporate domination. It was because of Fuller's fear of the U.S. government's restriction of commerce and because of his essentially unmitigated support for economic liberty that the chief justice wrote to a friend shortly after the decision, that "the *important* opinion [of the 1901 *Insular Cases*] is my dissent in [*Dooley v. United States II*] as you will see when you read it. The papers have not 'caught on.'"

But the newspapers did respond to the Court's decisions of December 2, 1901, and with mixed reactions. "The Philippines Are American, the Supreme Court Decides," ran the headline in the *San Francisco Examiner,* with the qualifying subhead, "$20,000,000 Decision Costs" — money that the government would have to refund on its previously levied taxes. The Spooner amendment, which granted the U.S. president the power to levy and collect taxes in the Philippines, was "not legislation defined by the Supreme Court." The *Examiner* also observed that while the *Fourteen Diamonds* case went against the government, the terms of the Treaty of Paris made it "hard to see how any distinction could have been drawn between the two territories." Neither did the insurrection make the Philippines foreign. "Nothing," the *Examiner* wrote in its editorial commentary, "could have a better effect in quenching the embers of the insurrection than the stimulus to industry that would be given by admission to the American market. If we can keep up freedom for a year the insurrectos [*sic*] will all be out of the jungle and raising sugar."

The *Examiner* quoted Representative Charles Grosvenor (R-Ohio) in its extensive story on the two cases: "The decisions taken together and added to the decisions of last spring, fully sustain all the points insisted upon by the Ways and Means Committee of the House of Representatives, and which became the position of the Republicans in Congress and the Administration." For Grosvenor, "The net result of the whole business is that by the treaty of Paris we acquired the islands without terms and with no stipulations controlling this Government in its relations to the new possessions." As he put it, "That while the treaty terminated the sovereignty of Spain and made the territory the property of the United States, yet it placed no limitations on the power of Congress to legislate on the new territory as it might deem wise and for the best interest of the islands. . . . The Supreme Court, after these great contests have ended, placed the court where Webster, and Burton and Lincoln and the Republican platform of

1860 placed it." The *Examiner* ran only a short piece on the Democratic response, however, namely, that the party should adhere to the Democratic doctrine of free trade among areas "covered by the sovereignty of the United States."

The *New York Daily Tribune*, published by Whitlaw Reid, an administration supporter, likewise celebrated the two "insular decisions." *Fourteen Diamond Rings* and *Dooley II* were "sweeping decisions" and "in complete harmony with the findings of that tribunal last May," the *Tribune* told its readers. "It is confidently predicted in the best informed circles in Washington that the present colonial policy of the government is now permanently eliminated as an issue of national politics." The *Tribune* noted that there were now three "United States" for the purposes of the U.S. Supreme Court: the states; incorporated territory; and unincorporated territory.

"The liberty then given to the government to deal with the new possessions as expediency may require" was not compromised, according to the *Tribune*. Rather, it "is reaffirmed as the one point then left in doubt — namely, the power of Congress to impose duties in the outlying islands on goods sent from a state." The paper went on to explain, "The result is that Philippine goods have free entry into the United States until such time as Congress passes a tariff law applying to them." This was despite the "Senate resolution disclaiming intent to incorporate them into the United States, and also because of the state of insurrection. No justice, however, was led to take this view." The Court refused to differentiate the Philippines from Puerto Rico, the newspaper concluded.

Whereas the *Examiner* was exultant and the *Tribune* celebratory, the *New York Times* and *Washington Post* were deadpan. The *Times* featured the two decisions in an inside story of December 3: "Government Beaten in an Insular Case," read its headline on page three, in reference to *Fourteen Diamond Rings*. The *Times* summarized both cases and referred to Fuller's opinion in the *Rings* case with the headline "De Lima Case Governs" and summarized *Dooley II* with the headline "Like the Downes Case." The decisions affirmed the constitutionality of the Foraker Act, the *Times* noted; the Philippines were not foreign insofar as military government could levy tariffs "without the legislative authority of Congress."

The *Washington Post* also ran a matter-of-fact account of the

Court's two decisions. "Philippines Are Held to Be Domestic Territory," read one headline; "Decision Leaves Plenary Power in the Hands of Congress," read another. The *Post* simply summarized the decisions, quoted them at length, and commented that only $1.9 million of the $17 million in imports from the Philippines was dutiable — a number the *San Francisco Examiner* got wrong.

But the *Post* did report on the reaction in the Philippines. "Manila Goes Wild," read its headline the next day. Newspapers in the Philippines published extra editions, the *Post* told its readers, and "the decision [in *Fourteen Diamond Rings*] caused great excitement and jubilation among the merchants and general public here. Representatives of the principal business houses say it will revolutionize the entire trade of the Orient." In addition, "Spanish merchants are pleased, since Spanish goods have the same treaty rights as American goods."

A few newspapers looked sourly at the opinions. The *Chicago Record-Herald* pointed out that the Philippines "remain tariff free only so long as Congress refrains from imposing a tariff." The "ultimate effect" of the "acrobatic" Justice Brown's opinions was to leave "no essential difference between him and his four associates who support the government at all points." The paper believed the "stronger reasoning" to be with "the judges who believe that uniform federal laws should apply to all American territory, and the subject still remains to be discussed as a question of policy before Congress. That body will find itself in a very peculiar and embarrassing position if it takes to enacting discriminating tariff legislation for the Philippines." The *Record-Herald* then asked: "If not for the Philippines, why not for any other territory of the United States?" And, "If for any other territory why not for any separate state of the Union?"

The *Philadelphia Record* also took a grim view of the Court's two December decisions. It noted that the justices, once again, "do not agree among themselves, and the people of the United States . . . cannot be expected to understand the why and wheretofore." The *Record* also thought that legislation would have to settle matters: "Congress will be obliged to turn its attention to legislation for the Philippines, since the military authority of the Administration to govern and make laws for the archipelago has ceased to exist," the *Record* wrote in an editorial on December 4, 1901.

It was right. That summer, Congress passed an organic act for the Philippines — the Act of July 1, 1902.

———

The Supreme Court's decision in *Neely v. Henkel*, a ruling on a Cuban case that some scholars include among the *Insular Cases* (see "A Note on the *Insular Cases*" at the end of the book), stands as a contrast to the decisions on the United States' other island acquisitions in the aftermath of the Spanish-American War. Unlike the cases involving Puerto Rico, the Philippines, and Hawai'i, *Neely v. Henkel* applied to Cuba, which Spain had relinquished to the United States but not "ceded" to the United States as were the other island territories by the terms of the Treaty of Paris.

Neely v. Henkel — there were actually two cases by this name, the second being decided on the basis of the first — concerned Cuba's request for the extradition of Charles F. W. Neely. Neely, a resident of New York, was charged with embezzling $14,000 from the Cuban post office during the U.S. occupation of Cuba. William Henkel, U.S. marshal for the Southern District of New York, had arrested Neely, and Neely sought his release. Attorneys for Neely and the U.S. government argued the case before the U.S. Supreme Court on December 10 and 11, 1900 — only a week before the Court began hearing the arguments in *Goetze v. United States* and the other *Insular Cases*. The Court issued its decision in *Neely v. Henkel* on January 14, 1901, in the midst of hearing the arguments on the other *Insular Cases* of 1901.

John D. Lindsay and De Lancey Nicoll of Nicoll, Anable & Lindsay represented Neely. Lindsay and Nicoll contended that Neely could not be extradited to Cuba, since Article I of the Treaty of Paris provided that Spain was to relinquish all claim to Cuba and that the island was "to be occupied by the United States . . . so long as such occupation shall last, assume and discharge the obligations that may under *international law* result from the fact of its occupation, for the protection of life and property" (emphasis added). Since there was no extradition treaty between the United States and Cuba, Neely's lawyers argued, the U.S. government had no grounds in international law on which to proceed.

Neely's attorneys argued that Cuba was already an independent republic, so the U.S. occupation of Cuba constituted a violation of international law. The U.S. occupation of Cuba effectively constituted war
against Cuba, the attorneys argued, since it went beyond the terms of
the treaty. But because only Congress had the power to declare war,
the U.S. occupation of Cuba beyond the terms of the Treaty of Paris
was contrary to the U.S. Constitution. The attorneys further pointed
out that the Cuban judicial system as it then existed stood in violation
of the Sixth, Seventh, and Eighth Amendments of the U.S. Constitution were Neely to be extradited to Cuba.

Assistant Attorney General James M. Beck presented the U.S. government's argument. Beck contended that the United States was only
temporarily occupying Cuba, by the terms of the Treaty of Paris and
consistent with the United States' rights as a belligerent and as a party
to a treaty of peace. The United States had the power to extradite
Neely, Beck claimed, because of "the inherent right of the United
States as a sovereign nation to extradite a fugitive criminal to a foreign
country." The U.S. government was "justified" to remove a criminal
"from one part of the United States to a territory which is subject to
our jurisdiction, and over which we are for the time being exercising
full sovereignty." Cuba was a part of the United States "internationally." But "constitutionally it was not."

In addition, Beck pointed out that the Cuban government was
never recognized prior to U.S. occupation, that the United States
never recognized the Cuban insurgents as belligerents, and that the
clause in the Teller Amendment "that the Government of the United
States hereby recognize the republic of Cuba as the true and lawful
government of the island" had been stricken out before it had been
passed by Congress and signed by President McKinley. Cuba was thus
territory of the United States only temporarily, and the United States
consequently had the power to extradite Neely.

Beck further noted that although the courts in Cuba were military
courts, they were *civil courts* set up by the U.S. military government;
they were not *courts-martial*. The judges presiding over the courts
were not military officers, and the law they were to apply was not U.S.
martial law but Cuban law.

Neely's lawyers submitted a supplemental brief that argued that if
what Beck had argued was true, then Cuba was not "foreign." And if

Cuba were not foreign, then the Act of June 6, 1900, did not authorize Neely's extradition. Furthermore, if Cuba were "land appertaining to the United States" as a temporary territory by reason of conquest and treaty provision, then all agencies of the U.S. government (per *Callan v. Wilson*) had to "observe constitutional limitations" with respect to "the fundamental rights of life, liberty, and property."

Justice Harlan presented the unanimous opinion for the Supreme Court.

Harlan argued that the 1898 Treaty of Paris, the Teller Amendment, and McKinley's presidential addresses had all established Cuba as a foreign nation. Harlan quoted McKinley's address of December 6, 1898, in which he stated that "until there is complete tranquility in [Cuba] and a stable government inaugurated, military occupation will be continued." The U.S. pledge of Cuban independence, moreover, "is of the highest honorable obligation, and must be sacredly kept," as Harlan quoted McKinley. Harlan further noted that by the Act of June 6, 1900, Congress had extended the powers under the Treaty of Paris, including the right of extradition to Cuba of "those who, having committed crimes there, fled to this country to escape arrest, trial and punishment." For Harlan, "it was competent for Congress, by legislation, to enforce or give efficacy to the provisions of the treaty made by the United States and Spain with respect to the island of Cuba and its people." The simple facts that Cuba was a foreign nation and that Neely was a U.S. citizen, Harlan argued, did not mean that the Act of June 6 was unconstitutional by depriving Neely of constitutional protection.

Harlan concluded that the establishment of U.S. occupation in Cuba granted by the Treaty of Paris did not contradict the Teller Amendment's provision for a free and independent Cuba. He ruled that Congress and the executive could, through the powers of joint resolutions, duly passed legislation, and official addresses, determine the status of another state. Specifically, the United States could exercise temporary — and virtually open-ended — control over areas outside the United States. Neely had to be returned to Cuba.

The newspapers in the states uniformly applauded the Supreme Court's decision.

Although the Court unanimously decided *Neely v. Henkel*, Harlan's ruling stands at odds with his dissent in *Downes* just months later; with Justice Brown's opinions in *De Lima* and *Dooley I*, both of which Harlan joined; and with Chief Justice Fuller's lead opinion in *Fourteen Diamond Rings* and Fuller's dissent in *Dooley II*, both of which Harlan also joined. Whereas Harlan held in the other *Insular Cases* of 1901 that presidential pronouncements and executive actions — namely, the imposition of the wartime tariffs and the tariff of the Foraker Act — were *contrary* to the uniformity clause and the prohibition against taxes on exports (per the decision in *Dooley v. United States I*), Harlan was willing to accept them as justification for the U.S. government's authority to extradite Neely to Cuba. It is not clear, then, how Harlan could hold that Cuba was *foreign* for the purpose of extradition and yet still be subject to U.S. legislation and sovereign power, as James E. Kerr observes in his study of the *Insular Cases*. Harlan's strict constructionism, manifest in the other *Insular Cases* of 1901, was not in evidence in *Neely v. Henkel*.

Contributing to the Court's decision may have been the size of the scandal caused by Neely. Solicitor General Richards commented that Neely's crime "became a scandal that attracted the attention of the civilized world and gravely compromised the honor and good name of this Government. The public interests, as well as the fair fame of the Republic," Richards stated, "imperatively require that the said Neely shall be extradited to Cuba with the least possible delay. . . . Undue delay in bringing him to justice would further compromise this Government and injure it in the estimation of the Cuban people and of the world at large."

Or, Harlan and the Court may have gone along with the U.S. government's position because they regarded the question of Cuban independence as being constitutionally settled by reason of the Teller Amendment and the president's pronouncements, no matter the reality of the United States' sovereign authority over Cuba. Whatever the reason, Harlan and the Court's unanimous decision in *Neely v. Henkel* contrasts with the positions of Harlan, Fuller, Brewer, and Peckham in the other closely decided 1901 tariff cases — so much so that Justice White referred to *Neely v. Henkel* as precedent for his concurring opinion in *Downes v. Bidwell*.

———

Three members of the Supreme Court, Justices Shiras, Brewer, and Peckham, did not contribute written opinions to any of the ten *Insular Cases* of 1901, even if the record shows that they actively participated in the oral arguments before the Court. But their positions on the tariff issue still mattered greatly, given the divisions on the Court over how the Constitution was to apply to the new island territories.

George Shiras Jr. was born in Pittsburgh in 1832, the son of a wealthy brewer. He was reared as a Presbyterian and grew up on an orchard after the age of five, where his father resided after making an early retirement. Shiras attended Ohio University, transferred to Yale, where he graduated Phi Beta Kappa, and then enrolled in the Yale Law School. He made a very successful career representing the iron and steel industry and the railroad companies of the Pittsburgh area and western Pennsylvania, industries that were booming at the time. In 1881, Shiras had a chance to serve in the U.S. Senate, since his politics were independent from those of the Pennsylvania Republican political machine. But he declined to pursue the office, notwithstanding the wishes of the state legislature. Then, when Shiras was sixty years old, with a law practice of thirty-seven years and with no experience on the bench or in political office, President Harrison nominated him to the Supreme Court when Justice Joseph Bradley died in early 1892; Harrison sought a respected member of the Pennsylvania bar and an independent Republican. Shiras, although relatively unknown outside the state, was well regarded in political and legal circles and had important support from Pennsylvania industrialists and Yale alumni. Although Pennsylvania's two Republican senators initially opposed Shiras's appointment, their opposition backfired, and the Senate confirmed Shiras unanimously.

David Josiah Brewer, the nephew of former Supreme Court justice Stephen J. Field, grew up in Wethersfield, Connecticut, in an upper-middle-class family. His father, a Congregationalist minister, served as a chaplain following missionary work in Smyrna, Georgia, where Brewer was born in 1837. Brewer attended Wesleyan and Yale before reading law with his uncle David Dudley Field (the brother of Stephen Field) and attending the Albany Law School. Brewer then headed west to Leavenworth, Kansas, where he was elected judge for Leavenworth County in 1862. Voters proceeded to elect Brewer, a social conservative and devout Christian, to the Kansas Supreme Court in 1870 and reelected him in 1876 and 1882. The following year President Arthur appointed Brewer to the Eighth Circuit Court of Appeals. President Harrison appointed Brewer to the Supreme Court in late 1889.

Brewer was yet another economic libertarian, much like his uncle Justice Field. Indicatively, Brewer wrote the lead opinion in *In Re Debs* (1895), a case involving Socialist leader Eugene V. Debs in which the Court upheld President Cleveland's emergency action to end the great Pullman strike of 1894 and denied Debs's petition for habeas corpus. "The strong arm of the National Government," Brewer held, "may be put forth to brush away all obstructions to the freedom of interstate commerce or the transportation of the mails." Brewer showed "unvarying opposition . . . to the most minimal restrictions upon freedom of contract," one observer commented. Indeed, Brewer had earlier agreed to the Supreme Court's majority opinions in the *Income Tax Case*, the *Sugar Trust Case*, and *Allgeyer v. Louisiana* (1897).

Although Brewer did not write an opinion of his own in the *Insular Cases*, Republican newspapers nonetheless scolded him for siding with the Democrats and the anti-imperialists in the May and December decisions. After the May decisions, Brewer wrote Fuller to be sure to "stay on the court till we over-throw this unconstitutional idea of colonial supreme control." Later, Brewer would oppose the Roosevelt administration's wresting of Panama from Colombia.

Justice Rufus Wheeler Peckham, another believer in laissez-faire government, came from a respected, upper-class Protestant family from Albany, New York, where his father served as Albany County district attorney, on the New York Supreme Court and Court of Appeals, and as a Democratic member of Congress. The son followed the father. Peckham read law in his father's office, became active in Albany County politics, and served as Albany Country district attorney in 1869. He was elected to the New York Supreme Court in 1883, and in 1886 was elected to the New York Court of Appeals, the state's highest court. Peckham represented railroads and other corporations in his private practice, but was also an active party man. As a reform-minded Republican he opposed the Tammany Hall and Tweed Ring Democrats. President Cleveland nominated Peckham to the Supreme Court after William Hornblower and Frederic Coudert (the father) both declined the appointment. Although the Senate, led by David Hill (R-N.Y.), had previously refused to confirm Hornblower's nomination, Hill, who had led the opposition, had no objection to Peckham's appointment to the bench. Peckham received the nomination in December 1895.

Peckham is best known as the author of the doctrine of "substantive due process." Although the idea that the Fourteenth Amendment amounted to an absolute protection of economic liberty dates from Justice Field's dissents in the *Slaughterhouse Cases* (1873) and *Munn v. Illinois* (1877), it was Peckham who first combined in writing the Fourteenth Amendment's right to due process and the freedom of contract. Peckham articulated the substantive due process doctrine in his opinion for a unanimous Court in *Allgeyer v. Louisiana* (1897). He stated that the right under the Fourteenth Amendment guaranteeing due process to citizens of all the states applied also to a person's right to be "free in the enjoyment of all his facilities," including the right "to enter into all contracts which may be proper, necessary, and essential" for his or her purposes. This, as the judicial scholar Melvin Urofsky points out, "sanctified" commercial relations with constitutional protection. Peckham expressed the doctrine again in a dissent in a Utah case (*Holden v. Hardy*, 1898), where he challenged the police power of the Utah government to regulate mining conditions. Later, Peckham wrote the controversial opinion of the Court in *Lochner v. New York* (1905). In the minds of Peckham and the other justices in the *Lochner* majority, the Fourteenth Amendment protected persons in their right to contract; and bakeshop owners and employees did not stand as exceptions to this principle.

———

The decisions of the *Insular Cases* of 1901 leave a remarkable record.

In *Downes v. Bidwell* the Supreme Court ruled that Congress could, through its plenary authority, govern territory of the United States contrary to constitutional provisions — in this case the uniformity clause of taxes, imposts, and duties. In *De Lima v. Bidwell* (as well as in *Goetze v. United States, Dooley v. United States I,* and *Armstrong v. United States*), the Court ruled that the executive branch did not have power to tax trade between the territories and states following the treaty annexing the island territories to the United States. The same applied to the imposition of tariffs on the recently annexed territory of Hawai'i (*Crossman v. United States*). Then the Court established that the McKinley administration *did* have the executive authority to tax imports into militarily occupied regions from ports in the several states prior to the island territories being officially annexed to the

United States (*Dooley v. United States I* and *Armstrong v. United States*). And in *Huus v. New York & Porto Rico Steamship Co.*, the Supreme Court held that trade with Puerto Rico, Hawai'i, and other U.S. territories was coastal trading for the purposes of U.S. maritime shipping laws.

Then, in *Fourteen Diamond Rings v. United States*, the Court held that the same principle of the *De Lima* ruling applied to the Philippines, despite the guerrilla war. But in *Dooley v. United States II*, the Court confirmed that trade to the territories from the states was, for the purposes of the Constitution, no different than trade into the states from the territories. Congress could therefore act in seeming violation of the uniformity clause and the export clause, under its authority from the territories clause, and it could also contravene the prohibitions against taxation on exports from the states and against favoring one port over another with respect to interstate trade.

In sum, the *Insular Cases* of 1901— and especially the seminal case of *Downes v. Bidwell*— represented a continuation of the tariff battles that had been fought in Congress over the Foraker Act, even between different parts of the Republican Party, centered on the conflict between beet-sugar growers, domestic cane-sugar growers, and other protectionist interests on the one hand, and the McKinley administration, the Sugar Trust, free-trade interests, and foreign investors on the other hand. So when the Foraker Act passed Congress, Coudert Brothers and other law firms took the matter to the courts, where a decision by the U.S. Supreme Court stood as the final opportunity for the establishment of free trade between Puerto Rico, the other new territories, and the states. The *Insular Cases*— or, as they were also called, the "Porto Rican cases"— mattered so much precisely because they were about much more than just the Foraker Act or Puerto Rico. As White remarked after the decisions in *Downes* and the other cases of May 1901, "Why, if we had decided them that way [i.e., that the Constitution fully applied to the new island territories], this country would not have been a nation!"

But in *Neely v. Henkel*— though chronologically preceding the other *Insular Cases*— a unanimous Court held that Cuba, although under full U.S. sovereign control, could be treated as a foreign country for constitutional purposes. Cuba may have been territory "appertaining" to the United States, but it had neither been incorporated into the United States, nor had the Constitution been extended to Cuba. Congress and the executive could therefore treat Cuba as being wholly foreign to the United States.

In view of these closely decided, controversial, and complex decisions — with the exception of *Neely v. Henkel* and *Huus v. New York* — any single change in personnel could potentially alter the delicate balance on the Court. The *Downes* decision "can hardly be considered final," John G. Carlisle noted, and many commentators agreed with him. "A decision even of the Supreme Court of the United States which becomes a law by the *mere turning of the finger of one man out of nine* cannot be regarded as a very satisfactory judgment," commented the *Seattle Daily Times* on May 28, 1901 (emphasis in original). "A single change in the Supreme Court bench would completely upset this opinion," it added. The *New York Herald*'s headline similarly proclaimed, "The *Downes* Decision Rested on a Foundation of Sand." The *Herald* remarked that "no great constitutional opinion of that tribunal has rested on a basis more insecure . . . [one that is] opposed by the largest minority of which the Court is capable. . . . [E]ven the majority could not agree in the reasoning by which it was reached." And the *St. Louis Post-Dispatch* commented, "The decision . . . [in *Downes*] will probably emphasize and intensify rather than settle the political issues arising from the acquisition of our new possessions."

So we have to look beyond 1901 — especially since a number of constitutional provisions remained to be tested. Among the "questions not decided" discussed by political and legal experts, the U.S. attorney general, and journalists were trial by jury, indictment by grand jury in cases of felony, the Fifteenth Amendment's right to vote, U.S. citizenship, and whether Puerto Rico would ever qualify for statehood and "all the privileges . . . warranted by the protection of [the] United States flag."

CHAPTER 6

Commerce, Citizenship, and Other Questions

All the insular dependencies of the Union and Alaska are probably destined never to be incorporated into the Union as States, because it is best for them and for the Union that they should permanently remain in a relationship of dependence on the Union. . . . Under a well-balanced and expert administration by the American Union, as their Imperial State, they can have that distinct community life which their isolated position makes necessary.

ALPHEUS SNOW, *Administration of Dependencies,* 1902

The Supreme Court's ten decisions of 1901 were slender reeds on which to support the United States' expansionist policies and control of the new island territories. *Slender* because a majority on the Court fully upheld the U.S. government in only three of the cases (*Downes v. Bidwell, Dooley v. United States II,* and *Neely v. Henkel*), and because the Court split five-to-four in eight of the ten cases. *Reeds* — plural — because no one clear doctrine emerged from the *Insular Cases* of 1901. No single position, not Brown's extension theory, not White's Incorporation Doctrine, and not Fuller and Harlan's doctrine of the Constitution applying *ex proprio vigore,* achieved the support of even five justices on the bench.

Then, too, it was not clear what other new areas the United States was going to annex. As Attorney General Griggs had argued in the U.S. government's brief in *Goetze v. United States* — and was quoted by the chief justice in his dissent in *Downes* — the U.S. government needed broad powers, since it might in the future acquire "Egypt and the Soudan [*sic*], or a section of Central Africa, or a spot in the Antarctic Circle, or a section of the Chinese Empire." (The latter reference turned out to be well-founded: McKinley had ordered 5,000 U.S. troops into the mainland of China in 1900 on the pretext of protecting U.S. lives and property, although they were actually there to suppress the Boxer Rebellion and head off the Russian colonization of

Manchuria.) The United States might well acquire more land around the world, since Griggs, President Roosevelt — who took office only three and a half months after the May 27 decisions, following the death of President McKinley — Secretary Root, Secretary of State John Hay, Senator Lodge, and other nationalists saw the United States as part of an expanding empire. By this logic, the United States had to be free to treat additional areas and their inhabitants as the White House and Congress judged best.

Observers outside the government also thought further U.S. expansion likely. "It is clear that the United States may, from its peculiar trade relations and from the growth of its foreign commerce, be led at any moment into the acquisition of control of additional territory," James Young of the University of Pennsylvania wrote in early 1902, "whether for the purposes of protecting trade routes, the opening of new routes, the guarantee of markets, or the preservation of order." John G. Carlisle of Curtis Mallet remarked, "The possession of the Philippine Islands, Cuba, Hawaii, the Caroline Islands, the Ladrone Islands [i.e., Marianas Islands] and Puerto Rico will not satisfy the aggressive spirit of imperialism; in fact, it will, according to the uniform experience of other nations, stimulate the desire for new acquisitions and we will almost certainly go on." U.S. expansion would continue "unless checked by the armed opposition of other powers, until we have fastened upon the United States a black and yellow horde of conscript citizens to debauch the suffrage and sap the foundations of our free institutions."

With further expansion possible and with many constitutional questions left resolved with respect to the new territorial inhabitants, the issues of the *Insular Cases* were still very much on the table. As the *New York Herald* wondered, can the *Downes* decision "be said to settle even the one special point it decides, to say nothing of the momentous issues it throws into dispute? In short, can it endure permanently and withstand the attacks that time and its own weakness are sure to bring? We think not."

Those in the McKinley administration, other expansionists, and many Republicans may have been gratified by the Supreme Court's decisions in *Downes v. Bidwell* and *Dooley v. United States II*, but they had lost the other cases with the partial exceptions of *Dooley v. United States I* and *Armstrong v. United States*. They could hardly afford to rest on their laurels.

President Roosevelt, Secretary Root, Philippine governor Taft, and Senator Lodge — lawyers all — and other leading Republicans therefore sought to reaffirm and entrench the constitutional status of the United States' new island territories. So when Justice Horace Gray announced his resignation on July 9, 1902 — Gray had suffered a small stroke earlier in the year and would pass away only two months later — Roosevelt wanted to be sure of his first appointment to the U.S. Supreme Court.

Roosevelt and Senator Lodge — the president's close friend, though ten years Roosevelt's senior — selected Oliver Wendell Holmes Jr. for the nomination. Holmes was from Massachusetts, like Horace Gray, sixty-one years old, and chief justice of the Massachusetts Supreme Judicial Court. He was also a celebrated and extremely able writer, a distinguished and thrice-injured Civil War veteran, a Harvard graduate, and, like Lodge and Roosevelt, a member of Harvard's elite Porcellian Club; he was also the class poet. Holmes was from an old, established Boston family and, most famously, the son of Oliver Wendell Holmes, a well-known writer and medical doctor. Following a three-year service in the Union army, Holmes studied law at Harvard and then practiced law with, and became partner in, the Boston firm of Shattuck, Holmes, and Munroe. He was also a member of the "Metaphysical Club," an informal discussion group of intellectual friends, along with William James, John Dewey, and Charles Sanders Peirce. From 1870 to 1873, Holmes edited the *American Law Review*, and he published a set of his essays in the volume *The Common Law* (1881). When Dean C. C. Langdell and President Eliot of Harvard subsequently invited him to become a professor of law, Holmes agreed to take the position. But only months after he started teaching, Holmes accepted a position on the Massachusetts Supreme Judicial Court. In 1899, he became chief justice.

The president had his doubts about Holmes. Although Roosevelt liked Holmes's independence and consideration "for the men who most need that consideration" — notwithstanding the criticisms from "big railroad men and other members of large corporations" — he was worried about Holmes's position on the island territories, as he confided to "Cabot" — who was also chairman of the Senate Committee on the Philippines — in a letter of July 10, 1902:

The majority of the Court, who have . . . upheld the policies of President McKinley and the Republican party in Congress, have rendered a great service to mankind and to this nation. The minority — a minority so large as to lack but one vote of being a majority — have stood for such reactionary folly as would have hampered well-nigh hopelessly this people in doing efficient and honorable work for the national welfare, and for the welfare of the islands themselves, in Porto Rico and the Philippines. No doubt they have possessed excellent motives and without doubt they are men of excellent personal character; but this no more excuses them than the same conditions excused the various upright and honorable men who took part in the wicked folly of secession in 1860 and 1861.

Now I should like to know that Judge Holmes was in entire sympathy with our views, that is with our views and mine and Judge Gray's. . . . I should hold myself as guilty of an irreparable wrong to the nation if I should put in his place any man who was not absolutely sane and sound on the great national policies for which we stand in public life.

Lodge promptly reassured the president that Holmes was safe on expansion and a good Republican: "I am absolutely for Holmes unless he should be adverse on the Porto Rican cases, which I am informed he is not," he wrote the president on June 5, 1902. So Roosevelt arranged a private meeting with Holmes at the president's home in Oyster Bay, Long Island, to discuss the appointment. During the visit, on July 25, Roosevelt offered Holmes the job, and Holmes accepted.

Chief Justice Fuller congratulated the president on the choice of Holmes. "I am delighted that you approve my choice," Roosevelt wrote back to Fuller. "You may rest assured that I shall do my best to give you fit associates on the bench."

Only months later, however, the president found himself in almost exactly the same position. George Shiras announced his decision to resign, effective February 1903, and Roosevelt again had to replace one of the justices on the side of the Supreme Court's narrow majority in *Downes*. The president immediately thought of Taft, whose political views and judgment he greatly respected. "You exactly appreciated the situation caused by the Supreme Court decisions and the reasons for the course we took," Roosevelt wrote Taft in September 1902. "It is delightful to have such an understanding without making explanations. Explanations by wire go into the record which Congress promptly calls for and makes public and then the explanations are likely to defeat themselves."

Roosevelt wanted to nominate Taft, but the president remained "puzzled" over the appointment; he needed Taft in the Philippines as much as he wanted him on the bench. "My own feeling is that you had better take the judgeship," he telegraphed "Will" on October 18. "Nothing can be more important than to strengthen in every way the Supreme Court. But I have immense confidence in your judgment and in your knowledge of the situation in the islands and of the men who can take your place; and I shall accept your decisions as wise whichever way it comes. Please cable me as soon as you make up your mind." On October 26, 1902, Roosevelt telegraphed Taft once more: "On January first there will be a vacancy on the Supreme Court, to which I earnestly desire to appoint you. It is in my judgment of utmost importance to get our strongest men on the Court at the very earliest opportunity. No one can quite take your place in the Philippines, but . . . [y]ou can at this juncture do in so far better service on the Supreme Court than any other man."

Taft was grateful for the "Great Honor" shown to him by his "dear President," he replied. But he had to decline because of the "most critical" economic circumstances in the Philippines. Although Roosevelt was "disappointed of course," he was also "at a loss whom to appoint to the bench in the place I meant for you. Everything else must give way to putting in the right man; but I can't make up my mind who *is* the right man" (emphasis in original).

Four weeks later, Roosevelt was no closer to a choice. "I am awfully sorry, old man, but after faithful effort for a month to try to arrange matters on the basis you wanted I find that I shall have to bring you home and put you on the supreme Court. I am very sorry." But Taft decided that he should stay on as Philippine governor. The commissioners and prominent Filipinos had "absolute confidence" in the governor and found him "indispensable," and Taft believed that his departure would have "deplorable effects" on the difficult situation in the Philippines. Roosevelt relented: "All right, you shall stay where you are. I will appoint someone else to the court."

That someone else was former secretary of state William R. Day, who had led the U.S. peace delegation in Paris after the Spanish-American War and who was then serving on the Sixth Circuit Court of Appeals. Day, a Republican from Ohio, grew up in a wealthy Protestant family in the small town of Ravenna, the son of a justice on the Ohio Supreme Court. After studying law at the University of Michigan for a year, Day settled in Canton, Ohio, where he became a successful criminal and trial lawyer, got involved in local politics, and became a close friend of and adviser to William McKinley. When McKinley became president, he appointed Day as first assistant secretary of state. By the spring of 1898, Day was effectively serving as secretary of state in the U.S. government's negotiations with Spain over the Cuban rebellion. McKinley asked Secretary of State Sherman to resign once the war started and in May 1898 promoted Day in his place. Although Day had little enthusiasm for territorial expansion, he cautiously supported the McKinley administration, given his loyalty to the president. When the war ended, McKinley appointed Day to the Sixth Circuit.

"I am sure that Day will make a good judge," Taft telegraphed Roosevelt on January 27, 1903. Day had a "very level head," Taft wrote, and "great common sense"; he was "a good lawyer"; and he was "orthodox on all the questions in which we are interested. He is a loyal man, a safe man, and will never do anything on the bench to discredit the President responsible for his appointment."

Taft's judgment was sound. Oliver Wendell Holmes and William R. Day generally supported the decisions in *Downes* and *Dooley II* in the cases that followed over the next two decades, cases involving other commercial issues and, especially, the application of the due process clauses of the Fifth and Sixth Amendments in criminal proceedings. But the president's two appointees did not always or unambiguously support the Roosevelt administration, and Holmes's and Day's positions on how the Constitution applied to the inhabitants of the United States' new island territories would evolve over time. Roosevelt would later view both appointments as failures.

————

The decisions in the *Insular Cases* of 1901 did not dispose of all revenue questions. Almost exactly three years after the *Downes* decision, on May 31, 1904, the Court issued its decision in an Alaskan revenue case, *Binns* v. *United States*. The plaintiff, Joseph Binns, charged that the license fees charged to those practicing various trades and occupations in Alaska violated the Constitution's uniformity clause because the proceeds of the licensing of the fees for Binns to sell liquor went to the U.S. Treasury (which served as the treasury of Alaska, the territory having no treasury or treasurer of its own).

Justice Brewer ruled for an undivided Court — Harlan took no part in the decision — that Congress and the U.S. government had plenary authority to impose excise taxes or license fees, especially because the revenues were to be used to defray the expenses of administering the territory of Alaska. Such legislative authority came not from Congress's power to tax but from its power over the territories of the United States (Brewer cited the concurring opinions of Justice White and Justice Gray in *Downes v. Bidwell*).

It was "unnecessary to consider the decisions in the *Insular Cases*," Brewer wrote, since, as Justice White said in *Downes v. Bidwell*, Alaska was incorporated and since the act of May 17, 1884, organized as a "civil and judicial district" of the United States. Although the U.S. assistant attorney general was at pains to distinguish license fees from general taxes — since fees were collected for the privilege of doing business and constituted the exercise of "the police power for the regulation and restriction of a dangerous business" — Brewer viewed the license fees as "local taxes" and therefore revenue measures.

Brewer cited Chief Justice Marshall's ruling in *Loughborough v. Blake* in support of the point that Congress could tax the inhabitants of the territories and Washington, D.C., alike: Congress had the power to legislate "as a local legislature" for the District of Columbia and, by implication, for any particular territory of the United States. Congress's imposition of internal taxes on Alaskan trades and occupations did not violate the uniformity clause because of Congress's authority under the territory clause.

What is notable about the decision is that Brewer agreed to allow the imposition of taxes on Alaskan commerce *despite the fact that Alaska was an incorporated territory*, as Christina Duffy Burnett points out. The Incorporation Doctrine thus did not brightly distinguish between Congress's plenary authority over the unincorporated territories and its constitutionally limited power in the incorporated territories, as Burnett astutely observes. Congress had the authority to raise such revenues from license fees, Brewer emphasized, since Brewer and the unanimous Court clearly regarded these revenues as "local taxes" — not unlike those collected for Puerto Rico under the Foraker Act — given that the Alaskan government was unable to pay for itself, even with the revenues from the license fees. But Congress could *not* impose license fees should those revenues accrue to the U.S. Treasury, rather than to the territorial government.

Furthermore, Brewer, joined by Chief Justice Fuller and Justice Peckham, now appeared to abandon the *ex proprio vigore* doctrine of the 1901 *Insular Cases* and to accept the exercise of Congress's plenary power over territories. The chief justice, Brewer, and Peckham now seemed to be moving away from Fuller's earlier dissent in *Dooley II*, away from Carlisle's argument on behalf of the plaintiffs in *Dooley I* and *Dooley II*, and away from Edward Whitney's argument for the second, fuller definition of the United States.

The reason for the inapplicability of the Incorporation Doctrine to Alaskan local license fees was that by May 31, 1904, the Supreme Court no longer had a single doctrine with respect to the island territories, as revealed in the Supreme Court's decisions in *Dorr v. United States* and *Kepner v. United States*, issued on the same day as *Binns* (see chapter 7). In other words, by mid-1904 the Supreme Court had begun to distinguish among the constitutional provisions as they applied to the island territories, rather than applying the Constitution on an "all-or-nothing" basis. All the justices on the bench except for John Marshall Harlan now seemed to agree to such a division of constitutional protections. And the tariff was one area where the justices now seemed to agree. While Puerto Rico achieved free trade with the states a year after *Downes*, in May 1902, the tariff remained controversial in the Philippines. Governor Taft, working on behalf of the Philippines, opposed extending constitutional protections to the islands. "It would be a great mistake" to extend the Constitution to the Philippines, Governor Taft told the House Committee on Insular Affairs on February 25, 1902, "first, because if the Constitution is extended to those islands you will extend the provisions of the Dingley bill to every part of those islands and will build a tariff wall around those islands against the countries with which those islands do most business." Second, "If you extend the Constitution, you probably extend the right to jury trial and you probably extend the right to bear arms. Both of those rights . . . should be withheld from the people until they learn a self-restraint that can only be learned after practice, and the advantage of the example of self-government which, by a gradual course, we hope to give them."

But the president still sought to further reduce the Dingley Tariff as it applied to the Philippines. Roosevelt was "bitterly disappointed by the failure of Congress to pass the bill for the further reduction in the Philippine tariff," he wrote Taft on April 22, 1903. "It is most unfortunate that sugar and tobacco should be the articles which agricultural states, notably of the west, feel that they have an interest in protecting." Congress, however, refused to reduce trade by more than 25 percent below the levels of the Dingley Tariff in the Act of July 1, 1902 (in contrast to the 85 percent reduction in the Foraker Act). In fact, the Philippines would not get any significant relief from the tariff until the passage of the Payne-Aldrich Tariff of 1909, which allowed for free trade up to a set quota, depending on the product.

In addition, Democrats and western Republicans in Congress, seeking to discourage investment in large-scale commercial agriculture in the Philippines, also blocked Roosevelt's and Taft's plans for encouraging foreign investors by restricting the size of landholdings and the sale of Philippine public lands. "The requirements that *no corporation shall own more than 2500 acres stops absolutely the investment of new capital in the sugar industry and in the tobacco industry*," the Philippine commission wrote Secretary Root in its November 1902 report (emphasis added). These were "burdensome restrictions [in the Act of July 1, 1902] upon the investment of capital in lands and mines in these islands." The commissioners thus recommended that the "limitations ought to be removed entirely or be increased so as to allow the acquisition of at least 25,000 acres of land." (The Roosevelt administration especially sought control over the Friar lands, owned by the Catholic Church and amounting to about 400,000 acres of the richest land in the Philippines, located among the different islands.) Congress, however, would not budge; members were worried about new competition arising in the Philippines that could undermine existing domestic sugar producers and threaten the well-being of those Americans in the sugar industry and other sectors of the economy.

As a consequence of the stalemate between the Roosevelt White House and Congress over the tariff, the Court once more had to adjudicate the tariff issue in the Philippines — one year after the *Binns* decision, and the first Philippine case since *Fourteen Diamond Rings*. In *Lincoln v. United States* and *Warner, Barnes & Co. v. United States*, the plaintiffs, Henry W. Peabody & Co. (Frederick W. Lincoln, the plaintiff, was a principal in Peabody) and Warner, Barnes & Co., Ltd., a British firm, challenged the U.S. government's collection of duties on goods shipped from New York into Manila between April 11, 1899, the date of the peace treaty, and October 25, 1901. Lawyers for Coudert Brothers filed suit on behalf of Peabody & Co. and Warner, Barnes & Co., and the U.S. Supreme Court heard and decided the two cases as a single case.

Solicitor General Henry Hoyt, the successor to Richards, argued that the duties levied under the authority of a presidential order of July 12, 1898, were a military necessity, since the suppression of the Philippine rebellion demanded the use of the war powers. Hoyt contrasted the "settled and serious rebellion" against the United States then taking place in the Philippines to the circumstances of *Dooley I* (which determined that the military tariff was invalid in Puerto Rico in that same period, since the United States had "title and peaceful possession and there was no military necessity") and the *Fourteen Diamond Rings* case (which determined that the Philippines were "domestic territory, notwithstanding the insurrection, in title and in possession").

On April 3, 1905, Justice Holmes presented the Court's unanimous opinion. Holmes observed that the presidential order of July 1898 establishing the tariffs made reference to the war with Spain only, and *not* to the Filipino insurrection, which did not begin until six months later. The presidential order, Holmes wrote, was not "a power in blank for any military occasion which might turn up in the future. It was a regulation for and during an existing war, referred to as definitely as it has been named." The Supreme Court's ruling in *Fourteen Diamond Rings* therefore applied; the Philippine insurrection was not "of sufficient gravity to give to the Islands the character of foreign countries within the meaning of a tariff act," in contrast to the circumstances in *United States v. Rice* — where the Supreme Court had ruled that Castine could be treated as a foreign port for tariff purposes, since Britain actually occupied it during the War of 1812.

The decisions in *Lincoln; Warner, Barnes* attracted little notice, only brief pieces in the *New York Daily Tribune* and *New York Times*.

But Holmes's ruling disclosed the Court's now-unanimous endorsement of the earlier split decisions in *Fourteen Diamond Rings* and *Dooley I:* Justices White and Brown, together with Day and Holmes in place of Justices Shiras and Gray, joined the majority to protect commerce against the executive branch's imposed tariff. And Holmes and Day, like the other seven justices, rejected the Roosevelt administration's claims of military necessity.

The rejection did not go unnoticed. Philippine governor Taft privately wrote Justice Brewer of his displeasure: the decision advantaged "a lot of Englishmen who had been at the bottom of the [Filipino] insurrection." Brewer politely wrote back to Taft, effectively avoiding the issue and remarking that Chief Justice Fuller, Justice Harlan, Justice Peckham, and he "had paid no attention to the case at all and let the other five run it." Taft answered, then "certainly the other five ran it into the ground."

Taft and the Roosevelt White House wanted a rehearing of *Lincoln; Warner, Barnes.* The U.S. solicitor general and attorney general drafted petitions and presented them to the Court, which agreed to rehear the case on January 18 and 19, 1906. In the rehearing, the U.S. attorneys contended that Congress had, in fact, already "approved, ratified, and confirmed" the president's executive orders and the actions of the Philippine Commission to impose a war tariff by passing the Spooner Amendment of March 2, 1901, and the Act of July 1, 1902. "The most obvious distinction between the status of Porto Rico and the Philippines, after cession is in the fact that Port Rico was at the time of cession in full peaceable possession, while a state of war had continued in the Philippines," Secretary Root wrote Taft in a telegraph of June 8, 1901. Congress had therefore knowingly ratified the continuation of the president's war powers, given that the Philippine insurrection was already under way in March 1901 and July 1902. It was up to the Supreme Court to settle "the question whether Congress ratified the collection of the sums sought in these suits," the U.S. attorneys argued.

On May 28, 1906, the Supreme Court issued its decision in the rehearing of *Lincoln; Warner, Barnes.* Chief Justice Fuller wrote the lead opinion this time, joined by six other justices, in which he upheld the previous ruling. Fuller observed that while Congress may have *appeared* to ratify the Philippine war tariffs in the "ambiguous language" of the Act of July 1902, Congress needed to do so *explicitly* if it wanted to approve of tariffs on goods imported into the Philippines — and not to simply lump these particular wartime tariffs together with the normal taxes paid on foreign goods imported into the Islands. "The instances are many," Fuller commented, "where Congress out of abundant caution has ratified what it did not need, or was afterwards found not to have needed ratification." Congress could have done so here. The chief justice further noted that *Dooley I* had already established "the right to levy duties . . . on goods brought from the United States ceased on the exchange of ratifications [with the Treaty with Spain]."

Justice McKenna dissented, joined by Justice White. McKenna wrote that he had previously erred by adhering to stare decisis — that is, the precedent of *Fourteen Diamond Rings*. McKenna was now convinced that Congress *had* approved of the tariffs imposed on the whiskey and other goods shipped from New York to the Philippines when it passed the Act of July 1, 1902.

In short, the Supreme Court supported the application of the uniformity clause in the absence of specific legislation to impose taxes (and thereby superseding the application of the clause in the territories). Though the Philippines may have been unincorporated, firms doing business with the islands could not be discriminated against, notwithstanding the U.S. government's war powers or Congress's seeming intent per the Spooner Amendment and Act of July 1, 1902. Although a clear majority on the Court still rejected the U.S. government's war powers argument and still refused to defer to Congress, the rare rehearing resulted in two justices changing their positions to support the U.S. government. The consequence of the Court's decision was that the U.S. government had to return about $8 million to Coudert Brothers' clients and other trading companies.

———

The U.S. attorney general who argued unsuccessfully for the U.S. government in *Lincoln* received some consolation: on December 17, 1906, President Roosevelt appointed William H. Moody to the Supreme Court (after U.S. senator and former attorney general Philander Knox and William Howard Taft — again — rejected the nomination) to succeed Justice Brown, who decided to retire.

Moody was a Massachusetts lawyer, politician, member of Congress, secretary of the navy, and U.S. attorney general. He was born in 1853 in Newbury, Massachusetts, to an upper-class Episcopalian family. He was firmly Republican and a supporter of U.S. expansion (and a big baseball fan). It also happened that Moody was a good friend and confidant of President Roosevelt; both were vigorous outdoorsmen and frequently rode horses together in Rock Creek Park in Washington, D.C., and they had also traveled together to the American West in April and May 1903. As a member of Congress, moreover, Moody had led a delegation to Cuba in 1901 to secure the U.S. naval base on Guantánamo Bay, and as navy secretary, he had established the U.S. naval base on Subic Bay in the Philippines. Moody tempered his nationalism with progressive positions on social issues, however — with what some saw as radicalism — of his willingness to prosecute business trusts and support organized labor.

Once the government lost the rehearing of *Lincoln*; *Warner, Barnes,* Taft went to Congress for legislation to allow the U.S. government to collect the duties on imports levied under the executive order of July 12, 1898, lasting until the passage of the Act of July 1, 1902. "There is very grave danger," Taft wrote Edgar D. Crumpacker (R-Ind.) of the House Committee on Insular Affairs on June 25, 1906, "that under the decision of the Supreme Court and its construction of Section 2 of the Act of July 1st, 1902, claims may be successfully presented and judgment obtained for the whole fifteen million dollars or more collected and expended in governing the Philippines for two years." Taft thought that there was "not the slightest real equity existing in favor of these elements," and that if Congress could "in any way defeat these claims, it should do so."

Congress complied with Taft's and the administration's wishes. On June 30, 1906, it passed legislation that now made the unconstitutionally extracted duties legal. Although both Peabody & Co. and Warner, Barnes & Co. were entitled to keep their recovered moneys, Congress pulled the rug out from other companies — and other clients of Coudert Brothers — who were suing or in a position to sue to retrieve their duties (the U.S. government had collected a total of about $3 million from Philippine trade with the states). Coudert Brothers again brought suit, challenging the new law as being unconstitutional because it was retroactive legislation and therefore prohibited under the due process clause. The Supreme Court took the case on appeal, and the Court decided *United States v. Heinszen & Co.* on May 27, 1907.

Justice White, who had dissented in the rehearing of *Lincoln, Warner, Barnes*, wrote the Court's opinion for the six-to-two majority which upheld the U.S. government. White argued that the new law was *not* a violation of the right to due process or an illegal taking of property. The Court had already established Congress's plenary authority over the territories in the preceding *Insular Cases*. Congress could therefore rewrite the tariff laws as they applied to trade with the Philippines if it so chose.

Justice Harlan added a short concurring opinion in which he argued that Congress's act should simply be interpreted as the withdrawal of the right of the U.S. government to be sued over its collection of duties. Justices Brewer and Peckham dissented without an opinion; Justice Moody, who had not been present for the oral argument in the cases, did not take part.

With its decision in *United States v. Heinszen*, the Supreme Court once more acknowledged Congress's authority over revenue questions, consistent with its rulings in *Downes v. Bidwell, Dooley* v. *United States II*, and *Binns v. United States*. Although the Court had previously supported the notion that the Philippines were part of the United States for tariff purposes, it deferred to Congress and the executive branch when confronted with their combined resolution to impose duties on trade between the Philippines and the several states.

The personnel on the Supreme Court changed considerably over the next several years. Justice Peckham died two years later, in October 1909; Justice Brewer died on March 28, 1910; Chief Justice Fuller died on July 4, 1910; Justice Moody resigned for health reasons (acute rheumatism) on November 20, 1910; and Justice Harlan died on October 14, 1911. As a consequence, President Taft, although only a one-term president, had the privilege of being able to fill six seats on the Supreme Court — five associate justices and one chief justice.

President Taft appointed Horace Lurton in place of Peckham. The Senate confirmed Lurton a week later, on December 13, 1909. Taft appointed Charles Evan Hughes in October 1910 in place of Brewer, and in December 1910 the president promoted Justice White to chief justice — the first associate justice ever to be promoted to chief justice. In late 1910 Taft appointed Willis Van Devanter and Joseph Lamar as replacements for Justices White and Moody, and the new associate justices took their seats in early January 1911. Taft then appointed Mahlon Pitney in Harlan's place. The only justices left from the Court of *Downes*, *De Lima*, and *Dooley I* and *Dooley II* were Chief Justice White and Justice McKenna.

Horace Harmon Lurton was a former officer in the Confederate army and a prisoner of the Union army, a southern Democrat, and almost sixty-six years old — the oldest appointee until then to take a seat on the U.S. Supreme Court. Lurton was born in Newport, Kentucky, to an upper-middle-class family and served in both the Tennessee and Kentucky Infantries in the Confederate army. After studying law at Cumberland University, Lurton worked in a private practice in Clarksville, Tennessee, served as chancellor of Tennessee's Sixth Chancery Division, and was appointed to the Sixth Circuit Court of Appeals in 1893. Roosevelt, though a Republican, thought well of him: Lurton "is right on the Negro question," the president wrote Lodge on September 4, 1906, when Lurton was earlier being considered for an appointment to the Supreme Court. "He is right on the power of the Federal Government; he is right on the insular business; he is right about corporations; and he is right about labor. On every question that would come before the bench he has so far shown himself to be in much closer touch with the policies in which you and I believe than even White."

Charles Evan Hughes had been governor of New York (1906–1910) and would become a Republican candidate for the presidency (1916), U.S. secretary of state (1921–1925), and chief justice of the Supreme Court (1930–1948). The son of a Baptist minister, Hughes was born in Glens Falls, New York, and graduated from Brown University at the age of nineteen. After attending Columbia Law School and practicing law for several years, Hughes became a professor at Cornell University Law School at the age of twenty-nine. As a result of his efforts as chief counsel of a New York state committee to investigate the insurance industry, an investigation that exposed the corruption in the business and financial world and led to numerous reforms, Hughes was elected governor of New York — defeating William Randolph

Hearst. Hughes's nomination to the Supreme Court in 1910 met with almost universal approval, and he was unanimously approved in the Senate. Although President Taft was going to appoint Hughes as chief justice, six members of the Senate Judiciary Committee at the last moment persuaded Taft to appoint Edward D. White instead.

Willis Van Devanter was born in Marion, Indiana, received his law degree at the University of Cincinnati at the age of twenty-two, and then moved west at the age of twenty-five to practice law. After practicing law for the city of Cheyenne, Wyoming, and the railroads, and after serving as the right-hand man of the territorial governor of Wyoming, Van Devanter was appointed chief justice of the Wyoming territorial Supreme Court at the age of thirty. When Wyoming was admitted as a state in 1890, he became chairman of the state Republican Party and then served on the Eighth Circuit Court of Appeals. Van Devanter was quiet, a skilled negotiator, a tireless worker, and a conservative on most issues. He was also the first of the "Four Horsemen" — one of the four justices to oppose President Franklin D. Roosevelt's New Deal programs.

Joseph Rucker Lamar was a successful corporate lawyer from Augusta, Georgia. He grew up in an upper-middle-class family, briefly studied law at Washington and Lee, served in the Georgia state legislature, and, in 1902, was appointed to the state supreme court. Lamar, who became acquainted with Taft when the president visited Augusta in 1908 and 1909, was highly recommended by retired justice Henry B. Brown and by the president's military aide and mutual friend, Archie Butt. The Senate confirmed Lamar unanimously, even though he was a southern Democrat and not well known outside Georgia. Like other Taft appointees, Lamar was an economic conservative and moderately progressive on business regulation, labor, and a handful of other issues. And like Justice White's promotion to chief justice, Lamar's appointment reflected the post–Civil War reintegration of Southerners in high-ranking positions in the U.S. government.

Taft promoted White to chief justice for several reasons; one was Taft's enthusiasm for White's decisions in the *Insular Cases*. Walter Pratt, a biographer of White as chief justice, observes that White's opinions in these cases attracted Taft because of the leeway the Incorporation Doctrine granted Congress and the U.S. president. Robert Highsaw, another White biographer, agrees: "White's opinions in the *Insular*

Cases . . . demonstrated an implicit flexibility that contrasted sharply with the rigid position taken by Chief Justice Fuller in his dissents."

White's other political and economic views, together with his personality, further commended him to Taft. White was an excellent administrator, particularly good at the social niceties and compromises necessary for smoothing professional dealings; he was adept at handling the growing caseloads; and he was respected by his peers. He was also a hard worker. White wrote 245 opinions between 1900 and 1910, totaling 2,070 pages — an output exceeded only by that of Chief Justice Fuller.

"I bet [President Taft] will appoint Hughes [as chief justice], who has given up a chance of being Republican nominee for the Presidency, but I know nothing," Holmes wrote his English friend Sir Frederick Pollock in late 1910. Holmes added: "I think White who is next in Seniority to Harlan (too old, etc.) the ablest man likely to be thought of." Holmes continued: "I know no first rate man except White. His writing leaves much to be desired, but his thinking is profound." White was also Holmes's closest friend on the Court.

Yet Taft could have easily chosen not to nominate White as chief justice, given that White was a Democrat, a former member of the Confederate army, and a Catholic. White also was older, where the issue of age apparently persuaded Taft not to appoint Elihu Root or Joseph H. Choate to the position, both of whom were also sixty-five at the time. (Harlan recommended that his friend Taft appoint Day as chief justice, calling Day "a first-class lawyer — sagacious, cautious, as firm as a rock, and eminently wise in consultation.") But the president appointed White, the oldest man ever to be appointed chief justice (although Charles Evan Hughes and Harlan Fiske Stone were each subsequently appointed chief justice at older ages). At the same time, White's advanced age worked in the president's favor: Taft had his own long-standing ambition to become chief justice of the U.S. Supreme Court, and had he appointed a much younger man such as Hughes as chief justice — Hughes was then in his forties — Taft would never have had the opportunity to later become chief justice. Toward the end of his presidency, in fact, Taft frequently asked of White's health and of the chief justice's plans for retirement.

Mahlon Pitney grew up in New Jersey, graduated from Princeton in the same class as Woodrow Wilson, practiced law in Dover (N.J.), and then, in 1894, was elected to the New Jersey legislature. In 1900 Pitney became president of the New Jersey Senate; he was appointed to the New Jersey Supreme Court in 1901. Pitney attracted President Taft for his defense of property rights, opposition to organized labor, effectiveness as an associate justice and chancellor, and genial disposition. Taft nominated him on February 12, 1912, and the Senate confirmed him after a rancorous, three-hour debate, with several Republicans crossing the aisle to oppose Pitney's appointment.

The newly constituted Court also had to address issues of property in relation to the Fifth Amendment's taking clause in *Ochoa v. Hernandez*. Justice Pitney presented the Court's unanimous opinion in *Severo Ochoa v. Ana Maria Hernandez y Morales*, decided on June 13, 1913. Pitney ruled that the Court invalidate an order by the military governor of Puerto Rico that had retroactively shortened the period for the acquisition of property by prescription. Pitney ruled that the military governor had denied due process to the defendants (who owned 105 acres of land over which the appellants, Ochoa et al., had obtained fraudulent title), since the governor had ordered a change in the law that had restricted the length of time during which the rightful owners could reclaim their title. The Court agreed with the Puerto Rican Supreme Court that the defendants had been denied due process in the deprivation of their property.

The ruling in *Ochoa v. Hernandez* suggests, then, that due process with respect to the taking of property was within the "fundamental powers" of the Constitution that applied to unincorporated territories. Seen in conjunction with the *Lincoln*; *Warner, Barnes* cases, the *Ochoa* ruling affirmed the Court's protection of property, consistent with its decisions in *De Lima v. Bidwell, Dooley I, Goetze v. United States, Crossman v. United States, Armstrong v. United States*, and *Fourteen Diamond Rings*.

In a later Philippine case, *Board of Public Utility Commissioners v. Ynchausti & Co.* decided on March 1, 1920, the Court denied the application of the Fifth Amendment's takings clause, however.

In *Board v. Ynchausti*, the Supreme Court under Chief Justice White unanimously decided to reverse a lower court ruling and to rule that vessels trading along the Philippine coast and among the islands were obligated to carry Philippine mail without charge. The uncompensated carriage of mail by coastal traders in the Philippines had been the tradition under Spanish law and the practice under both the U.S. military government and the Philippine government set up by the United States in the Act of July 1, 1902. Coastal traders nonetheless sued on the grounds that the Philippine Bill of Rights made the coastal trade's uncompensated carriage of the mails tantamount to the taking of private property.

Chief Justice White did not deny the validity of the Bill of Rights under the Philippine government. He argued, however, that the Bill of Rights had to be applied according to the "nature and character of the powers conferred by Congress upon the government of the Islands." There was "no doubt that the Philippine government had the power to deal with the coastwise trade so as to permit its enjoyment only by those who were willing to comply with the condition as to free mail carriage," White wrote. In fact, legislation passed by the U.S. Congress in 1904 gave the Philippine government explicit power to regulate coastwise trade. Furthermore, the U.S. Congress enjoyed "sovereignty" over the Philippines, given the status of the Philippines as "territory not forming part of the United States because not incorporated therein." White cited *Downes v. Bidwell, Hawaii v. Mankichi, Dorr v. United States, Dowdell v. United States,* and *Ocampo v. United States* — I discuss the last three cases in the next chapter — as establishing the point beyond any doubt.

In short, the Court as a rule protected commerce, but when faced with explicit congressional action, as it did in *United States v. Heinszen* and with the provision of free mail carriage by coastal traders in *Board v. Ynchausti,* deferred to Congress. And the Incorporation Doctrine gave the Supreme Court discretion over how it would decide the U.S. Constitution and its amendments applied to the "nature and character" of the laws governing the island territories.

———

Other cases adjudicated by the Supreme Court after the *Insular Cases* of 1901 provided a fuller vision of how the Constitution applied to the inhabitants of the United States' island territories.

One of the unsettled issues after the cases of 1901 was citizenship. On January 4, 1904, the Court issued its decision in *Gonzalez v. Williams,* a case that concerned the citizenship of a young Puerto

Rican woman, Isabel González — the Supreme Court record anglicized the name — who had been detained by New York port authorities upon entering the United States. Fred Coudert filed suit for her release (and took the case pro bono, González being indigent).

Chief Justice Fuller wrote for the unanimous Court that the immigration laws of the United States extended to Puerto Rico. Since the Treaty of Paris had ceded the island to the United States, Puerto Ricans no longer had allegiance to Spain, and González could thus not be defined as an alien according to the text of the Immigration Act of 1891. Thus she had to be released from detention. But Fuller made it clear that the Court did not establish that Puerto Ricans were U.S. citizens; the ruling only established that González was not an alien according to immigration law, and that she could travel unhindered between the U.S. mainland and Puerto Rico.

As a result, *Gonzalez v. Williams* did nothing to alter the Foraker Act's definition of a "citizen" as simply "a person owing allegiance to a government and entitled to protection from it" — a definition devoid of the notions of membership, representation, or political participation. Puerto Ricans would not be formally classified as "U.S. citizens" until 1917, in fact, and in 1954 Congress wrote into law the new category of persons created by Coudert in his arguments on behalf of González: that of "U.S. national" (although one writer remarked that it might be better to call these persons "appurtezens" in light of the Court's language in its opinions, since "the term citizen has been derived from the word city").

The case attracted little notice. The *New York Daily Tribune* and *New York World* merely summarized the decision in brief stories inside their newspapers.

———

The Court addressed the relationship between the U.S. Supreme Court and the subsidiary territorial courts in *Kent v. Porto Rico*, decided on November 18, 1907. James Kent, who had been convicted of embezzlement by the Supreme Court of Porto Rico, appealed the decision to the U.S. Supreme Court on the grounds that the Puerto Rican court did not have jurisdiction, and that the Fifth Amendment protected against Kent's self-incrimination.

Justice White wrote the unanimous opinion for the Court that the appeal from the Supreme Court of Porto Rico relied on a federal question, and that the plaintiff's assertion of a federal right was "frivolous — that is without color of merit." White held that the U.S. Supreme Court could *not* review the final judgment by the Supreme Court of Porto Rico: the fact that the appellant was prosecuted according to the boundaries of judicial districts set up by Puerto Rican law — boundaries in conflict with those established by the Foraker Act of April 12, 1900 — did not merit the review of the U.S. Supreme Court. White further rejected the argument that the appellant's rights under the Constitution had been denied him, since Kent's confession had been voluntary. As long as Kent's confession was made "without compulsion or undue promise or inducement, and [was] entirely voluntary," then no Fifth Amendment rights had been violated. In short, the issues in *Kent v. Porto Rico* furnished no basis for the Supreme Court to exercise its jurisdiction.

The Supreme Court reaffirmed that the courts in the insular territories, as those in territories more generally, were the creation of Congress and did not come under the jurisdiction of the judiciary and of Article III of the U.S. Constitution.

———

In *Municipality of Ponce v. Roman Catholic Apostolic Church in Porto Rico*, decided on June 1, 1908, the Supreme Court had to rule on whether the Catholic Church was a legal personality and was, in consequence, entitled to the ownership of the local cathedral. The cathedral had been built partly with municipal funds, and the city of Ponce wanted to claim its ownership. The case had clear implications for the fate of the Catholic Church and its property throughout Puerto Rico, the Philippines, and other U.S. territories.

Chief Justice Fuller wrote the unanimous opinion for the Court. He argued that Puerto Rico had been "de facto and de jure American territory" since April 11, 1899, and that the U.S. Supreme Court was bound to recognize the "legal and political institutions" of Puerto Rico according to the terms of Article VIII of the Treaty of Paris.

Fuller accepted the arguments made by the plaintiff's attorneys, Coudert Brothers, on behalf of the Bishop W. Jones and the Catholic Church of Porto Rico that the Catholic Church was a judicial person and that it had been so recognized both internationally and by the

U.S. courts in earlier cases following the Louisiana Purchase. The funds given or allotted to the Catholic Church by the municipal government of Ponce were therefore irrevocable. The town of Ponce could not dispute the legitimate ownership and possession of property by the Catholic Church; the church's ownership was inviolable.

The Supreme Court's decision in *Ponce v. Roman Catholic* reveals that the Court recognized the particular conditions of Puerto Rico in upholding preceding Spanish law on the Roman Catholic Church and endorsing the Supreme Court of Porto Rico's original jurisdiction over conflicts involving Catholic property on the island. As in the "Louisiana" territory and the territory of Orleans, Congress and the Court protected the Catholic Church. In the words of Justice Reed in the U.S. Supreme Court's decision in *Kedroff v. St. Nicholas Cathedral* (1952), "Ours is a government which by the 'law of its being' allows no statute, state or national, that prohibits the free exercise of religion." But there "are occasions" — and here Reed cited *Ponce v. Roman Catholic* — "when civil courts must draw lines between the responsibilities of church and state for the disposition or use of property."

Ponce v. Roman Catholic may thus be seen as an early example of the "multiculturalist defense" — that Puerto Rico's distinctive culture merited protection under an interpretation of the Constitution, contrary to the establishment clause, not unlike some of the earlier exceptions granted to Louisiana.

———

On January 4, 1909, the Court issued its decision on habeas corpus in *Kopel v. Bingham* — the first time it had addressed habeas corpus since *Neely v. Henkel.* Theodore A. Bingham, police commissioner of the city of New York, arrested Abraham Kopel, who had been charged with embezzlement in Puerto Rico and then fled to New York. Kopel sued for a writ of habeas corpus from the New York Supreme Court. Both the New York Supreme Court and the Court of Appeals affirmed the authority of the Puerto Rican governor's warrant. Kopel then appealed to the U.S. Supreme Court on the basis of Article IV, Section 2, Clause 2 ("A Person charged in any state with Treason, Felony, or other Crime, who shall flee from Justice, and be found in another State, shall on demand of the executive Authority of the State from which he fled, be delivered up, to be removed to the State having Jurisdiction of the

Crime"). But since Puerto Rico was not a state, how could Bingham detain Kopel, and how could Puerto Rico demand his extradition from the state of New York as a fugitive from justice?

Chief Justice Fuller wrote for the unanimous Court that Kopel was to be extradited to Puerto Rico. Fuller addressed two questions in his opinions: whether "the Governor of Porto Rico had power and authority to make a requisition upon the Governor of the State of New York for the arrest and surrender" of Kopel; and whether "New York had power and authority to honor such requisition" and, accordingly, issue a warrant for the arrest of Kopel and his surrender to Puerto Rico. While Fuller recognized that the Constitution referred only to the states, he noted that in 1793 Congress "made provision for the demand and surrender of fugitives by the governors of the territories as well as of the states, and it was long ago held that power to extradite fugitive criminals, as between state and territory, as complete as between one state and another."

Was, then, Puerto Rico a territory of the United States — consistent with Congress's earlier legislation?

Fuller argued that it was. A territory, as defined in *Ex Parte Morgan* (1883), was "a portion of the country not included within the limits of any state, and not yet admitted as a state into the Union, but organized under the laws of Congress with a separate legislature, under a territorial governor and other officers appointed by the President and Senate of the United States." Fuller then quoted from *In re Lane* (1890), which involved an offense "within that part of Indian territory commonly known as 'Oklahoma,'" and which defined "territories" as

> that system of organized government, long existing within the United States, by which certain regions of the country have been erected into civil governments. These governments have an executive, a legislative, and a judicial system. They have the powers which all these departments of government have exercised, which are conferred upon them by act of Congress, and their legislative acts are subject to disapproval of the Congress of the United States. They are not, in any sense, independent governments; they have no Senators in Congress and no Representatives in the lower house of that body, except what are called "Delegates," with limited func-

tions. Yet they exercise nearly all the powers of government, under what are generally called "organic acts," passed by Congress, conferring such powers on them.

The chief justice noted that Puerto Rico "became a domestic country, . . . and has been now *fully organized* as a country of the United States by the Foraker Act" (emphasis added). And a citizen of Puerto Rico "was not an alien immigrant," per *Gonzalez v. Williams.* Puerto Rico was thus "a completely organized territory, although not a territory incorporated into the United States." The Puerto Rican governor could requisition Kopel, and New York was to honor his request.

With the ruling in *Kopel v. Bingham,* though, the Supreme Court completed the circle: territories could be either *unorganized* or *organized,* and either *incorporated* or *unincorporated,* as the Puerto Rican judicial scholar Efrén Rivera Ramos points out. Organized territories did not have to be incorporated (Puerto Rico); unorganized territories were not necessarily unincorporated (Alaska); territories could be both organized and incorporated (Hawai'i); and they could be both unorganized and unincorporated (Guam, American Samoa). Congress and the Supreme Court could decide which was which and assert the U.S. government's plenary authority in each of the four categories.

———

Another of the *Insular Cases* forced the Court to determine the applicability of the Eleventh Amendment. In *People of Porto Rico v. Rosaly y Castillo,* decided on February 24, 1913, the Supreme Court ruled on whether the Government of Porto Rico — the official title — was immune from suit. The Puerto Rico District Court had earlier found for Rosaly and Castillo, who were suing for the recovery of property, rents, and profits. Felix Frankfurter and the attorney general of Puerto Rico, Wolcott H. Pitkin, argued on behalf of the Puerto Rican government and appealed the district court's decision on the basis of the Eleventh Amendment — that "the Judicial power of the United States shall not be construed to extend to any suit in law or equity, commenced or prosecuted against one of the United States by Citizens of another State, or by Citizens or Subjects of any Foreign State."

Chief Justice White wrote the unanimous opinion for the Court. He argued that the Government of Porto Rico *had* immunity from suits from its citizens, and that Puerto Rico, just like Hawai'i and the other organized territories of the United States, was sovereign insofar as it enjoyed immunity from suit. The Foraker Act was adopted by Congress for the creation of "a government conforming to the American system with defined and divided powers, legislative, executive and judicial," White wrote. The entitlement of Puerto Ricans "with power to sue and be sued" in the Organic Act was not an oversight of Congress; nor was it intended to "destroy the government which it was [the Organic Act's] purpose to create." The Eleventh Amendment thus also applied to Puerto Rico and, by extension, the other island territories of the United States.

———

The Supreme Court's record in the years after the original *Insular Cases* decisions of 1901 reveals two major findings. One is that the Court applied several of the protections and guarantees of the U.S. Constitution to the inhabitants of the U.S. island territories. In both *Lincoln*; *Warner*, *Barnes* cases (1905, 1906), for instance, the Court upheld the uniformity clause, contrary to the wishes of the Roosevelt and Taft administrations and to their claims of military necessity.

The Court also held that the Puerto Rican territorial government could extradite criminals from the states (Art. IV, Sec. 2, Cl. 2) in its decision in *Kopel v. Bingham* (1909) — just as other governments of incorporated territories and the states could demand the extradition of fugitive criminals from other territories or states. (Recall that *Neely v. Henkel* [1901] established that the power of extradition to areas "appurtenant to" but not belonging to the United States was an inherent power of sovereignty.)

In *Ponce v. Porto Rico* (1908), too, the Court agreed to support the "legal and political institutions" of Puerto Rico as specified in the terms of the Treaty of Paris, even though the use of public funds in support of the Catholic Church might seem to violate the establishment clause (since Puerto Rico, although under Congress's plenary authority, favored the establishment of a particular religion — the Roman Catholic Church). (In earlier cases adjudicating disputes over Mexican land grants in the American Southwest, however, the Supreme Court had felt no compunction to honor particular provisions spelled out in the Treaty of Guadalupe-Hidalgo.)

The Court's decision in *Ochoa v. Hernandez* (1913) protected Puerto Ricans from their government's taking of land. Implicitly, citizens in all the other territories of the United States enjoyed the same protections. Even in the instance of the Court's unanimous opinion in *Board of Public Commissioners v. Ynchausti*, which could be interpreted as a denial of the application of the takings clause, Chief Justice White never asserted that the takings clause of the Fifth Amendment did not apply to the Philippines because it was an unincorporated territory. (Presumably White would have made the argument if he thought it bore on the Court's opinion.) Instead, White and the unanimous Court merely suggested that there were limits to the takings clause. And the long-standing tradition of coastal traders carrying the Philippine mail, a practice explicitly continued in the Philippine Organic Act of July 1, 1902, was a reason the Court could temper its support for the protections of the Fifth Amendment.

The Court also decided that the Eleventh Amendment's protection of sovereign immunity applied to the territorial governments established in the United States' island territories, per its decision in *Porto Rico v. Rosaly* (1913). If the Puerto Rican government enjoyed immunity from suit, then presumably the same held for the government of the Philippines. (Guam and American Samoa, although also in the possession of the United States at the time, were wholly administered by the U.S. Navy in the first half of the twentieth century.)

The second finding challenges the first: the Court often itself decided which constitutional provisions applied and which did not, where Congress's own actions were typically controlling. In *Binns v. United States*, the Court allowed Congress to impose fees on trade in Alaska, although the funds were being withheld for the purpose of the Alaskan government and although Alaska was recognized to be an incorporated territory. And in *United States v. Heinszen* (1911), the Court supported Congress's legislation that made it illegal for companies to recover the duties collected on tariffs levied on trade between the Philippines and the several states — notwithstanding the Court's earlier rulings in the two *Lincoln; Warner, Barnes* cases. This is to say that the Court possessed considerable discretion over how it interpreted the provisions of the Constitution to the territories of the United States; the Court itself could read the tea leaves.

But the Court was not nearly so expansive in its interpretation of the United States and application of the Constitution in a number of other cases coming after the 1901 *Insular Cases* — cases that addressed the rights of territorial inhabitants with respect to criminal defense. Here, the Court showed progressively less flexibility and increasing support for the government of the United States and those of the territories when acting against the criminally accused.

CHAPTER 7

Law and Order in the Territories

Under our flag you can not have a republic and an empire. You can not have self-government and a government by force. One or the other will triumph. Either the republic will go down and the empire survive, or we will at once retrace our steps to the old ground and anchor our ship of state to the declaration and to the doctrine that all governments derive their just powers from the consent of the governed.
SENATOR R. F. PETTIGREW, *The Course of Empire,* 1921

The most controversial post-1901 *Insular Cases* concerned the Fifth and Sixth Amendments' guarantees of due process for criminal defendants, particularly with respect to the right to trial by jury, the right to indictment by grand jury in cases of felony, and the prohibition on persons being put twice in jeopardy. In these decisions, the Court reinforced the Incorporation Doctrine and buttressed the power of the U.S. and territorial governments in their prosecution of crimes — and especially political crimes — in the United States' new territories.

———

The Court announced its first decision involving the application of the Constitution's guarantee of criminal due process to the United States' insular territories on June 1, 1903, in *Hawaii v. Mankichi*. Osaki Mankichi, a day laborer, was charged with the manslaughter of a Chinese man. But since Mankichi had not been indicted by a grand jury and since a nonunanimous jury had found him guilty (nine of the twelve jurors), Mankichi appealed to the Hawaiian Supreme Court on the basis of the Fifth and Sixth Amendments. When the Hawaiian Supreme Court affirmed the lower court's judgment, Mankichi appealed the decision to the U.S. Supreme Court.

Mankichi's attorneys (Fred Coudert, Paul Fuller, and three other associates at Coudert Brothers) argued that Article IX of the Newlands Resolution — which annexed the Hawai'ian Islands as a U.S. territory — specified that the governing laws of Hawai'i would apply *unless they violated the U.S. Constitution.* It surely appeared so with Mankichi's guilty verdict.

The prosecution, for its part, made the claim that when passing the Newlands Resolution, Congress did not intend to extend jury trial to the Hawai'ian islands or to interfere with local legislation. The U.S. government's lawyers argued that Mankichi and his attorneys were interpreting the Newlands Resolution verbatim, which in their view took the case out of its context and made little sense.

A closely divided Supreme Court upheld the judgment of the Hawaiian Supreme Court. Justice Brown wrote the lead opinion, joined by Justices Holmes and Day. Brown held that Congress did not intend to interpret the words "not contrary to the Constitution" literally, certainly not to the extent that such an interpretation would lead to "unjust consequences" or "disastrous" results for a population "unfamiliar" with all the provisions of the U.S. Constitution. "Surely such a result could not have been within the contemplation of Congress."

Brown then conceded that "most, if not all the privileges and immunities contained in the bill of rights of the Constitution were intended to apply from the moment of annexation." He added, however, "We place our decision of this case upon the ground that the *two rights alleged to be violated in this case* [trial by jury and grand jury indictment in criminal cases] *are not fundamental in their nature, but concern merely a method of procedure*" (emphasis added). Hawai'ian practice was long-standing procedure that "sixty years of practice had shown to be suited to the conditions of the islands, and well calculated to conserve the rights of their citizens to their lives, their property and their well-being."

Justice White concurred, joined by Justice McKenna. White argued that Hawai'i was not incorporated, and that Mankichi could therefore be convicted under Hawai'ian law — the Newlands Resolution notwithstanding. The Fifth and Sixth Amendments "were not applicable to that territory," White stated, because even if the resolution of annexation made the islands subject to "the sovereignty of the United States, neither the terms of the resolution nor the situation which arose from it served to incorporate the Hawaiian Islands into the United States and make them an integral part thereof." The decision in *Downes v. Bidwell* was dispositive for White: "The minutest examination of the [Newlands] resolution fails to disclose any provision declaring that the islands are incorporated and made a part of the

United States or endowing them with the rights which would arise from such relation." White recognized that there were "fundamental provisions of the Constitution, which were by their own force applicable to the territory with which Congress was dealing"; he did not specify what those other constitutional provisions were, however.

Chief Justice Fuller dissented, joined by Justices Harlan, Brewer, and Peckham. Fuller believed that the fundamental rights of the Constitution included those of a jury trial and indictment by a grand jury in cases of felony. "This is *not* a question of natural rights, on the one hand, and artificial rights on the other, but of the *fundamental rights* of every person living under the sovereignty of the United States in respect to that Government. And among those rights is the right to be free from prosecution for crime unless after indictment by grand jury, and the right to be acquitted unless found guilty by the unanimous verdict of a petit jury of twelve" (emphasis added). The Newlands Resolution, Fuller remarked, "is plain and unambiguous, and to resort to construction or interpretation is absolutely uncalled for. To tamper with the words is to eliminate them." Fuller further observed that Justice Day, who sided with Brown in the majority, was the same person who earlier, as U.S. secretary of state, had written the constitutional guarantees into the Newlands Resolution.

Harlan also dissented strongly on his own: "It has been announced by some statesmen that the Constitution should be interpreted to mean, not what its words naturally, or unusually, or even plainly import, but what the apparent majority of the people, at a particular time, demand at the hands of the judiciary." But Harlan could neither "assent to any such view of the Constitution," nor "approve of the suggestions that the status of Hawaii and the powers of its local government are to be 'measured' by the resolution of 1898, without reference to the Constitution." It was "impossible" for him "to grasp the thought that that which is admittedly contrary to the supreme law can be sustained as valid."

Harlan observed, too, that had Mankichi been convicted in the territory of Arizona or in any of the organized territories, or in Washington, D.C., "and if he had been then sentenced to be hanged, and was hanged, the judge of the court pronouncing the sentence would have been guilty of judicial murder. Of that the decisions of this court leave no room for doubt." Harland added, "If the principles now announced should become firmly established, the time may not be far distant when, under the exactions of trade and commerce, and to gratify an ambition to become the dominant political power in all the earth, the United States will acquire territories in every direction . . . whose inhabitants will be regarded as 'subjects' or 'dependent peoples,' to be controlled as Congress may see fit." He concluded that were the logic of the Supreme Court majority to hold, there "will be engrafted upon our republican institutions, controlled by the supreme law of a written Constitution, a *colonial* system entirely foreign to the genius of our Government and abhorrent to the principles that underlie and pervade the Constitution" (emphasis in original).

The Supreme Court's decision in *Hawaii v. Mankichi* is noteworthy for several reasons. One reason is that *Hawaii v. Mankichi* was the first case involving the United States' insular territories since the decisions of December 2, 1901. And like most of the previous *Insular Cases*, the Court split on the decision "by the usual vote of five to four," as the *New York World* reported on June 5, 1903. A second reason is that the Court upheld the power of the U.S. government to govern an island territory as it so chose, only this time not with respect to the tariff but with respect to due process in criminal trials — specifically the right to a jury trial and to indictment by grand jury.

A third reason is that for three of the five justices in the majority, the decision was not made on the basis of the Incorporation Doctrine, but on the basis of the U.S. Supreme Court's own authority to judge which provisions of the Constitution applied to the U.S. territories and which did not; the fact that Hawai'i had been incorporated and organized by the Newlands Resolution did not matter. Brown was able to marshal a three-person plurality because the two new appointees to the Court, Justices Holmes and Day, both joined Brown's opinion.

Holmes's prior correspondence with Sir Frederick Pollock hinted at Holmes's agreement with Brown's position. Pollock wrote Holmes, his friend and longtime correspondent, about a recent issue of the *Harvard Law Review* that contained articles on the new island territories. "I don't feel competent to discuss the Constitution of the U.S. in its possible application to the Salvage Yles [*sic*]," Pollock wrote on February 22, 1899, "but I have no doubt that [Christopher C.] Langdell's view is right in point of policy and will have to be made so in law." (Langdell held the first, narrow view of the United States, the same as did Justice Brown.) As Justice Harlan wrote in a letter to Fuller shortly after Holmes's appointment to the bench: "The indications in the papers are that [Holmes] is sufficiently 'expansive' in his views to suit those who think that it is the destiny of the United States to acquire & hold outlying possessions 'outside the Constitution.'" Harlan anticipated correctly.

Last, the decision in *Hawaii v. Mankichi* indicates that even with two years' time elapsed since the decisions of May 1901, the U.S. Supreme Court was no closer to a consensus on how the U.S. Constitution applied to the new island territories: not with respect to the tariff, not — now — with respect to jury trial or indictment by grand jury, and not when it came to the Incorporation Doctrine or any one judicial doctrine.

The popular press and expert opinion divided over the Court's ruling in *Hawaii v. Mankichi*, just as they had after the decisions of May 27, 1901. The populist *New York World* strongly criticized the Court's decision: "When the Supreme Court makes a decision by a majority of one, with the Chief-Justice and some of his ablest associates in the minority, it is permissible to doubt whether the judgment is the final voice of inspired wisdom." The dissenting opinions were made by "beyond question four of the strongest Justices on the bench," the *World* added, and "expressed in language much stronger than could properly be employed by a newspaper." It was "well known," the *World* unsparingly concluded, that "Justice McKenna is certainly not the strongest member of the court, that Justice Day was Secretary of State at the time the imperialist policy was adopted, and that he and Justice Holmes are the newest recruits to the bench. In such circumstances it is not at all inconceivable that the court may yet reverse itself on this question, as it has done on others."

The *New York Herald*, which had the largest circulation among U.S. newspapers at the time, was similarly harsh: "To grasp the momentous, if not revolutionary, sweep of this ruling, it is only necessary to realize that, as maintained by four of the nine members of the court, *it makes Congress, instead of the constitution, supreme and omnipotent with respect to personal rights and liberty, just as the previous decisions did in tariff matters, in all the insular domain now held or hereafter to be acquired by the United States*" (emphasis added). The *Herald* continued: "These guarantees of the national constitution thus swept aside are the prized and boasted bulwarks of Anglo-Saxon rights and freedom. They are designed to shield every accused person against tyranny or oppression, wrong or injustice — to guard against conviction for crime without guilt established beyond reasonable doubt by fair procedure and just trial. To this end there must be indictment by grand jury and unanimous verdict of trial jury."

The Republican *Philadelphia Inquirer*, in contrast, wrote approvingly of the Court's decision. Did the Newlands Resolution annexing Hawai'i eliminate "all laws that were contrary to the Constitution?" the paper asked. The Court's answer was no, the *Inquirer* replied, and for the Court to do so "would have been attended by so much inconvenience." The *Inquirer* continued: "The legal logic of the conclusion is open to attack, but it accords with good common sense and with the . . . changing demands of the national development." Other papers also supported the decisions. Still others covered the *Mankichi* decision without editorial comment (e.g., *New York Times* and *New York Daily Tribune*) or did not cover it at all in their news.

Frederic Coudert, Mankichi's attorney, thought the decision was "wrongheaded" and that it marked "an important departure in our Constitutional law." Judge Emlin McLain, writing in the *Harvard Law Review*, also thought that the Court had decided wrongly. "If it is admitted that the framers of the constitution contemplated the exercise by Congress of the power of providing territorial governments, it can hardly be conceived that they intended to give Congress unlimited power in this respect." McLain emphasized: "*It must be borne in mind that the protection of individual rights and property against the undue exercise of governmental power* was an ever-present motive in the framing of the state and federal constitution; and that the rights thus protected were not conceived as the rights of any particular persons but of all persons" (emphasis added). It was "hardly imaginable," McLain wrote, "that the framers," with the Declaration of Independence in mind, would have considered subjecting persons "to an arbitrary and unlimited power which they did not tolerate for themselves." Even were jury trial in Hawai'i or the Philippines "to some extent unsatisfactory," it was "likewise unsatisfactory" in the territories and other possessions of the United States, McLain pointed out.

But it may well be, as the judicial scholar Loren Beth more recently comments, that the decision in *Hawaii v. Mankichi* simply reflected "the judges' own feelings about the territory in question: all constitutional rights were to be extended to those in which the people were sufficiently advanced to deserve them, while in more backward areas only limited rights were considered possible." Certainly there had been loud controversy and tense debate over the annexation of Hawai'i and the racial characteristics of the Hawai'ian population.

———

About a year later, on May 31, 1904, the Supreme Court decided *Kepner v. United States* — the same day that the Court issued its decisions in *Binns v. United States* (see chapter 6) and *Dorr v. United States* (see later in this chapter). In *Kepner v. United States*, a split Court decided in favor of the appellant, Thomas Kepner, a Manila attorney charged with and then acquitted of embezzlement. The Philippine military government appealed the decision to the Philippine Supreme Court, which convicted him in a second trial. Kepner then appealed to the U.S. Supreme Court on the basis of the Fifth Amendment's prohibition of double jeopardy. The Constitution, the U.S. military orders, the mandate of the Taft Commission, the text of the Act of July 1, 1902, and Spanish law *all* contained explicit prohibitions against double jeopardy.

Justice Day wrote the opinion for the Court, joined by Chief Justice Fuller and Justices Harlan, Brewer, and Peckham. Day argued that the reversal by the appeals court *did* violate Kepner's constitutional rights that he (Kepner) not be put twice in jeopardy. Day disputed the solicitor general's contentions that due process of law obtained in the Philippines and that Kepner's conviction should therefore be overturned. Day argued, instead, that Kepner's case was an issue of a person being put in double jeopardy in the face of explicit protections to the contrary. Kepner's appeal on the grounds of double jeopardy was therefore justified. Day emphasized that he was not questioning or usurping Congress's plenary powers.

Justice Holmes dissented, joined by Justices White and McKenna. Holmes argued that the second trial marked a continuation of the first jeopardy. Holmes effectively denied the premise of the Fifth Amendment, in effect, by writing that "there is no rule that a man may not be tried twice in the same case." Holmes was also results-oriented; he worried about the policy consequences of the majority's opinion. The majority decision would fasten "upon the country a doctrine covering the whole criminal law, which . . . will have serious and evil consequences. At the present time in this country there is more danger that criminals will escape justice than that they will be subject to tyranny."

Justice Brown wrote a separate dissent in which he argued that "Congress could constitutionally authorize" the review of Kepner's case, since the review by the Philippine Supreme Court was consistent with how the judicial proceedings on the Philippines Islands were understood.

The Court decided a second double jeopardy case, *Mendezona y Mendezona v. United States*, at the same time and on the same grounds as *Kepner*. Justice Day noted that Secondino Mendezona was to be discharged and that the Philippine Supreme Court's judgment was to be reversed for the reasons stated in *Kepner*. Justices White, McKenna, Brown, and Holmes all again dissented for the reasons they had given in *Kepner*.

Although the Court's majorities in *Kepner* and *Mendezona* might suggest that the Court — albeit a split Court — viewed double jeopardy as one of the fundamental constitutional provisions to be protected in the United States' new unincorporated territories, the decisions involved a question of statutory interpretation — specifically the laws established by the U.S. Congress and in the Philippine Bill of Rights that explicitly protected Filipinos from double jeopardy. Still, the *Kepner* and *Mendezona* decisions suggest that Justice Day, Roosevelt's new appointee on the Court, appeared to be siding with Chief Justice Fuller and Justices Harlan, Brewer, and Peckham — those who held that the Constitution applied *ex proprio vigore* — while Justice Holmes, in contrast, appeared to be supporting the expansion-minded administration.

———

In *Dorr v. United States*, decided the same day, Justice Day showed that he in fact did *not* hold that the Constitution applied *ex proprio vigore*. The question in *Dorr*, like that in *Hawaii v. Mankichi*, concerned the applicability of the Fifth Amendment's guarantees of a jury trial and indictment by grand jury in the Philippines.

Fred L. Dorr was one of two publishers and editors of a Manila newspaper, the *Manila Freedom*, who had been denied a jury trial in the determination of his guilt for an act of libel. Dorr and the other editor, Edward F. O'Brien — the plaintiffs — had printed "TRAITOR, SEDUCER, AND PERJURER" in large type in the newspapers and, in smaller type, "Wife would have killed him" and "Legarda pale and nervous." The prosecution claimed that Dorr and O'Brien's headlines had libeled Don Benito Legarda, who was a prominent Filipino and a member of the Philippine Commission. The "malicious defamation" published by the two men was contrary to the law established by the commission.

Dorr, however, sought to have a jury trial since he had been found guilty without being tried by a jury of his peers. And since the United States had annexed the Philippines upon the ratification of the 1898 Treaty of Paris, per the Court's ruling in *Fourteen Diamond Rings* with respect to tariff laws, the U.S. Constitution was the sole government authority in the Philippines.

Justice Day wrote the lead opinion, joined by Justices White, Brown, McKenna, and Holmes. Day began by citing *De Lima v. Bidwell* and *Downes v. Bidwell* as precedents. The decisions in "the so-called 'Insular Cases,'" Day argued, made "superfluous any attempt to reconsider the constitutional relation of the power of the government to territory acquired by a treaty cession to the United States." Congress had authority over the territories acquired by the United States, and it was up to Congress to incorporate them as it judged best. "Until Congress shall see fit to incorporate territory ceded by treaty into the United States," Day wrote, "we regard it as settled [in *Downes v. Bidwell*] that the territory is to be governed under the power existing in Congress to make laws for such territories and subject to such constitutional restrictions upon the powers of that body as are applicable to the situation."

Day then used a results-oriented argument to deny the right to a jury trial:

If the right to trial by jury were a fundamental right which goes wherever the jurisdiction of the United States extends, or if Congress, in framing laws for outlying territory belonging to the United States, was obliged to establish that system by affirmative legislation, it would follow that, *no matter what the needs or capacities of the people*, trial by jury, and in no other way, must be forthwith established, although the result may be to work injustice and provoke disturbance rather than to aid the orderly administration of justice. If the United States, impelled by its duty or advantage, shall acquire territory *peopled by savages*, and of which it may dispose or not hold for ultimate admission to Statehood, if this doctrine is sound, it must establish there the trial by jury. To state such a proposition demonstrates the impossibility of carrying it into practice. (emphasis added)

Congress needed to be able to exercise discretion over which constitutional provisions were to apply to the territories, Day remarked, and the procedural rights of jury trial were not fundamental to territorial residents: "The Constitution does not, without legislation and of its own force, carry such right [i.e., trial by jury] to territory so situated."

Justice Peckham concurred separately, joined by Chief Justice Fuller and Justice Brewer. Peckham, in a very brief opinion, simply disputed the authority of the *Downes* precedent cited by the majority. *Downes*, Peckham held, was not relevant. "The Mankichi case is, however, directly in point, and calls for an affirmance of this judgment." Peckham argued that he (along with the chief justice and Justice Brewer) was simply following the precedent of *Hawaii v. Mankichi*.

Harlan wrote the sole dissent. Harlan, in contrast to the three concurring justices, "did not believe now any more than when *Hawaii v. Mankichi* was decided" that the rights to grand jury indictments and jury trials were anything other than fundamental. The purpose of the Constitution was to protect the life, liberty, and property of all, regardless of race or nativity. Harlan condemned the majority opinion for the reason that Day's ruling "in effect adjudges that the Philippine Islands are not part of the 'land,' within the meaning of the Constitution, although they are governed by the sovereign authority of the United States and although their inhabitants are subject in all respects to its jurisdiction — as much so as are the people in the District of Columbia or in the several states of the Union." According to the principles of the majority as Harlan saw it, "Neither the Governor nor any American civil officer in the Philippines, although citizens of the United States, although under oath to support the constitution, and although in those distant possessions for the purpose of enforcing the authority of the United States, can claim, of right, the benefit of the jury provisions of the Constitution, if tried for crime committed on those Islands." Less than a week later, on

June 4, 1904, Harlan privately wrote Day that he believed that "the Constitution was horribly mangled" in the *Dorr* decision.

Dorr, together with *Binns v. United States* and *Kepner v. United States*, received a mixed response in the press. Some newspapers prominently featured the cases; other papers had stories placed well inside their pages; and still others omitted covering the case altogether. A few newspapers, such as the *New York Herald*, carried both news stories and editorials in their papers of June 1; a handful of other papers, such as the *Buffalo Evening News and Telegraph*, ran only editorials and no straight news stories. Other newspapers, meanwhile, among them the *New York Daily Tribune*, *New York Times*, *New York World*, and *Washington Post*, ran news stories without editorial commentary.

The *Buffalo Evening News and Telegraph*, a Republican paper, agreed with the decision in *Dorr*. The practice of jury trial had been "established in England and America" and "cannot be worked among half-civilized races." The Court's decision was "so clearly the common sense view that one is constrained to wonder how there could be a contrary opinion in the Court." The *Philadelphia Inquirer* also agreed: "Trial by jury is a boon granted by legislation, and not inherent in its flag." The idea that the Constitution applied "for all of the Federal Territory," the *Inquirer* added, was the now-discounted theory of John Calhoun and of Chief Justice Taney in *Dred Scott v. Sandford*.

The *New York Herald* disagreed. It quoted extensively from Justice Harlan's "masterly dissenting opinion" in its editorial of June 1. For the *Herald*, "the constitutional doctrine affirmed by a bare majority in this and the preceding insular cases . . . puts Congress above the constitution throughout a large part of the national domain." The *Herald*'s editors disapproved of the fact that Congress "may abolish the jury system, as has practically been done in the Hawaiian case, and nullify all other guarantees of personal rights and liberty" (although the *Herald* mistakenly reported that *Dorr* had been decided by a five-to-four vote). The *New York Daily Tribune* merely observed that the three cases (*Dorr*, *Binns*, and *Kepner*) stood "in curious contradiction."

But the cases were more than just contradictory. Rather, the eight-to-one decision in *Dorr v. United States*, coming on the heels of the Court's controversial decision in *Hawaii v. Mankichi* and at the same time as its decisions in *Binns*, *Kepner*, and *Mendezona*, marked a turning point in the history of the *Insular Cases*.

Strikingly, Fuller, Brewer, and Peckham had switched sides. As the *Tribune* observed, it was "surprising to find three of the 'anti-imperialist judges' leaving the Filipinos without jury trial even for independent reasons of their own." Although "Brown, White, McKenna and Day are still firm for the plenary power of the government on the question of jury trial, . . . there is a new alignment" among the other justices. "Justice Holmes, Brewer, Peckham, and Chief Justice Fuller, after holding that a man cannot be put twice in jeopardy, curiously enough decide that he is not entitled to the jury trial established by the same Constitution," the *Tribune* commented (although the newspaper mistakenly reported that Justice Holmes held that a man cannot be put twice in jeopardy, when it was Justice Day who sided with the chief justice and Justices Harlan, Brewer, and Peckham). "The balance of power is [now] held by Justice Holmes, the successor of Justice Gray," the *Tribune* concluded, "one of the majority in holding that the Constitution did not extend ex proprio vigore to the islands."

The judicial scholar Owen Fiss suggests several reasons for the switch, one he concedes he cannot account for. Fiss considers the argument that Holmes's friendship with Fuller may have influenced the change, since Holmes and the chief justice were good friends. Fiss recognizes, of course, that friendship and mutual respect are not usually enough to cause a defection such as this, especially among justices of the Supreme Court—typically independent, proud, and accomplished persons. Then, too, Harlan was close to Fuller, but obviously Harlan did not prevail, just as Taft was close friends with Harlan— they even vacationed in the same town on the Saint Lawrence River in Quebec—but unable to convince Harlan to agree to his views. Even in the unlikely event that Holmes had swayed Fuller, moreover, this still does not explain the switch by Justices Brewer and Peckham.

The recent history of U.S. foreign relations may better explain the change, Fiss remarks. By 1904, Cuba was no longer under direct U.S. sovereignty, and the United States had effectively ended its recent costly war in the Philippines (although some guerrilla resistance continued). "The whole question of the Philippines is now a dead issue," Charles Francis Adams Jr. wrote. "The discussion attracts no sort of attention," he continued, "and, when it is brought to the fore, people turn away from it with a sense of weariness." (Adams, who was one of the most notable anti-imperialists of 1898–1900, was also the brother of Brooks Adams and the historian Henry Adams, and the direct descendent of John and John Quincy Adams.) And both houses of Congress and both political parties were reluctant to support further U.S. territorial annexation.

In addition, the Roosevelt administration had been able to achieve Panama's independence from Colombia — Panama had been a province of Colombia up to that time — secure the canal area, and establish military sites in Panama. All this had been accomplished while avoiding the exercise of U.S. sovereignty over Panama and its people. This is to say that the recent history of Panama indicated that there might be other ways to spread U.S. influence besides the establishment of territorial governments in areas under U.S. sovereignty. Fiss suggests that Fuller, Brewer, and Peckham may thus have realized that the United States was not going to acquire more territory in the foreseeable future. As a result, the three justices may have decided to moderate their positions on how the Constitution was to apply to the U.S. island territories.

An alternative explanation offered by Fiss is that the three "anti-imperialist judges" may have thought that the Court's decisions in *Kepner, Mendezona, Gonzalez v. Williams,* and *Fourteen Diamond Rings* already revealed consensus to restrict Congress's plenary power over the island territories and to protect the territorial inhabitants with at least some constitutional protections. Even Judge Cooley, the well-known commentator on the Supreme Court, conceded that "citizens of the Territories as well as citizens of the States may claim the benefit" of the protection of "the securities for personal liberty which are incorporated in the Constitution" and that "were intended as limitations of its power of any and all persons who might be within its jurisdiction anywhere." The three justices may also have appreciated the convenience of the Incorporation Doctrine, Fiss also proposes, given the discretion that the doctrine gave the Court in contrast to the rigidity of the doctrine of *ex proprio vigore*.

Yet arguably the most important reason for Fuller, Brewer, and Peckham's switch from their "anti-imperial" position was that the *Dorr* decision was careful to distinguish between commerce, on the one hand, and criminal justice, on the other hand.

Justice Day was at pains in his opinion to point out to his colleagues that *Dorr* was about *criminal law* and *not* about *commerce* — not unlike Justice Brewer's emphasis in *Binns v. United States* that the decision was about local Alaskan taxes and not about the tariff, contracts, or commerce itself. Commercial regulation was not at issue in *Dorr*, Day reassured his colleagues. Rather, "the practical question" was if "Congress, in establishing a system for trial of crimes and offenses committed in the Philippine Islands," had to legislatively provide for "a system of jury trial." Only here, with respect to due process in criminal proceedings, could Congress have "a free hand in dealing with these newly acquired possessions," Day wrote.

This was not the case, Day implied, with respect to taxation, property, or other economic issues. Here, Congress did not have a free hand. In fact, Day in other passages of his opinion stressed the limits to congressional power. The source of the limit of the power under the territory clause, Day quoted from Justice Curtis's dissent in *Dred Scott v. Sandford*, was one Curtis found "in common with all the other legislative powers of Congress." This was the Constitution's "express prohibitions on Congress not to do certain things; that, in the exercise of the legislative power, Congress cannot pass an ex post facto law or bill of attainder, *and so in respect to each of the other prohibitions contained in the Constitution*" (emphasis added). Day then quoted from Brown's lead opinion in *Hawaii v. Mankichi*: "We would go farther and say that *most, if not all, the privileges and immunities contained in the Bill of Rights of the Constitution were intended to apply from the moment of annexation*; but we place our decision of this case upon the ground that the two rights alleged to be violated in this case [right to trial by jury and presentment by grand jury] *are not fundamental* in their nature, but concern merely a method of procedure" (emphasis added).

Day also cited Justice Bradley from the *Mormon Church Case*: "Doubtless Congress, in legislating for the territories, would be subject to those fundamental limitations in favor of personal rights which are formulated in the Constitution and its amendments." Finally, Day quoted Justice White's concurring opinion in *Downes*, which recognized that there were "inherent, though unexpressed, principles which are the basis of all free government, which cannot be with impunity transcended. . . . [E]ven in cases where there is no direct command of the Constitution which applies, there may nevertheless be restrictions of so fundamental a nature that they cannot be transgressed, although not expressed in so many words in the Constitution."

In short, Justice Day's repeated qualifications to his opinion may have reassured Justice Peckham, Chief Justice Fuller, and Justice Brewer that the ruling in *Dorr* posed no threat to property rights or the ability of persons or associations to conduct commerce. All three justices had, after all, throughout their careers been strong advocates of economic liberty and laissez-faire capitalism.

Fuller's commitment to the protection of commerce was evident not only in his opinions in the *Sugar Trust Case* and *Income Tax Case*, as noted earlier, but also manifest in his dissent in *Downes v. Bidwell*, where Fuller condemned the majority's support of the Foraker Act for reason of the threat that it posed to commerce. The levy on trade between Puerto Rico and the states "is clearly a regulation of commerce, and a regulation affecting the States and their people as well as this territory and its people," Fuller wrote. And the commerce clause embraced "the entire internal as well as foreign commerce of the country." Chief Justice Fuller cited the Court's ruling in *Stountenburgh v. Hennick* as well — as had John G. Carlisle in his argument for Dooley, Smith, & Co., and Carlos Armstrong — on the point that trade between territories and states was protected under the Constitution. "The logical result" of the majority opinion, Fuller concluded, "is that Congress may prohibit commerce altogether between the States and the territories, and may prescribe one rule of taxation in one territory, and a different rule in another." Neither did "the fact that the proceeds are devoted by the act to the use of the territory make national taxes local." To tax trade was to — unconstitutionally — regulate commerce.

This was also the chief justice's view in his dissent in *Dooley II*, joined by Justices Harlan, Brewer, and Peckham, where he also stressed the implications of the *Insular Cases* on the regulation of commerce. It was further consistent with the Court's majority opinions in *De Lima v. Bidwell*, *Goetze v. United States*, *Crossman v. United States*, and *Armstrong v. United States*.

Justice Peckham was no less adamant. Only a few years earlier, in *Allgeyer v. Louisiana* (1897), Peckham was explicit about the importance of economic liberty in his opinion for the unanimous Court:

> The liberty mentioned in [the due process clause] means not only the right of the citizen to be free from the mere physical restraint of his person, as by incarceration, but the term is deemed to embrace

the right of the citizen to be free in the enjoyment of all his facul-
ties; to be free to use them in all lawful ways; to live and work
where he will; to earn his livelihood by any lawful calling; to pursue
any livelihood or avocation, and for that purpose to enter into all
contracts which may be proper, necessary and essential for that
purpose to his carrying out to a successful conclusion the purposes
mentioned above.

Like Chief Justice Fuller, Peckham was a Jacksonian Democrat who
sought to protect economic liberty at all costs.

Although Justice Brewer was no Jacksonian Democrat, he was a
staunch defender of laissez-faire capitalism—much like his uncle, Justice Stephen Field (as noted earlier). Brewer took absolute positions
against any restrictions on commerce. He, together with Justice Field,
had joined Chief Justice Fuller's majority opinion in the *Income Tax
Case* (*Pollock v. Farmers Loan & Trust Company*)—an unpopular decision by the Court—and had also joined the Chief Justice's opinion for
the Court in the *Sugar Trust Case* (1895). Brewer, too, was part of the
Court's unanimous opinion written by Justice Peckham's opinion in
Allgeyer v. Louisiana (1897), as discussed above. And in 1903, Brewer
concurred with Chief Justice Fuller's dissent in the *Lottery Case* (*Champion v. Ames*), in which Fuller wrote that the interstate transport of
lottery tickets *was* protected under the commerce clause and that
Congress, therefore, could not legislate against such commerce.

Justice Peckham could safely concur with Justice Day, then, since
Day had repeatedly stressed that *Dorr* was *not* about the regulation of
commerce. But he had to reject *Downes* as precedent. *Downes v. Bidwell*, Peckham reminded his colleagues, was about the recovery of
"duties [that Downes had] paid under protest upon the importation
into the City of New York of certain oranges from the port of San
Juan." In view of Day's reminder that the *Mankichi* decision concerned
the rights to a jury trial and to indictment by a grand jury *only*, then,
the former "anti-imperialist" justices could now accept the ruling in
Hawaii v. Mankichi as binding precedent. Reassured, Peckham, Fuller,
and Brewer could now concur with Day's opinion for the Court.

This hypothesis — that by mid-1904 eight of the nine justices on
the bench agreed to distinguish among the constitutional provisions
that applied to the United States' territories — may explain several

other anomalies of the post-1901 *Insular Cases* as well: why the five-to-four majority in *Fourteen Diamond Rings* became a unanimous decision in *Lincoln*; *Warner, Barnes*, and an eight-to-two decision upon the rehearing a year later; why Justice Brewer could rule as he did in *Binns v. United States*, despite his position in the previous *Insular Cases* of 1901 (see chapter 5); and why Justices Brewer and Peckham still dissented in *United States v. Heinszen & Co.*, although all other justices deferred to Congress's authority. It may also account for the contrast between the Court's rulings on double jeopardy in *Kepner* and *Mendezona*, decided the same day as *Dorr*, and its decision in *Trono v. United States* of December 4, 1905. Justice Peckham's opinion for the five-to-four majority in *Trono* held that the appellant was not put twice in jeopardy. Justices Brewer, Day, and Brown joined Peckham's opinion. Justices Harlan, McKenna, and White, with the chief justice, dissented.

But with the switch of the three justices, Justice Harlan now stood alone in support of the position that the Constitution applied *ex proprio vigore*.

The *Dorr* decision poses two additional puzzles. One is why Justice Brown agreed to Day's lead opinion, since the Incorporation Doctrine played a prominent role in the ruling and since it was "settled that the Constitution is the only source of authority for any branch of the federal government" — even though the argument runs counter to Brown's extension theory (which held that *Congress* had to extend the Constitution for it to apply). In addition, Justices White and McKenna, both of whom also opposed Brown's extension theory, joined Day's opinion. So why did Brown not write a concurring opinion — especially since Day had already supported the rights of the plaintiffs not to be put twice in jeopardy in the *Kepner* and *Mendezona* decisions, whereas Brown had dissented in each case?

I think the credit goes to the skill and diplomacy with which Justice Day crafted his opinion in *Dorr* — the same skill that he had used to secure the concurrence of Fuller, Brewer, and Peckham and that Justice Harlan referred to in his endorsement of Day for the position of chief justice. Fiss suggests that Brown simply missed the references to incorporation in *Dorr*; but I would argue that the text of Day's opinion shows, instead, that the references to the Incorporation Doctrine in *Downes* were carefully balanced by Day's repeated citations of Brown's own opinions. Recall, too, that Day had sided with Brown in

Hawaii v. Mankichi, and that he on several occasions in *Dorr* referred to and quoted from Brown's lead opinions in *Hawaii v. Mankichi*, *Downes v. Bidwell*, and *De Lima v. Bidwell*. But Justices White and McKenna had only *concurred* in the former two cases, of course, and actually *dissented* in the latter case.

In addition, Day used language in his summary of precedents supporting his opinion that echoed the language of Brown's extension theory. The decisions in *Seré v. Pitot* (1810), *American Insurance Company v. Canter*, *Dred Scott v. Sandford*, and *Downes v. Bidwell*, Day wrote, "sustain the right of Congress to make laws for the government of territories, without being subject to all the restrictions which are imposed upon that body when passing laws for the United States, *considered as a political body of states in union*" (emphasis added). In short, Day's solicitude to Brown's own opinions may have worked to secure his agreement — just as Fuller's careful drafting of the *Fourteen Diamond Rings* opinion seemed to have secured Brown's agreement in the "Philippine case."

A remaining puzzle in *Dorr* is why Day, who sided with Fuller, Brewer, Peckham, and Harlan in *Kepner* and *Mendezona*, argued *against* Dorr's appeal to the right for a jury trial. Owen Fiss may be right that Day, the new justice on the bench, could have still been feeling his way around; it is certainly possible that Day did not have his views on the political and constitutional relationship between states and the new island territories fully worked out. Alternatively, however, it may be because the double jeopardy cases were a matter of the interpretation of statutory law (since the Philippine Bill of Rights, which was included as part of the Philippine Organic Act of July 1, 1902, explicitly prohibited putting the accused in double jeopardy). *Dorr*, in contrast, concerned constitutional interpretation about whether or not the Constitution guaranteed a jury trial and indictment by grand jury, since the organic act contained neither guarantee.

—————

About a year later, on April 10, 1905, the Supreme Court issued its decision in *Rassmussen v. United States*. The decision affirmed the *Downes* and *Dorr* rulings and further entrenched the Incorporation Doctrine. Alaska, which had a district government but not a territorial government — that would happen in 1912 — was incorporated and could be distinguished from the newer, organized, and unincorporated island territories.

Alaskan authorities found Fred Rassmussen guilty of keeping a "disreputable house" — that is, a brothel — and fined him $500. Rassmussen — spelled "Rasmussen" by Chief Justice Taft in his opinion in *Balzac v. Porto Rico* (1922), the constitutional commentator Charles Warren, the *Washington Post*, and others — claimed that his conviction was unconstitutional, since under the Alaskan territorial code trials could be held for misdemeanors with only six persons on the jury.

The question for Justice White, who wrote for the seven-justice majority, was whether Congress could deprive an Alaskan inhabitant of the protections guaranteed by the Sixth Amendment. White answered in two parts. First, White argued that under the rulings in *Dorr v. United States, Hawaii v. Mankichi*, and *Downes v. Bidwell*, Congress had the authority to incorporate territory if it chose to do so. "Until Congress shall see fit to incorporate territory ceded by treaty into the United States, we regard it as settled by [*Downes*] that the territory is to be governed under the power existing in Congress to make laws for such territories, and subject to such constitutional restrictions upon the powers of that body as are applicable to the situation."

White then compared the texts of the two treaties annexing Alaska and the Philippines to find out whether Alaska was in fact incorporated, or "is simply held, as the Philippine Islands are held, under the sovereignty of the United States as a possession or dependency." Here White found that Article IX of the Treaty of Paris left it up to Congress to determine the "civil rights and political status of the native inhabitants" of the Philippines, whereas Article III of the 1867 treaty with Russia stated that "the inhabitants of the ceded territory . . . shall be admitted to the enjoyment of all the rights, advantages, and immunities of citizens of the United States, and shall be maintained and protected in the free enjoyment of their liberty, property and religion." Alaska was therefore incorporated, White argued, just as Congress clearly intended (and consistent with Gray's concurring opinion in *Downes*).

The second part of White's answer addressed whether the Sixth Amendment was applicable to congressional action, since Alaska, though incorporated, did not have an *organized* territory (although in

Binns Justice Brewer claimed that Alaska's district government *did* mean that Alaska had an organized government). White ruled that the Alaskan law on jury trial was "unsound" and in "irreconcilable conflict with the essential principles" of U.S. constitutional government. Congress had already extended the Constitution and its statutes to the continental territories and the District of Columbia; these areas were part of the United States, and whether or not they were organized was immaterial to the point at hand. White therefore reversed the judgment against Rassmussen and ordered a new trial.

Justice Harlan wrote the first of two concurring opinions. Harlan stated that he chose not to restate the arguments he had previously made in his dissents in *Downes*, *Hawaii v. Mankichi*, and *Dorr*. But he did remark that the terms of the 1867 cession by Russia placed the inhabitants of Alaska under all the guarantees and protections of the Constitution. Harlan therefore agreed with White that Rassmussen warranted a twelve-person jury trial, but he again rejected the Incorporation Doctrine and its premise that "the supremacy of the Constitution depends on the will of Congress."

Justice Brown added a second — bitter — concurring opinion. "I should be doing an injustice to myself if I failed to express myself upon the doctrine of incorporation," he wrote. "My position regarding the applicability of the Constitution to the newly acquired territory is contained in [my] opinion in *Downes v. Bidwell*. . . . It is simply that the Constitution does not apply to the territories acquired by treaty until Congress has so declared, and that, in the meantime . . . it may deal with them regardless of the Constitution except so far as concerns the natural rights of their inhabitants to life, liberty, and property." Brown further commented that White's claims that whether or not a territory was incorporated determined if the Constitution applied in all its force were just not true. It "was not the opinion of the Court" in *Downes*, and "it was certainly not the opinion of the justice who announced the conclusion and judgment of the Court; it was wholly disclaimed by the four dissenting justices. . . . It was simply the individual opinion of three members of the Court."

The ruling in *Hawaii v. Mankichi* made this clear, Brown stated: Hawai'i was annexed "as part of the territory of the United States and subject to the sovereign dominion thereof" according to the Newlands Resolution; "there was plain incorporation by Congress of these islands." Despite this incorporation, however, Congress and the Court accepted that Hawai'ian inhabitants could be legally tried and convicted, "though not in compliance with the Fifth and Sixth Amendments." And "now we are asked to introduce a new classification of 'incorporated' territories," Brown wrote, "without attempting to define what shall be deemed an incorporation. The word appears to me simply to introduce a new element of confusion, and to be of no practical value."

The decision in *Rassmussen* thus represented both a continuation and a culmination of the Court's decisions on the Fifth and Sixth Amendments. Whereas Day had been careful and diplomatic in his opinion in *Dorr*, White took no prisoners; he made it clear that there was no basis by which to determine the U.S. government's authority over its territories *other* than the Incorporation Doctrine. And there were no nods to the extension theory. Yet both Day and Holmes nevertheless joined White in support of the Incorporation Doctrine, as did Chief Justice Fuller and Justices Brewer and Peckham. Day and Holmes thus appeared to have withdrawn their support for the extension theory as manifested explicitly in *Hawaii v. Mankichi* and more ambiguously in *Dorr*. Fuller, Brewer, and Peckham likewise joined White's lead opinion and therefore appear to have accepted the Incorporation Doctrine — despite the fact that they had just concurred in *Dorr* and previously joined Justices Brown and Harlan in *De Lima*, *Goetze*, *Crossman*, *Armstrong*, *Dooley I*, *Fourteen Diamond Rings*, *Binns*, *Kepner*, *Mendezona*, and, only a week earlier, *Lincoln; Warner, Barnes*.

Rassmussen thus marked the final victory of the Incorporation Doctrine over the extension theory and the first, minimal view of the United States. After *Rassmussen*, the extension theory never again rivaled the Incorporation Doctrine as the constitutional basis for Congress's authority over the island territories with respect to the due process rights of the accused.

Justice White was triumphant. Court reporter Charles Henry Butler describes the occasion: "As [White] came towards me, the breeze from the open window blowing out his gown, he was flourishing the proof sheets of his opinion in one hand and shaking the fist of the other at me, it seemed. Then he exclaimed in a voice that was probably heard by all who were on the other side of the screen: 'Butler, now *Downes* vs. *Bidwell* is the opinion of the Court and I want you to make it so appear in your report of this case.'" Butler recalled, "To Justice White it was as great a victory as winning his first case in the Supreme Court would be for a youthful attorney; and he was bound that everybody should know that his views as to incorporation or non-incorporation of acquired territory in the United States had become the law of the land."

The pro-administration *Washington Post* was the only newspaper among those I surveyed to cover the decision. In a long, inside story of April 11, 1905, the *Post* first summarized the "court's" opinion and then discussed "Justice White's Opinion" (as though they were separate opinions); the *Post* reported neither concurring opinion.

Although White's Incorporation Doctrine may have won out over the extension theory as the Court's doctrine on how the Constitution would apply to the territories, the victory of the Incorporation Doctrine still left open *which* constitutional provisions and *which* individual protections applied to the residents of the unincorporated territories, as seen in the last chapter and in cases over the rights of criminal defendants.

———

The next term on December 4, 1905, the Court decided another double jeopardy case, *Trono v. United States*. Valentin Trono and two other men were tried for killing Benito Pérez "with great cruelty and evident premeditation . . . by means of blows given with the butts of guns, . . . cooperating one with the other." The three men were convicted of assault and sentenced to pay compensation to Pérez's heirs. They appealed to the Philippine Supreme Court, which reversed the judgment and convicted them of the more serious crime of homicide. Trono appealed to the U.S. Supreme Court on the basis that he had been twice put in jeopardy.

Justice Peckham wrote the opinion for the Court, split five to four, and was joined by Justices Brewer, Brown, and Day; Holmes concurred without writing an opinion. Peckham addressed whether the Supreme Court of the Philippines violated the Act of July 1, 1902 (which specified that "no person for the same offense shall be twice put in jeopardy of punishment"). Peckham distinguished *Trono* from *Kepner* on the basis that Trono and the other defendants had *themselves* appealed the case to the Philippine Supreme Court, whereas the *gov-*

ernment had made the appeal in *Kepner*. But if the person who is convicted appeals the conviction, Peckham asked, does the new trial put the party in the same position as if no trial had taken place? Or does the new or corrected verdict only go as far as the accused himself extends it? Although precedents in lower court decisions supported both interpretations, Peckham argued that "the better doctrine is that which does *not* limit the court or jury, upon a new trial . . . and we see no reason why he should not, upon a new trial, be proceeded against as if no trial had previously taken place" (emphasis added). Peckham affirmed the decision of the Supreme Court of the Philippines.

Justice Harlan dissented. He once more argued that the U.S. Constitution was the supreme law of the land, and that the Philippines were part of the United States following the ratification the Treaty of Paris. Persons had to be indicted by a grand jury and offered a jury trial by their peers, unless they were charged under conditions of war or public danger.

Harlan also agreed with Justice McKenna's separate dissent. McKenna, joined by Justice White, held that the accused were entitled to the benefit of the jeopardy clause. After an acquittal for the trial of murder, McKenna argued, the accused could not be again tried in a U.S. appellate court for that crime or one any more serious than the one he or she was convicted of in the Court of the First Instance (the title of the Philippine lower court). McKenna further pointed out that the trial-court system established by the U.S. president and Congress in the Act of July 1, 1902, prohibited double jeopardy. It was not even necessary to determine if the Bill of Rights was or was not "the law of the islands without congressional legislation," then, since Congress had already explicitly prohibited double jeopardy in the Philippines.

Fuller dissented without offering an opinion.

The right not to be put twice in jeopardy came up again in *Grafton v. United States*, decided on May 27, 1907. Private Homer Grafton was tried before a general court-martial in the Philippines and then acquitted of "unlawfully, willfully, and feloniously" killing two Filipinos while he served on afternoon guard duty. Grafton was subsequently prosecuted in the provincial court, found guilty of homicide, and sentenced to twelve years in prison. He appealed to the Philippine

Supreme Court, which affirmed the provincial court's judgment in a four-to-three decision and denied Grafton's plea of double jeopardy. Grafton therefore appealed to the U.S. Supreme Court on the basis of being put in double jeopardy.

Justice Harlan wrote the Court's unanimous opinion. A civil court could not retry a court-martial, Harlan pointed out; the two had separate jurisdictions. Since the court-martial in the Philippines *did* have jurisdiction over Grafton, the fact that the civil court convicted him with what amounted to the same charge of an unlawful killing of a named person — even though the precise charges were different in the two venues, "homicide" versus "assassination" — meant that Grafton had been put twice in jeopardy. Because Grafton was tried twice for the same offense and because territorial courts derived their authority from the U.S. Congress — unlike the federal courts in the states, which came under the authority of the judiciary clause — Harlan reversed the decision of the Philippine Supreme Court and discharged the appellant from custody.

————

Three years later, the Supreme Court addressed the application of the Eighth Amendment's prohibition of cruel and unusual punishment in *Weems v. United States* (1910). Paul Weems was an officer of the U.S. government of the Philippine Islands who was convicted of falsifying the cost of two items with a total value of 612 pesos. Weems was fined 4,000 pesos for the crime and sentenced to *cadena temporal,* a punishment that lasted "a minimum of twelve years and one day," and called for "a chain at the ankle and wrist of the offender, hard and painful labor, no assistance from friend or relative, no marital authority or parental rights or rights of property." And even after serving a twelve-year sentence, the convict was subject to restrictions on his mobility and the ability to make good his name. Weems appealed his conviction on the basis that his sentence subjected him to "cruel and unusual punishment," per the Eighth Amendment ("Excessive bail shall not be required, nor excessive fines imposed, nor cruel and unusual punishments inflicted").

Justice McKenna wrote the Court's opinion in the five-to-two decision of May 2, 1910 (Justices Lurton and Moody did not take part in the decision; Lurton had not yet taken his seat on the bench, and Justice Moody was ill). McKenna argued that the punishment imposed on Weems constituted cruel and unusual punishment, since the Philippine Bill of Rights — and the Philippines were the first of the new territories to receive a bill of rights — used the exact same language as the U.S. Bill of Rights. The Eighth Amendment had to apply to Weems, McKenna reasoned, if the Philippine Bill of Rights were to have any meaning. The provisions of *cadena temporal* clearly constituted "cruel and unusual punishment," McKenna held, even if the Eighth Amendment does not specify exactly what constitutes cruel and unusual punishment.

Justice White dissented, joined by Justice Holmes. White argued that the punishment of *cadena temporal* was already well established in Philippine law as a sentence for public officials convicted of knowingly entering false statements on the public record. White further argued that the "cruel" and "unusual" provisions of the Eighth Amendment were not being violated: Weems's punishment was no worse than many other harsh sentences that had been imposed by American and British courts, which applied the same common law that had been the origin of the Eighth Amendment.

The Court thus not only overturned Weems's conviction but also established that Filipinos — and the inhabitants of other U.S. territories by implication — came under the protections of the Eighth Amendment.

———

A year later, on April 3, 1911, the U.S. Supreme Court decided yet another double jeopardy case from the Philippines, *Gavieres v. United States*. Vincent Gavieres was charged with "calumniating, outraging and insulting" a public official, as well as "being drunk or intoxicated" and behaving "in a drunken, boisterous, rude, or indecent manner in any place or premises to the annoyance of another person." But since Gavieres had been convicted twice for the same incident (once by a Manila municipal court and once by a military court-martial), and since the Act of July 1, 1902, protected persons in the Philippines from being put twice in jeopardy, the Court had to decide if Gavieres had been denied protection from double jeopardy.

Justice Day gave the Court's opinion for the eight-person majority. Day upheld the Philippine Supreme Court, which had ruled that the two charges were *not* the same offense. A conviction on one charge did not prevent prosecution on the other. Day distinguished *Gavieres* from *Grafton* — in which the Court had ruled that Grafton could not be prosecuted both before a military court-martial and a civil court — on the basis that in *Grafton*, the civil court derived its authority from the same governmental power as the court-martial, whereas this was not the case in *Gavieres*. The insult to the public official under Philippine code (one conviction) "was not within the terms of the offense or prosecution" of drunken and disorderly conduct under the Manila city ordinance (the other conviction).

Harlan dissented without writing an opinion.

In sum, a review of the Court's decisions in the several double jeopardy cases suggests that the Court had wide discretion as to how it interpreted the prohibition on double jeopardy in the Philippine Bill of Rights. We see the close rulings in *Kepner*, *Mendezona*, and *Trono* (two in favor of the constitutional guarantee and one opposed), but then the wilder swing between the Court's decisions in *Gavieres v. United States* (an eight-to-one vote upholding the Philippine and U.S. governments) and *Grafton v. United States* (a unanimous decision upholding the rights of Private Grafton). Given that the Act of July 1, 1902, protected Filipinos against double jeopardy, the Court ruled on the merits of statutory law rather than on constitutional principle.

———

Six weeks later, on May 15, 1911, the Supreme Court decided *Dowdell v. United States*, which concerned the Sixth Amendment's guarantee that the accused be able to confront his witnesses and be informed of the nature and cause of the accusation. Although the U.S. Supreme Court had not granted Filipinos the right to a jury trial or indictment by grand jury in felonies, the Court had not up to this point determined whether other criminal due process rights applied to the U.S. territories.

Louis Dowdell, a supply officer with the Philippine Constabulary, and two other men were charged with conspiring to steal public funds for their own use. The three men took a safe containing Philippine government money, sunk it in deep water, and concealed their crime from their superior officers. The Supreme Court of the Philippines convicted Dowdell, who appealed because he had multiply been denied due process: he had not met his witnesses face-to-face, a guarantee contained in the Philippine Bill of Rights as well as in the Sixth Amendment (the accused having the right "to be confronted with the witnesses against him"); he was not present at every stage of his trial; he was improperly arrested, since information taken from him had not been verified by oath or affidavit; there had been no indictment by grand jury; and he was not tried by a jury of his peers.

Justice Day issued the opinion of the Court for the eight-person majority; the Philippine Supreme Court, he argued, had acted wholly within its power. Day proceeded through Dowdell's arguments one at a time: there had always been exceptions to the right of the accused to confront his witnesses; there was precedent for the accused not being present at the testimony of witnesses; Dowdell had not made any objection when first brought to trial with respect to information not being verified by oath or affidavit; the Act of July 1, 1902, which established the government in the Philippines, did not mandate indictment by grand jury; and the objection that Dowdell had been not tried by a jury had already been addressed in *Dorr*.

Justice Harlan dissented without writing an opinion.

The decision in *Dowdell* thus not only upheld the unincorporated status of the Philippines — and, by extension, the other U.S. island territories — but when coupled with the Court's decision only six weeks earlier in *Gavieres v. United States* suggested the support of the newly constituted Supreme Court (with the new justices appointed to the bench between 1909 and 1911, as discussed in chapter 6) for the Republican Taft administration. It is hard to imagine all the dissenters in *Downes v. Bidwell* and *Hawaii v. Mankichi* — Justice Harlan excepted — agreeing to deny Filipinos the protections under the Fifth and Sixth Amendments, as did eight of the nine justices in *Gavieres* and *Dowdell*, as James Kerr points out in his study of the *Insular Cases*. But the ruling in *Dowdell* is also fully consistent with the agreement on the Court to support the police powers of the U.S. and territorial governments in administering territorial inhabitants. Such a view makes sense of the discrepancy between the rulings in *Grafton* and *Gavieres*, moreover: in each case the U.S. Supreme Court upheld the forces of law and order in the territories — in the former case, Grafton was a U.S. soldier, whereas in the latter case, Gavieres was a Filipino charged with "calumniating, outraging and insulting" a public official.

———

The Supreme Court on May 5, 1914, decided another case of due process in criminal proceedings — this time on the issue of the preliminary finding of probable cause — in *Ocampo v. United States.* Martin Ocampo and others owned, published, and wrote for a Manila newspaper, *La Renacimiento.* Ocampo was charged with libeling a member of the Philippine Commission, Dean C. Worcester (similar to the circumstances in *Dorr v. United States,* where Dorr was charged with libeling another member of the Philippine Commission). Ocampo appealed his conviction by the Philippine Supreme Court to the U.S. Supreme Court on the grounds that his arrest and trial had been without a preliminary finding of probable cause and therefore violated the Philippine Bill of Rights, which stated "That no person shall be held to answer for a criminal offense without due process of law" and "That no warrant shall issue but upon probable cause, supported by oath or affirmation." Both clauses paralleled the Fifth Amendment's guarantee that "no person shall . . . be deprived of life, liberty, or property without due process of law," and the Sixth Amendment's guarantee that "in all criminal prosecutions, the accused shall . . . be informed of the nature and cause of the accusation; [and] be confronted with the witnesses against him."

Justice Pitney wrote the unanimous opinion for the Court. Pitney found that the actions of Philippine authorities against Ocampo were consistent with the provisions authorized by the Philippine Commission (the Manila Charter, enacted August 1, 1901). With respect to indictment by grand jury, moreover, "the Constitution does not, of its own force, apply to the Islands." In addition, the requirement of a grand jury indictment was not within the guarantee of the "due process" clause. Pitney cited *Hawaii v. Mankichi, Dorr v. United States,* and *Dowdell v. United States* as precedents and also noted that the Philippine Supreme Court could increase its punishment and find the accused guilty of more serious charges upon an appeal — just as the U.S. Supreme Court had done in *Trono v. United States* (where the double jeopardy appeal was denied in large part because the plaintiff himself had made the appeal after being convicted of a lesser charge). "In short,"

Pitney concluded, "the appellate jurisdiction of the Supreme Court of the Philippine Islands in criminal cases is not confined to mere errors of law, but extends to a review of the whole case." Pitney and the Court again emphatically rejected the idea that the U.S. Constitution applied *ex proprio vigore.*

With the decision in *Ocampo* coming on the heels of *Dowdell, Rassmussen, Dorr,* and *Hawaii v. Mankichi,* we see that the Supreme Court progressively restricted the sphere of civil liberties allowed criminal defendants in the United States' territories.

———

The Court completed its rejection of the Constitution applying *ex proprio vigore* and its acceptance of the Incorporation Doctrine with its unanimous decision in *Balzac v. People of Porto Rico.* This case concerned two prosecutions of libel against Jesús M. Balzac, the editor of a newspaper published in Arecibo, Puerto Rico, for Balzac's description of the governor of Puerto Rico, Arthur Yager. "Like an abortion of hell expired by the fiery billows of infamy," Balzac had written, "this prototype of ignominy came among us as the diabolical incarnation of despotism." Yager was a "tyrant," a "dictator," a "calumnimator of people," an "assassin of democracy," and a "hyena studded with maledictions."

Balzac, as a result, was indicted for libel. But when Balzac was denied a jury trial, he appealed the verdict to the Supreme Court of Porto Rico. When that court denied his plea, Balzac appealed to the U.S. Supreme Court on the basis of the Sixth Amendment's right to a jury trial.

It was a different Supreme Court that decided the case. Chief Justice White, Justice Lurton, and Justice Lamar had all died, and Justice Hughes had resigned. The only member of the Court remaining from the original *Insular Cases* of 1901 cases was Justice McKenna. And President Harding's new chief justice was none other than William Howard Taft — the man who had promoted White to chief justice, former U.S president, former governor of the Philippines, a chief architect of the United States' territorial policies, and someone who had sought to be chief justice of the U.S. Supreme Court for much of his life. Three new associate justices sat on the bench alongside the new chief justice: James C. McReynolds, Louis Brandeis, and John Clarke.

James McReynolds was a southerner and archconservative. He was opposed to smoking; he thought the use of nail polish vulgar; he could be very rude; and he was anti-Semitic to the point of refusing to acknowledge fellow justices Brandeis and (later) Benjamin Cardozo. McReynolds was born in Elkton, Kentucky, and grew up in an upper-middle-class family. After attending Vanderbilt University and studying law at the University of Virginia, he practiced in Nashville and then taught law at Vanderbilt. When McReynolds failed to get elected to Congress, then-president Taft appointed him as assistant attorney general, where McReynolds was in charge of (and succeeded in) prosecuting the tobacco trust; President Wilson later appointed him U.S. attorney general. But when McReynolds became ineffective by making enemies among his fellow cabinet members and U.S. senators, Wilson appointed him to the Court to replace Lurton (who was also from Tennessee). McReynolds was another of the "Four Horsemen."

Louis D. Brandeis was by all accounts brilliant, liberal, imperious, and a passionate reformer. Brandeis, born to a wealthy family, grew up in Kentucky and Germany. After receiving his Harvard law degree at the age of twenty, he practiced law and, at the same time, participated in a variety of social, economic, and political causes. Brandeis attacked the commercial life insurance industry and persuaded savings banks to start selling life insurance. He was also a committed Zionist, among the American leaders of the nineteenth-century movement to form a Jewish state in Palestine. When President Wilson nominated Brandeis to the Supreme Court, however, the Senate subjected him to a difficult five-month nomination struggle. Seventy-four witnesses testified for and against the Brandeis appointment, accompanied by thousands of pages of submitted materials. Seven former presidents of the American Bar Association thought him unfit for the job, as did Taft and Root. The Senate eventually confirmed Brandeis, forty-nine to twenty-two.

John H. Clarke grew up in Ohio, where he also studied and practiced law. Clarke was a railroad lawyer, a Catholic, and a Democrat. He was also a reformer and a populist, who supported the direct election of U.S. senators, home rule for American cities, and the disclosure of politicians' campaign finances. Wilson appointed Clarke to the federal court and subsequently, based on Clarke's distinguished record as a Progressive, appointed him to the Supreme Court to replace Hughes.

The new chief justice wrote the Court's opinion in *Balzac v. Porto Rico*. "Few questions," Taft observed, "have been the subject of such discussion and dispute in our country as the status of our territory acquired from Spain in 1899. The division between the political parties in respect to it, the diversity of the views of the members of this court in regard to its constitutional aspects, and to the constant recurrence of the subject in the Houses of Congress, fixed the attention of all on the future relation of this acquired territory to the United States." Thus far, Taft summarized, the U.S. Supreme Court had already established that the foreign territory acquired by the United States could be classified into two categories: territory incorporated into the United States, in which case the entire Bill of Rights and provisions of the Constitution applied; and territory not incorporated into the Union, in which case Congress could govern the outlying territories subject to some but not necessarily all the provisions of the Constitution and its amendments.

Distinguishing *Balzac v. Porto Rico* from the previous *Insular Cases*, such as *Hawaii v. Mankichi*, *Dorr v. United States*, *Rassmussen v. United States*, and *Dowdell v. United States* was whether Congress's plenary power extended over persons explicitly designated as "U.S. citizens," since the Jones Act of 1917 made Puerto Ricans U.S. citizens. Furthermore, other provisions of the Jones Act appeared to indicate that Puerto Rico was now territory incorporated into the United States.

Two earlier cases prepared the ground for Taft's decision in *Balzac v. Porto Rico:* the Supreme Court's per curiam decisions in *Porto Rico v. Tapia* and *Porto Rico v. Muratti*. In these cases, jointly decided on January 22, 1918, the Court confronted the application of the Fifth Amendment to Puerto Rico under the conditions of the newly passed Jones Act.

The question in *Porto Rico v. Tapia* was whether Carlos Tapia, accused of a felony *after* the passage of the 1917 Jones Act, could be held without indictment by a grand jury. Tapia appealed the Puerto Rican district court's decision, arguing that the Jones Act effectively incorporated Puerto Rico since it made Puerto Ricans U.S. citizens and extended U.S. laws with respect to the mail, "revenue, navigation, immigration, national banking, bankruptcy, federal employers' liability, safety appliance, extradition, and census laws." But the U.S. District Court in Puerto Rico discharged Tapia, ruling that he could not be detained without presentment or indictment by grand jury as provided in the Fifth Amendment to the Constitution of the United States. So the prosecution appealed to the U.S. Supreme Court.

In *Porto Rico v. Muratti*, the felony was committed *before* passage of the Jones Act, but Muratti was prosecuted *after* the passage of the act. José Muratti also appealed the district court's conviction to the Supreme Court of Porto Rico on the basis of the Fifth Amendment. The Supreme Court of Porto Rico determined the plea good: the Constitution was "in full force and vigor in Porto Rico, and especially said Fifth Amendment." The prosecution then appealed to the U.S. Supreme Court.

The Supreme Court reversed both lower court decisions. In *Porto Rico v. Tapia*, the Court cited *Downes v. Bidwell, Hawaii v. Mankichi, Dorr, Rassmussen, Kopel v. Bingham, Dowdell,* and *Ocampo* as dispositive. Then on the basis of the *Tapia* decision and the "authorities therein cited," the Court also reversed the Supreme Court of Porto Rico's ruling in *Muratti*. The constitutional historian Charles Warren (writing before the 1922 decision in *Balzac*) called the Supreme Court's decision in *Porto Rico v. Tapia* "the capsheaf" — that is, the crowning or finishing part — "of the doctrine of incorporation."

In *Balzac v. Porto Rico*, Chief Justice Taft first addressed the question of jurisdiction, since the Judicial Code Act of September 6, 1916, changed the appellate jurisdiction of the Supreme Court. Taft held that, yes, the U.S. Supreme Court did have appellate jurisdiction over the Puerto Rican Supreme Court. Taft then considered the question of whether the Puerto Rican statute that did not grant the right to a jury trial in cases of misdemeanor was actually called into question in the case of libel. Did the Sixth Amendment, or at least that part that requires the accused to have "the right to a speedy and public trial, by an impartial jury of the state and district wherein the crime shall have been committed," apply to Puerto Rico?

The chief justice held that the right to a trial by jury did apply to the territories of the United States, consistent with precedents set on the right to trial by jury in Utah (*Reynolds v. United States*), the District of Columbia (*Callan v. Wilson*), Alaska (*Rassmussen*), and, in fact, all territories of the United States (*Dred Scott v. Sandford*). But Taft added that the right to a jury trial did *not* apply to territories that belonged to the United States but were not incorporated into the Union, citing *Dorr v.*

United States, *Hawaii v. Mankichi*, and *Downes v. Bidwell*. "The *Dorr* case," Taft argued, "shows that the opinion of Mr. Justice White of the majority, in *Downes v. Bidwell*, has become the settled law of the Court." Taft quoted directly from *Dorr*: "The power to govern territory, implied in the right to acquire it, and given to Congress . . . does not require that body to enact for ceded territory, not made part of the United States by congressional action, a system of laws which shall include the right of trial by jury, and that the Constitution does not, without legislation and of its own force, carry such right to territory so situated."

What, though, of the effect of the Jones Act, the organic act for Puerto Rico, which placed Puerto Rico under the Constitution by the terms of Section 1891 of the Revised Statutes of the United States? Balzac's attorneys argued that Puerto Rico should be distinguished from the Philippines, since U.S. law repeatedly distinguished between the two island territories. According to Section 1891, "The Constitution and all laws of the United States which are not locally applicable shall have the same force and effect within all the organized Territories, and in every Territory hereafter organized as elsewhere within the United States." In contrast, the organic act for the Philippine Islands (the Act of July 1, 1902) expressly held that Section 1891 should *not* apply to the Philippines, whereas the Foraker Act of 1900 was entirely silent with respect to Section 1891.

A number of other provisions in U.S. law, moreover, treated Puerto Rico as an incorporated territory: (1) Puerto Rico had a district court of the United States, with the powers of the district and circuit courts of the United States; (2) appeals from the Supreme Court of Porto Rico were allowed to the U.S. Supreme Court in all cases that brought the Constitution into question; (3) young men from Puerto Rico could become cadets at West Point and midshipmen at Annapolis; (4) U.S. stamps had been on sale in Puerto Rico for about twenty years; (5) Puerto Rico constituted the second of five districts of navigable waters of the United States; (6) U.S. copyright statutes had been enforced in Puerto Rican courts; (7) the laws of the United States, not locally inapplicable, had been enforced in Puerto Rico; (8) the immigration laws of the United States applied to Puerto Rico; (9) the Federal Employer's Liability Act, Federal Safety Appliance Act, and Federal Bankruptcy Acts applied to Puerto Rico; and (10) Congress provided in 1919 that a population census was to be required to be taken in each state, the District of Columbia, Alaska, Hawai'i, and Puerto Rico.

Taft responded to all these points by simply noting that the Jones Act did not contain an *explicit* clause "to incorporate the island into the Union." Most notably, the Bill of Rights contained in the Jones Act mentioned every guarantee "*except those relating to indictment by a grand jury in the case of infamous crimes and the right of trial by jury in civil and criminal cases*" (emphasis added). "If [the Bill of Rights] was intended to incorporate Porto Rico into the union by this act, which would *ex proprio vigore* make applicable the whole Bill of Rights," Taft pointed out, "why was it thought necessary to create for it a Bill of Rights and carefully exclude trial by jury?"

"As for the fact that Porto Ricans were U.S. citizens," Taft added, "we find it entirely consistent with nonincorporation," since Puerto Ricans were no longer the subjects of Spain. And "it enabled them to move into the continental United States" and become "residents of any state there." "It is *locality*," Taft wrote, "that is determinative of the application of the Constitution, in such matters as judicial procedure, and not the status of the people who live in it" (emphasis added).

The chief justice explained the Incorporation Doctrine:

> It is well settled that these provisions for jury trial in criminal and civil cases apply to the territories of the United States, but it is just as clearly settled that they do not apply to territory belonging to the United States which has not been incorporated into the Union. It was further settled in Downes v. Bidwell, and confirmed by Dorr v. United States, that neither the Philippines nor Porto Rico was territory which had become incorporated into the United States, as distinguished from merely belonging to it; and that the acts giving temporary Governments to the Philippines and to Porto Rico had no such effect.

The differences between Puerto Rico, on the one hand, and Alaska or Louisiana, on the other hand — each was annexed territory that did not contain any explicit language of incorporation in its legislation or treaty, but which Congress interpreted as being incorporated in the United States — were, for Taft, a matter of practical politics. Here, Taft also took a results-oriented approach: "Alaska was a very different case from that of Porto Rico. It was an enormous territory, very

sparsely settled, and offering opportunity for immigration and settlement by American citizens." And the conditions in the Philippines
presented their own obstacles for incorporation. Thus to insist on jury
trial "no matter what the needs or capacities of the people," Taft
quoted from *Dorr*, would be to "provoke disturbance, rather than to
aid the orderly administration of justice."

Since Puerto Ricans were "trained to a complete judicial system
which knows no juries, living in compact and ancient communities,
with definitely formed customs and political conceptions," they were
not suited for trials by jury. Puerto Rico, like the Philippines and other
Pacific territories, was one of several "distant ocean communities of
a different origin and language from those of our continental people,"
Taft remarked.

As for the argument made by Balzac's attorneys that U.S. laws
treated Puerto Rico as an incorporated territory, Taft held that the
application of U.S. laws was insufficient on its own; incorporation was
not to be "left a matter of mere inference or construction." Incorporation was not to be done casually, even if in the period before the
Spanish-American War "the distinction between acquisition and
incorporation was not regarded as important, or at least it was not
fully understood and had not aroused great controversy." And Congress's purpose could well be merely inferred from "various legislative acts." But now, with the United States' new overseas possessions,
"incorporation is not to be assumed without express declaration, or
an implication so strong as to exclude any other view."

Taft thereby followed the *Tapia* and *Muratti* precedents and agreed
with the prosecution: (1) that the treaty-making power of the United
States was devoid of authority to incorporate foreign territory in the
absence of implicit or explicit congressional assent; (2) that the Treaty
of Paris left it to Congress to determine incorporation; (3) that the
Fifth and Sixth Amendments did not, by their own force, extend to
ceded territory without congressional action; (4) that the Fifth and
Sixth Amendments were not fundamental rights included within the
guaranty of the "due process" clause; and (5) that the only test of
whether or not ceded territory were incorporated is the expression
of Congress, an expression that Congress had not made with respect
to Puerto Rico and the Philippines.

The chief justice acknowledged that Balzac's words may have been "unconsciously humorous." But Balzac went "far beyond" the "exuberant expressions of meridional speech"; his words were libelous in their extremity and therefore in violation of the First Amendment. Taft affirmed the ruling of the Supreme Court of Porto Rico.

Justice Holmes concurred with the chief justice but did not write an opinion.

Puerto Rico thus remained an unincorporated territory according to the U.S. Supreme Court for the purposes of Balzac's petition on the grounds of being guaranteed the right to jury trial in the case of libel — notwithstanding that Puerto Ricans were designated as U.S. citizens under the 1917 Jones Act, that the Jones Act made Puerto Rican District Court cases subject to review by the U.S. Supreme Court, and that the act established that the commercial, financial, regulatory, and other laws of the United States were to apply in full to Puerto Rico. Puerto Ricans had already been residents of a U.S. territory for more than two decades, moreover, and the "origin and language" of Puerto Rico were arguably no more exceptional than those of New Mexico or Hawai'i.

More important, *Balzac* settled several questions about the application of the U.S. Constitution to the territories of the United States. Territorial inhabitants may have been explicitly designated as "U.S. citizens," but they were not necessarily full members of the American political community. Only *some* constitutional protections applied to the residents of the unincorporated territories — not all and not none — and trial by jury and indictment by grand jury were not among the protected provisions. The U.S. government, acting through Congress, could exercise sovereignty more or less indefinitely over people and areas outside the boundaries of the states; the United States *could* possess a colonial empire.

Balzac v. Porto Rico received little notice, with little or no newspaper coverage. The *New York Times*, for instance, had only a brief, page-three story noting that Puerto Ricans did not have the right to trial by jury in misdemeanors and that Puerto Rico had not been incorporated into the United States.

———

A look at the Supreme Court's decisions in the twenty years from *Hawaii v. Mankichi* in 1903 to *Balzac v. Porto Rico* in 1922 shows that slender reeds of the decisions in the 1901 *Insular Cases* were rooted in nurturing soil, thanks to the pro-expansionist Republican Party's dominant position in American national politics of the early twentieth century, the overwhelming influence of the United States in the Western Hemisphere and its growing global presence, and the quality of the justices that Presidents Roosevelt, Taft, and later, Wilson, and Harding appointed to the Supreme Court. The new justices on the Court supported the United States' emergence as a world power. The judicial support for U.S. policies was especially manifest in the Court's upholding of strong governmental authority in the new island territories — law and order for officials in Washington, D.C., Manila, and San Juan — evident in the decisions in *Hawaii v. Mankichi, Dorr v. United States, Dowdell v. United States, Ocampo v. United States,* and *Balzac v. Porto Rico.*

In a series of cases involving the rights of criminal defenders in the territories, the Supreme Court used the Incorporation Doctrine to deny persons the right to a jury trial (*Hawaii v. Mankichi, Dorr v. United States, Dowdell v. United States, Porto Rico v. Tapia, Porto Rico v. Muratti, Balzac v. Porto Rico*); the protection of indictment by grand jury in cases of felony (*Hawaii v. Mankichi, Dowdell v. United States, Tapia, Muratti,* and *Balzac*); the prohibition against self-incrimination; the right for the accused "to be informed of the nature and cause of the accusation" (*Ocampo v. United States*); the right of the accused to "enjoy . . . a speedy and public trial" by an impartial jury (*Balzac*); and the right of the accused "to be confronted with witnesses against him" (*Dowdell v. United States*). Twenty-one years after Justice White had articulated a three-person concurring opinion in *Downes v. Bidwell* — with more justices dissenting than joining White's elaboration of the Incorporation Doctrine — Chief Justice Taft relied solely on the Incorporation Doctrine for writing his opinion for a unanimous Court in *Balzac.* Even an officially designated "U.S. citizen" was not necessarily entitled to constitutional protections if she or he resided in territory of the United States.

The Court's record in criminal proceedings thus followed the path of the original set of *Insular Cases* of 1901, where Justice White first proposed the Incorporation Doctrine as the basis for the U.S. government's plenary authority over the new territories, even if in seeming violation of the Constitution's uniformity clause (*Downes v. Bidwell; Dooley v. United States II*); export clause (*Dooley v. United States II*); and preference clause — although the Supreme Court did not directly rule on the latter clause.

Other cases, too, which might seem to indicate that territorial citizens were equal to U.S. citizens and that territorial governments were the equal of state governments, can perhaps be better viewed as occasions in which the Supreme Court upheld the demands for law and order in its new possessions. So in *Neely v. Henkel* (1901) and *Kopel v. Bingham* (1909) the Court ruled that the governments the United States created in occupied Cuba and Puerto Rico could demand the extradition of fugitive criminals from the states or, by extension, from other territories of the United States (per Art. IV, Sec. 2, Cl. 2). Yet these two cases may be more about the Court enforcing the U.S. government's authority in Cuba and Puerto Rico — and by implication in other U.S. territories — than they are about the territories being the equivalent of states for the purposes of the extradition. The apparent anomaly of the *Grafton* case, where a unanimous Court upheld Homer Grafton's right to be protected from double jeopardy, can, as noted earlier, be better understood as another instance where the Court supported territorial control; the appellant was a U.S. soldier, after all. More, the ruling in *Porto Rico v. Rosaly* that the Puerto Rican government (and by implication other territorial governments) enjoyed sovereign immunity may also be better seen as the Court's support of the U.S. government's control of its territories.

Interestingly, Justices Holmes — who many see as a progressive and civil libertarian — was nonetheless willing to go along with the Court majority in its support of territorial control, per his opinions in *Hawaii v. Mankichi, Dorr, Dowdell, Ocampo,* and *Balzac v. Porto Rico.* His dissenting opinions in two of the double jeopardy cases, *Kepner* and *Mendezona,* and in *Weems* further reveal Holmes's support for upholding the U.S. government's authority vis-à-vis territorial inhabitants. Holmes may have been politically isolated on the Court on many constitutional issues, as the popular writer and columnist Max Lerner once remarked, but this was not true with respect to how the Constitution applied to the United States' new territories; here Holmes had plenty of allies on the bench, especially his friend and fellow intellectual aristocrat Justice White.

But the thirty-five *Insular Cases* offer lessons beyond the triumph of the Incorporation Doctrine proposed in the initial *Insular Cases* in issues of law and order.

One further lesson is that *the Court followed Congress's lead*. When Congress passed a particular law relevant to the territories (e.g., the Foraker Act), then the Court honored the legislation (e.g., *Downes, Dooley II*). In the absence of that expressed intent by Congress, the Court ruled in support of the uniformity clause and the protection of commerce (e.g., *De Lima v. Bidwell, Goetze v. United States, Crossman v. United States, Dooley v. United States I, Armstrong v. United States, Fourteen Diamond Rings v. United States*, and both *Lincoln; Warner, Barnes* cases). Similarly, when Congress made the duties extracted from trade with the Philippines legal — given that they were ruled unconstitutional in the two *Lincoln; Warner, Barnes* cases — the Court approved Congress's action in *United States v. Heinszen*.

Thus if the Philippine organic act specifically protected persons against being put twice in jeopardy, the Court interpreted the Fifth Amendment's protection against double jeopardy as applying to citizens of unincorporated territories as seen in the decisions in *Kepner, Mendezona*, and *Grafton* (although in *Trono* and *Gavieres*, the Court supported the Philippine government and the authority of territorial officials). Another provision of the Philippine Bill of Rights, part of the Act of July 1, 1902, protected Filipinos from "cruel and unusual punishment." Thus the Court guaranteed the protection of the Eighth Amendment's prohibition against cruel and unusual punishment (*Weems*). Or, when the U.S. Congress allowed the Philippine government to continue the practice of free carriage of mail by coastal traders, the Court accepted Congress's judgment (*Board v. Ynchausti*). If Congress were not entirely clear, however, as with the Senate's resolution continuing the McKinley administration's tariff on Puerto Rican trade and with Congress's "ambiguous language" of the Philippine organic act instating the Philippine war tariffs, then the Court used its discretion to protect commerce and support uniform tariff duties (e.g., *Fourteen Diamond Rings*, and the second decision in *Lincoln; Warner, Barnes*).

Congress's intent could also be expressed through treaty, not just by legislation. So in *Ponce v. Porto Rico* the Court agreed to support the "legal and political institutions" of Puerto Rico by the terms of the Treaty of Paris. Although the decision to support the Catholic Church seemingly violated the establishment clause, given that the territorial government of Puerto Rico favored the establishment of a particular religion, the U.S. Supreme Court honored the terms of the peace treaty. In contrast, the Supreme Court felt no compunction to necessarily honor the provisions of the Treaty of Guadalupe-Hidalgo in cases adjudicating disputes over Mexican land grants in the American Southwest.

Conversely, the Court was not infrequently willing to buck the wishes of the executive branch, as in *De Lima v. Bidwell, Goetze, Crossman, Dooley I, Armstrong, Fourteen Diamond Rings*, and both *Lincoln; Warner, Barnes* cases. The Court also ruled against the territorial and U.S. governments in *Kepner, Mendezona, Grafton, Weems*, and *Ochoa v. Hernandez*. If the Court was not willing to challenge Congress's explicit intent, it was willing to take on the White House and the territorial governments.

A second, additional lesson of the *Insular Cases* is that the *Incorporation Doctrine was itself flexible*. The Incorporation Doctrine was by no means a hard-and-fast guide for territorial policy. The Court could rigidly apply it, on the one hand, as did the chief justice in *Balzac v. Porto Rico* (interpreting the 1917 Jones Act) and did Justice White in his concurring opinion in *Hawaii v. Mankichi* (interpreting the Newlands Resolution); in neither case did the justices find text explicitly incorporating the territory— Puerto Rico in 1917, Hawaii in 1903— hence their decisions. But the Court could use its license to infer Congress's intent in the absence of explicit language, on the other hand. So Justice White held that Alaska was incorporated in his opinion for the Court in *Rassmussen v. United States*, even though there was no language expressly incorporating Alaska into the Union, as did Chief Justice Taft in *Balzac v. Porto Rico*. And even taking Alaska to be incorporated, this fact did not prevent Justice Brewer from approving Congress's imposition of "local taxes" for the purpose of funding the administration of Alaska — seemingly in violation of the decision in *Rassmussen*.

The Supreme Court's decisions in the *Insular Cases* reveal a maneuverability and complexity, then, that go well beyond simply the establishment and consolidation of the Incorporation Doctrine, or even of the affirmation of Congress's plenary authority over the United States' island territories. Yet this maneuverability and complexity emerged gradually. While there were clear and serious differences in the Court over the decisions of May 27 and December 2, 1901, and in its decision in *Hawaii v. Mankichi*, it was in the four simultaneously issued decisions of May 31, 1904 — *Binns v. United States, Kepner v. United States, Mendezona v. United States*, and *Dorr v. United States* — in which the justices revealed how they would now decide which constitutional provisions applied to the United States' territories and their inhabitants, and which did not. In subsequent years, the Court elaborated and entrenched these directions and distinctions in other territorial cases.

A third lesson is that the *Insular Cases* were not just about the loss of constitutional protection; the Court in some instances *did apply constitutional provisions to the territories and their inhabitants*. The Supreme Court guaranteed the Fifth Amendment's protection of due process with respect to the taking of property in *Ochoa v. Hernandez* — thus implicitly protecting persons in all other U.S. territories from governmental takings. The Court also interpreted treaties and legislation so as to guarantee personal and territorial rights, as seen with the prohibition against double jeopardy in *Kepner, Mendezona*, and *Grafton*, the prohibition against cruel and unusual punishment in *Weems*, and the protection of Puerto Rican society in *Ponce v. Roman Catholic*. In these and other cases, the Court very clearly — as other cases often showed — had the discretion *not* to interpret congressional legislation or the Treaty of Paris as reason to protect particular constitutional provisions.

The application of the Constitution to the governments in and people of the territories touches on a last lesson of the *Insular Cases*: the political debates and legal battles over how the Constitution applied to the U.S. territories foreshadow the more familiar and later "incorporation debate" — the issue of which provisions in the Bill of Rights are guaranteed under the Fourteenth Amendment. This was Justice Harlan's premise in all the *Insular Cases*, as we can see: that the Fourteenth Amendment encompassed — or "incorporated" — the individual protections of the U.S. Bill of Rights.

Harlan made this argument throughout much of his judicial career, in fact, as the judicial scholar Tinsley Yarbrough points out. In his dissent in *Hurtado v. California* (1887), Harlan stated that the identical language of the Fifth and Fourteenth Amendments was no accident, and that due process with respect to indictment by grand jury was among the guarantees provided by the Constitution because of the Fourteenth Amendment. In his dissent in *O'Neil v. Vermont* (1892), to give another example, Harlan argued that the protections of the Fourteenth Amendment included the Eighth Amendment's ban on cruel and unusual punishment. And in his dissent in *Plessy v. Ferguson* (1896), arguing against the segregation of African American railroad passengers, Harlan maintained that the passage of the Fourteenth Amendment, in conjunction with the ratification of the Thirteenth and Fifteenth Amendments, served to "protect all the civil rights that pertain to freedom and citizenship," including "the privilege of participating in the political control" of the United States.

In *Maxwell v. Dow* (1900), Harlan wrote that the Fourteenth Amendment included the guarantee of the Sixth Amendment's norm of a twelve-member jury. Later, in his dissent in *Patterson v. Colorado* (1907), Harlan stated that the First Amendment's protection of free speech came under the Fourteenth Amendment. And in *Twining v. New Jersey* (1908), he stated that the Fourteenth Amendment controlled the Fifth Amendment's prohibition on compulsory self-incrimination. For Harlan, there were no constitutional barriers to the full incorporation of the Bill of Rights under the Fourteenth Amendment.

This was, of course, Harlan's argument in the *Insular Cases* and, for a while, also that of Fuller, Brewer, and Peckham: that territorial annexation by the United States necessarily meant their incorporation under the laws and Constitution of the United States. This was the *ex proprio vigore* doctrine, which logically led to the notion that the Bill of Rights fully applied to the territories of the United States, no matter how distant or different in culture than the states and territories of the continental United States. Seven of the first ten *Insular Cases* — all except for *Downes, Dooley II,* and *Neely v. Henkel* — were decided on this basis, and so too were a number of others where the Court interpreted Congress's will and treaty provisions consistently with the Constitution applying *ex proprio vigore*.

Only Harlan was ahead of his time. The Fuller Court, the White Court, and the Taft Court essentially kept to the Supreme Court's ruling in the *Slaughterhouse Cases* (1873), instead: that the first eight amendments of the Bill of Rights were *not* "privileges or immunities of the United States" and thus did *not* come under the Fourteenth Amendment's privileges and immunities clause. Only later, in the 1950s and 1960s, did the Warren Court start incorporating the protections guaranteed by the Bill of Rights under the Fourteenth

Amendment's due process clause to the citizens of the states: the *First Amendment* rights of speech, press, and religion (*Fiske v. Kansas* [1927]); the *Fourth Amendment* rights to be free from unreasonable search and seizure (*Mapp v. Ohio* [1961]); the *Fifth Amendment* prohibitions against double jeopardy (*Benton v. Maryland* [1969]) and compelled self-incrimination (*Malloy v. Hogan* [1964], which overruled *Twining*); the *Fifth Amendment*'s due compensation for property taken for public use (*Chicago, Burlington & Quincy Railroad v. Chicago* [1897]; the *Sixth Amendment* rights to counsel (*Gideon v. Wainwright* [1963]), to a speedy and public trial (*In re Oliver* [1948]), to confrontation of opposing witnesses (*Pointer v. Texas* [1965]), and to a compulsory process for obtaining witness (*Washington v. Texas* [1967]); and the *Eighth Amendment* prohibitions against cruel and unusual punishment (*Robinson v. California* [1962]) and against excessive bail (*Schilb v. Kuebel* [1971]).

Harlan can thus be seen as Justice Hugo Black's direct predecessor. Black, more than any other justice on the Warren Court, also fundamentally believed that the Fourteenth Amendment incorporated the Bill of Rights.

CHAPTER 8

The *Insular Cases* and American Empire

Take up the White Man's burden—
Send forth the best ye breed—
Go bind your sons to exile
To serve your captive's need;
To wait in heavy harness,
On fluttered folk and wild—
Your new-caught, sullen peoples,
Half-devil and half-child.
RUDYARD KIPLING, "The White Man's Burden," 1899

Today, employees of clothing manufacturers in the Commonwealth of the Northern Marianas Islands may receive less than $3.05 an hour for their labor. That comes to about 60 percent of the U.S. minimum wage. Yet persons working for the Gap, Wal-Mart, Nordstrom, Tommy Hilfiger, Sears, Calvin Klein, the Limited, Liz Claiborne, Target, J. Crew, and other clothing manufacturers sew "Made in the U.S.A." labels into their garments. If the Northern Marianas is a territory of the United States and if the Northern Marianans, known as Chamorros, are U.S. citizens, though, how can labor policy in the Northern Marianas defy U.S. federal law?

On July 7, 2003, Hector "Gordo" Acosta Martínez and Joel Rivera Alejandro, both Puerto Ricans, were brought to trial for kidnapping and killing Jorge Hernández Díaz on the evening of February 11, 1998. The two men kidnapped Mr. Hernández and then, when they found out that authorities were investigating the kidnapping—contrary to their demands—retaliated by shooting Mr. Hernández, cutting off his head and limbs, and leaving his head and body parts on the roadside. U.S. prosecutors in Puerto Rico invoked the 1994 Federal Death Penalty Act and asked that both men be put to death. Had Mr. Martínez and Mr. Rivera been found guilty, they would have been executed by lethal injection in Terre Haute, Indiana. Yet the Puerto Rican Constitution of 1952, which established Puerto Rico as a commonwealth of the United States and represents a compact between Puerto Rico and the United States, prohibits the death penalty. How, then, can U.S. attorneys ask for the death penalty?

As of May 1, 2006, thirty-six troops from the United States' territories have died in Iraq while serving in the U.S. armed forces: twenty-two from Puerto Rico, three from the Virgin Islands, three from Guam, three from the Northern Marianas, and five from American Samoa. This total number of deaths comes to more fatalities than that of twenty-six of the fifty states. Yet in the summer of 2004, well after the war started, athletes from Puerto Rico, the Virgin Islands, Guam, and American Samoa — although not the Northern Marianas — for a little more than a two-week period competed against the United States in the Olympic Games. If residents of the U.S. territories are U.S. citizens, and American Samoans are U.S. nationals, who are fighting and dying for the United States of America, how can they, at the same time, be playing against the United States as foreign athletes in international competitions?

U.S. federal law does not seem to apply in the Northern Marianas, since wages can be below the U.S. minimum wage that applies in all the states and other territories. But by the terms of the covenant that established the Northern Marianas as a commonwealth and as a territory of the United States, employees in the Northern Marianas are not subject to U.S. minimum wage laws.

In contrast, U.S. criminal law appears to apply in Puerto Rico by virtue of the 1994 Death Penalty Act, despite Puerto Rico's constitution and its status as a commonwealth. Although the U.S. attorney general can also prosecute the citizens of states that have constitutions prohibiting the death penalty — twelve states and the District of Columbia also prohibit the death penalty — Article I, Section 1 of the Puerto Rican constitution states that Puerto Rico's "political power emanates from the people" and is to "be exercised in accordance with their will, within the terms of the compact agreed upon between the people of Puerto Rico and the United States of America." So Acosta and Rivera still faced the possibility of the death penalty — although they have since been acquitted — as have several other Puerto Ricans since.

Meanwhile, U.S. citizens of the territories can serve in the U.S. armed forces and also compete against other U.S. citizens in the

Olympics. In addition, women not only may serve in the U.S. military and represent "Puerto Rico" against the "United States" in athletic contests but also may compete for "Puerto Rico" and against women from the "United States" in international beauty pageants.

These paradoxes result from the fact that Puerto Rico, Guam, American Samoa, the U.S. Virgin Islands, and the Northern Marianas are territories of the United States. As U.S. territories, these islands are neither states of the United States nor independent nation-states. These oddities would simply not exist were the island inhabitants also members of states or citizens of (separate) nation-states. Neither would they exist in the absence of the *Insular Cases* and the Incorporation Doctrine allowing the U.S. government to exert sovereignty over persons in areas without political rights. Yet despite these and other notable incongruities, the territories seem to have vanished into insignificance, while the *Insular Cases* — a hundred years later — seem to be the artifacts of a distant past, a different world.

Territorial inhabitants have been U.S. citizens for decades; they enjoy most of the protections under the Constitution; and the rulings in the *Insular Cases* on the Fifth and Sixth Amendments denying criminal due process rights have largely been superseded by more recent Court decisions. Meanwhile, the Philippines have been independent for sixty years, and the United States years ago abandoned its two large military bases, Subic Naval Base and Clark Air Field; the U.S. Navy has stopped using Vieques Island off the east coast of Puerto Rico as a weapons proving ground; and the navy shuttered its Roosevelt Roads Naval Station on Puerto Rico on March 31, 2004.

Although the combined population of Puerto Rico and other U.S. territories has grown steadily from 3.4 million persons in 1980 to 3.8 million in 1990 and 4.2 million in 2000, it remains a small fraction of the total population of the United States. And only infrequently, with the closing of military facilities, the incidence of hurricanes and other natural disasters, electoral referenda — Puerto Rico in 1998 most recently — political scandals, and other extraordinary events, do the territories receive attention in the states.

Why, then, do the *Insular Cases* still matter, aside from their value of informing us of the territorial history of the United States, Supreme Court history, and the national politics at the time of the Spanish-American War and the years immediately following?

My answer is that the *Insular Cases* allowed for the emergence of two kinds of American empire. One was a *territorial empire*. The Supreme Court legitimated Congress's exercise of plenary power over the new island possessions — areas that a majority on the Supreme Court, a majority in Congress, U.S. presidents, and much of the American public agreed could be governed differently than had been the earlier and then-existing U.S. territories. The newly acquired islands could be held as territories indefinitely and granted only those constitutional rights and privileges consistent with the text of U.S. treaties and congressional legislation.

Notwithstanding the fact that Congress had exercised plenary power over the territories throughout the history of the United States, from the late eighteenth through the nineteenth century, novel in the *Insular Cases* was the breadth of the Court's decisions in *Downes v. Bidwell* and other cases. With the creation of the new category of "unincorporated" territories, the United States could now hold its island acquisitions at arm's length, apart from the American polity. And Congress, together with the Supreme Court, could decide whether to later bring the unincorporated territories into the Union, to keep them at arm's length, or to let them go.

The decisions in the *Insular Cases* thus endorsed the development of the United States into an international power, one like Great Britain, France, Germany, Russia, and Japan, each with its dependent territories or colonies. It was in the context of the United States becoming a world power that Rudyard Kipling in 1899 wrote "The White Man's Burden" (the chapter epigraph is the first of seven stanzas). For Kipling, the United States' duty was to use its new power responsibly, that is, to civilize, educate, and enrich less developed peoples.

This territorial empire persists.

The U.S. government currently exercises sovereignty over five territories: the Commonwealth of Puerto Rico, Guam, American Samoa, the U.S. Virgin Islands of Saint Thomas, Saint John, and Saint Croix, and the Commonwealth of the Northern Marianas Islands (formerly a U.S. trusteeship). Not only is this more territory than is controlled by any other country in the world, but more U.S. citizens live in Puerto Rico than in almost half of the fifty states (not counting the 4 million or so Puerto Ricans who live in the states and especially in and around New York, Miami, and Orlando); only China, with Hong Kong and Macau, has a larger territorial population. And the United States continues to hold these territories as unincorporated territories — although Puerto Rico and the Northern Marianas are also "commonwealths" — with little promise of eventual statehood.

The other empire created by the *Insular Cases* is the opposite of the first; the addition of the United States' new territories after the Spanish-American War effectively marked the *end of U.S. geographic expansion*. Since 1898, the United States has admitted five territories as states (Oklahoma, New Mexico, Arizona, Alaska, and Hawai'i) and annexed three island groups as unincorporated territories: the eastern Samoan islands (2,200 miles southwest of Hawaii and containing 60,000 inhabitants); the U.S. Virgin Islands (60 miles west of Puerto Rico with about 135,000 inhabitants); and the Northern Marianas (a 400-mile-long archipelago with about 80,000 inhabitants).

Over the same period, however, the United States also *reduced* the scope of its geographic sovereignty by granting Cuba its nominal independence in 1902 and then granting the Philippines its independence in 1946. Given the combined physical size and population of Cuba and the Philippines, and given the fact that the last five states admitted to the Union were previously incorporated territories, the United States never encompassed as large an area as it did between March 1899 and May 1902. The annexations of American Samoa, Virgin Islands, Northern Marianas, and — arguably — the Panama Canal Zone between 1903 and 1987 stand as minor exceptions to the larger reality that the United States of the twentieth and twenty-first centuries has more or less kept its same political geography. So even as the United States has become more powerful internationally, especially with the collapse of the Soviet Union and the end of the cold war, the geographic area inhabited by U.S. citizens and U.S. nationals has changed little.

Put another way, the United States has reaped relatively few territorial benefits — and has sought relatively few territorial benefits — from its remarkable victories in the global wars of the twentieth century. Despite winning World War I, World War II, and the cold war, the United States added no new territory except for the Pacific trust territories of the Marshall Islands and Palau. By way of comparison, France reacquired Alsace and Lorraine after World War I; the Soviet Union effectively added the "satellite" Eastern Europe nation-states and the four southernmost Kurile, or Tsushima, Islands to its domain after World War II; and West Germany reunited with the former East Germany — the German Democratic Republic — after the cold war. The "American Century," in the words of *Time* publisher Henry Luce in 1941, reveals a conspicuous absence of territorial spoils.

The United States' empire of the twentieth and twenty-first centuries has thus been one of a different sort. It has been based on the creation and maintenance of open markets, on the ability to project military force globally, on the cooperation of allied governments, and on the support of international institutions — many of them of the United States' creation. The decisions in the *Insular Cases* also established this second sort of empire.

A unanimous Supreme Court in *Neely v. Henkel* determined that Cuba was *foreign*, even though the United States defeated Spain on Cuban soil, even though the U.S. military occupied Cuba and exercised full authority over the island, and even though the McKinley administration and others both inside and outside the government sought to annex Cuba. Cuba achieved its independence, instead, with the passage of the Platt Amendment of 1901, which was appended to the new Cuban constitution. The lesson from Cuba was that the United States did not have to keep all the area that it acquired; the United States could also let territory go. Here, the Incorporation Doctrine also granted the United States this power to *divest* itself of territory under its possession — an idea first suggested to me by the legal historian Christina Duffy Burnett.

The text of "The White Man's Burden" suggests the logic for this second kind of empire as well, a fact obscured by the poem's title and Kipling's message — flattering to most Americans — that the United States was now on a par with Great Britain. But for all the acclaim and criticism that "The White Man's Burden" received for its message of imperialism, the poem makes painfully clear the difficulty, expense, and thanklessness of a territory-based empire — a fact pointed out by Senator Benjamin "Pitchfork Ben" Tillman (D-S.C.) and a few others at the time. Colonial administration, Kipling wrote, binds "sons to exile," demands "savage wars of peace," causes the ruling metropolitan power to have its hopes repeatedly dashed "to nought," and results in the imperial state receiving only the "blame of those ye better" and the "hate of those ye guard." There had to be a better way, and there was: informal empire.

This chapter and chapter 9 explain these distinct, dual legacies of the *Insular Cases*. This chapter investigates the scope and evolution of the U.S. government's authority over its several present-day territories, authority made possible by the decisions in the *Insular Cases*. Chapter 9 then turns to the emergence and features of the United States' informal empire, one in which the United States has been able to exercise global power in ways besides territorial expansion and acquisition. The chapter concludes by asking what the *Insular Cases* can tell us about constitutional law.

———

The idea of an American empire has been part of political thinking since the founding. In 1785, John Adams stated that the United States was "destined beyond a doubt to be the greatest power on earth"; a year later Thomas Jefferson proclaimed that the United States was to be "the nest from which all America, North and South, is to be peopled." From the founding, the nation's leading politicians and presidents believed in an American empire. As Senator Edward Everett of Massachusetts commented in the early nineteenth century — speaking for many — the westward advance of the United States was the progress of "the human family, led out by Providence to possess its broad patrimony." Thomas Hart Benton of Missouri, a future U.S. senator, strong supporter of western expansion, and future leader of the Democratic Party, likewise wrote in 1818 that the possession of the mouth of the Columbia River offered wonderful prospects for Asian trade. And Senator Henry Clay of Tennessee "had no doubt," the historian Reginald Horsman tells us, that the entire "continent, including Texas, was to be settled." (For Clay, as for most other Americans, Indian occupancy was not settlement.)

But the events of the late 1890s upended this process of geographic expansion, as the United States in a few short years transformed from being a continental republic (one kind of a nation) into being an overseas empire (another kind of a nation). "The relation of America to Europe and the world is profoundly modified by the new departure," one British newspaper observed. "Colonies mean a navy, a navy means naval bases and coaling stations, and naval bases are insecure unless they are backed up by the possession of a hinterland. This is the logic of imperialism," the *Westminster Gazette* remarked, "and it may lead the Americans as far as it has led us." (It gave a warning, though: "The entrance of the United States on the scene as a world power is already regarded as a highly disturbing factor by the European chancellories.")

Yet there can be little doubt that the *Insular Cases* led to "empire," if by "empire" we mean the extension of U.S. sovereignty over persons without voice in their annexation and without representation in their subsequent government. Cubans, Puerto Ricans, Filipinos, and the Chamorros of Guam were not party to the Treaty of Paris, and the inhabitants of the U.S. territories had no representation in the U.S. federal government. (The inhabitants of the continental U.S. territories in contrast were overwhelmingly émigrés from the existing states, who fully expected their districts and territories to later become states.) With its overseas empire, the United States *had* arrived as a world power. "It had thrown off its swaddling clothes," in the words of the *Chicago Record-Herald* following the Supreme Court's decision in *Downes v. Bidwell*. The United States had now "come forth full-powered, full-statured among the sovereign nations of the earth." As the naval strategist Mahan remarked at the time of the Spanish-American War, "Imperialism, the extension of national authority over alien communities, is a dominant note in the world politics of today."

Since the early twentieth century, in fact, the territories have been integral to the strategic development of the United States as a "full-powered, full statured" nation. During World War II the U.S. territories in the Pacific served as crucial military outposts in the war against Japan, whether as sites for launching attacks, monitoring enemy action, or stationing supplies and personnel. Although the Philippines, Hawai'i, Alaska, Midway, and Wake Island — the latter two are unincorporated and unoccupied U.S. territories — were vulnerable (obviously!) to Japanese aggression, the islands were also thereby able to buffer the mainland United States from its enemies. (Indeed, the *Enola Gay* flew from Tinian, in the Northern Marianas, then under U.S. possession, when it bombed Hiroshima and Nagasaki in August 1945.)

Throughout the whole "short twentieth century," from 1917 through 1989, the United States possessed Pacific island territories that enabled the U.S. military to effectively control the Pacific Ocean up to the Soviet Union's territorial waters. Those same territories also allowed the United States to control the South China Sea and the Philippine Sea in the latter part of the twentieth century and in the early twenty-first. And they of course allowed the United States to dominate the Caribbean and control access to the Panama Canal — thereby allowing the navy flexibility in how it employed its ships and facilitating interocean and bicoastal U.S. trade.

Despite the existence of this extended empire beyond the continental states and Hawai'i, the exact character of this overseas empire defies easy description. One reason for the difficulty is that the fact of an empire — the U.S. government's plenary authority over the territories — has been mitigated somewhat by the fact that the U.S. Supreme Court has effectively extended several of the constitutional protections it had earlier denied, and made territorial citizens U.S. citizens except for Samoans. Then, too, the U.S. government has granted significant degrees of self-government in these three island territories and in Puerto Rico, and it has now been more than fifty years since the U.S. Navy administered Guam, American Samoa, or the U.S. Virgin Islands. Meanwhile, the islands receive large annual subsidies from the U.S. government, further complicating the picture, and island residents can move to one of the states. This is *not* to say that this is "colonialism by consent," as the historian Raymond Carr suggests — there is too much opposition and animosity, on the part of many in Puerto Rico and Guam especially — but the facts of the subsidies, degree of self-government, and ability to reside in the states have obscured the nonrepresentative quality of U.S. sovereignty.

Another reason the United States' territorial empire defies easy description is the variation that exists in the governing arrangements of the several territories. Congress and the Court have shown flexibility when dealing with individual territories, with each territory — past or present — having a different "regime" of congressional statutes, constitutional law, and mutual understandings that govern the territories and their inhabitants — not unlike the variation in the British or the French administration of their colonies. The variation in government began when the territories were first annexed: the Division of Insular Affairs in the War Department oversaw the Philippines, Puerto Rico, and Alaska (until 1884); the War Department had control of the Panama Canal Zone; the Navy Department governed the U.S. Virgin Islands from 1917 until 1931, Guam from 1899 until 1950, and American Samoa from 1899 until 1952; and the Department of the Interior administered Hawai'i, Alaska after 1884, and then Puerto Rico, the U.S. Virgin Islands, Guam, and American Samoa.

———

Over the last several decades, the Supreme Court has issued decisions that have countered some of the rulings in the *Insular Cases*. Only a few years after the U.S. Congress passed Public Law 600 and Puerto Rico approved its new constitution to become the Commonwealth of Puerto Rico in 1952, the U.S. Supreme Court decided *Reid v. Covert* (1957) — a decision that undermined the judgments in the *Insular Cases*.

The circumstances of *Reid v. Covert* were that two military dependents stationed overseas were charged with murdering their spouses and were to be tried by a court-martial. The two women challenged the use of a court-martial instead of a civil court. Four justices out of the six-person majority — three justices dissented — argued that criminal justice demanded trial by jury, and that courts-martial constituted imperfect and deficient systems of justice. Justice Black, who wrote the lead opinion, argued for the plaintiffs' *personal* rights as U.S. citizens: "The prohibitions of the Constitution were designed to apply to all branches of the National Government and they cannot be nullified by the Executive or by the Executive and Senate combined" — that is, by force of treaty. The two defendants could not, therefore, be convicted according to the Uniform Code of Military Justice. (Chief Justice Taft in *Balzac v. Puerto Rico* had, in contrast, emphasized the importance of *locational* authority, not *personal* rights.)

The judicial scholar Gerald Neuman calls *Reid v. Covert* a "watershed decision," since it established constitutional protections of trial by jury to U.S. military dependents residing abroad and thereby implicitly reversed the rulings in *Balzac v. Porto Rico* — remember that Puerto Ricans were then also U.S. citizens — as well as, arguably, the rulings in *Hawaii v. Mankichi* and *Dorr v. United States*. Three years later, in *Kinsella v. Singleton* (1960), the Supreme Court extended the right to trial by jury for civilian dependents of military personnel in noncapital offenses.

In more recent cases involving Puerto Ricans, the Supreme Court has guaranteed territorial citizens further personal liberties under the First

Amendment (1993) and the Fourth Amendment (1979). In addition, the Ninth Circuit Court of Appeals upheld the right to an abortion — that is, the right to privacy — in a 1992 Guam case. And Arnold Leibowitz, an expert on territorial law, points out that the due process and equal protection clauses of the Fourteenth Amendment have been extended to the territories, just as they have been to the states.

Yet even as the Court has expanded the individual protections guaranteed territorial citizens, the U.S. government still exercises plenary authority over the territories and still withholds some constitutional protections to citizens of the territories. Congress may still impose tariffs on trade between the territories and the states, contrary to the uniformity clause; Puerto Rico is the only territory included within the U.S. customs area. And citizens of the territories are without the protections of citizens of the several states, contrary to the privileges and immunity clause ("The Citizens of each State shall be entitled to all Privileges and Immunities of Citizens in the several States" [Art. IV, Sec. 2, Cl. 1]).

Furthermore, the Supreme Court has not yet incorporated the Second Amendment (the right to bear arms) and Third Amendment (the prohibition of the forced housing of troops) in either the territories *or* the states. As for the Fourth Amendment right to protection from searches and seizures, the Supreme Court as recently as 1990 upheld the *Insular Cases* in *United States v. Verdugo-Urquidez.* Chief Justice William Rehnquist, who wrote the opinion for the Court, specifically cited the "*Insular Cases,*" as well as the individual cases of *Balzac v. Porto Rico, Ocampo v. United States, Dorr v. United States, Hawaii v. Mankichi,* and *Downes v. Bidwell* (among others) — all on the point that the Constitution does not apply everywhere the United States has sovereign power. As a result, the Rehnquist Court effectively overturned the 1979 ruling by the Court in *Torres v. Puerto Rico,* a decision under the Burger Court that protected a U.S. passenger from a search of a man's luggage without warrant or probable cause.

The Supreme Court has also declined to include the Fifth Amendment's right of indictment by grand jury in cases of felony against the territories or the states, and it has not yet overturned the ruling *Balzac v. Porto Rico.* Neither has the Court incorporated the Seventh Amendment guarantee of trial by jury in civil cases, but it has not done so for the several states. As with the nonincorporation of the Second and

Third Amendments, then, there is no discrimination against territorial citizens on this point. Nor has the Ninth Amendment's reservation of rights to the people been applied to U.S. citizens in the territories, although these persons are explicitly "U.S. citizens" and therefore presumably among the "people" of the United States whose rights are to be reserved to them under the Constitution.

Similarly, the Tenth Amendment's guarantee that powers not enumerated in the Constitution "are reserved to the States respectively, or the People" would seem to mean that the U.S. citizens of the island territories are entitled to the reserved powers under the Constitution and, again, presumably among the "people" of the United States. Yet the Supreme Court overturned a Virgin Islands divorce law in *Granville-Smith v. Granville-Smith* (1955), and invalidated the Guam legislature's establishment of its own supreme court in a 1977 case (on the grounds that Guam needed the expressed authority from the U.S. Congress to do so), both seemingly contrary to the Tenth Amendment.

Furthermore, the Fourteenth Amendment's proclamation that "all persons born or naturalized in the United States and subject to its jurisdiction thereof, are citizens of the United States and of the State wherein they reside" clearly does not include the citizens of the territories, since territorial inhabitants, although citizens of the United States, are obviously not also citizens "of the State wherein they reside." In other words, the Fourteenth Amendment does not state "*or* the State wherein they reside" (which would mean no dual citizenship and no federalism) or proclaim that "All persons . . . are citizens of the United States and of the State *or the Territory* wherein they reside" (which would mean full political rights for U.S. citizens of the island territories: full voting members of the House of Representatives and a full complement of U.S. senators).

Finally, it may be argued that the U.S. citizens of the territories come under the protections of the Fifteenth Amendment, as did Chief Justice Fuller in his dissent in *Downes:* that "the right of citizens of the United States to vote shall not be denied or abridged by the United States or by any State on account of *race, color,* or previous conditions of servitude" (emphasis added), since many territorial citizens are non-whites (although some 80 percent of Puerto Ricans in the 2000 census identified themselves as "white"). And while the Supreme Court ruled in the *Chinese Exclusion Case* (*Chae Chan Ping v. United States* 1889) and in *United States v. Wong Kim Ark* (1898) that the Fifteenth Amendment applied to whites and blacks only, *Chae Chan Ping* has subsequently been overruled. But the Fifteenth Amendment has still not been ruled to apply to the citizens of the territories.

In short, the decisions and lessons of the *Insular Cases* remain most relevant. The decisions in these cases have allowed the Constitution to be incompletely and inconsistently applied to U.S. citizens in the territories; the citizens of the territories are *not* U.S. citizens in the sense of being full members of a political community, as citizenship is commonly defined.

The condition of territorial citizens thus stands in stark contrast to other persons formerly marginalized by Congress and the Supreme Court. Despite the Court's long years of denying of civil rights to African Americans — for example, the rulings in *United States v. Reese* and *United States v. Cruikshank* (1876), the *Civil Rights Cases* (1883), *Plessy v. Ferguson* (1896), and *Williams v. Mississippi* (1898) — African Americans have been granted full political equality under the law. Despite the Court's previous rulings against American Indians from the founding forward — for example, *Johnson v. M'Intosh* (1823), *Cherokee Nation v. Georgia* (1831), *Cherokee Tobacco Case* (1870), *United States v. Kagama* (1886), *Lone Wolf v. Hitchcock* (1903) — American Indians enjoy the protections of both state citizenship and U.S. citizenship, as well as limited sovereignty as members of Indian tribes residing on reservations. And despite the Court's rulings in the *Chinese Exclusion Case*, *Fong Yue Ting v. United States* (1893), and other cases, immigration from China and other Asian countries is now handled no differently than immigration from other countries and regions.

Even residents of Washington, D.C. — who briefly had a territorial government from 1871 to 1874 — are guaranteed all rights under the Constitution and after the Twenty-third Amendment (1961) have three votes in the Electoral College (although still no representation in the House and Senate). And although the discussion here does not address the status of women in the territories or the evolution of women's citizenship in the United States, the claims here might also be said about women: that they have been made equals under the law and in the courts — even as the political reality for women, just like that for other previously marginalized groups, still lags behind that of white males.

In sum, the territorial empire established by the United States after the Spanish-American War and legitimated by the U.S. Supreme Court shows a distinct *spatial* dimension to judicial decision making, a characteristic apart from — although clearly related to and partially consistent with — the ascriptive dimensions of second-class citizenship identified by Rogers Smith and others. And this makes sense: Puerto Rico, Guam, American Samoa, the U.S. Virgin Islands, and the Northern Marianas each has its distinct set of cultures, religions, languages and dialects, and history. Certainly the people of each territory see themselves as separate political societies, unlike most U.S. citizens' identification with their own states of residence. Thus the ambiguous constitutional and political status of the territories and their citizens has parallels to the different constitutional and political situations of Indian tribes on reservations, Washington, D.C., and the inhabitants of former U.S. territories.

———

The other complicating component of the United States' territorial empire is the diversity in governing regimes established by the *Insular Cases*. These cases gave the U.S. government authority to vary its treatment of each territory, as seen in the comparisons of the Court's decisions in its cases from Cuba, Puerto Rico, the Philippines, Hawai'i, and Alaska. Neither the Supreme Court nor Congress mandated that all U.S. territories be treated alike.

The differences allowed by the Court in the *Insular Cases* have continued. Both American Samoa and the Northern Marianas have been granted exceptions from U.S. immigration law, for instance (and have also been allowed to restrict local landownership according to long-term residency and ethnicity requirements). Conversely, U.S. immigration policies as applied to the Virgin Islands (Virgin Islanders are black, with Danish-African background, as well as with some Indian and Puerto Rican heritage, and make up about 70 percent of the islands' population) and Guam (Chamorros make up less than 50 percent of the population and Filipinos account for about a third of the island's population) have heavily altered — many would say damaged — the integrity of the islands' indigenous populations.

In addition, the Northern Marianas have been able to avoid U.S. minimum-wage laws — as seen earlier in this chapter — according to the terms of the covenant that established them as a commonwealth and territory of the United States. Up to 10,000 migrant workers arrive in the Northern Marianas each year, mostly from the Philippines, and are vulnerable to abuses of various kinds, according to news reports, especially sexual abuse for workers in domestic service, nightclubs, and factories, and racial discrimination against teachers. But the compact between the Northern Marianas and the U.S. Congress leaves citizens of the Northern Marianas without full constitutional protections and shields employers. Another oddity of the Northern Marianas is that it has an upper house with highly skewed representation as a result of population imbalances among the islands that receive equal representation in the upper chamber.

Samoa, for its part, has an upper house whose members — that is, matai chiefs — do not have to be elected to serve in office. Samoa also has a court system — the matai system — independent of the U.S. federal courts. There are also severe restrictions on non-Samoans' purchasing real estate on the islands as there also are in the Northern Marianas. In addition, Samoa, along with the Northern Marianas, the U.S. Virgin Islands, and Guam, lies outside U.S. customs borders. Goods imported from other countries into Samoa and the other territories, besides Puerto Rico, are not subject to U.S. duties, whereas goods exported from these territories to the states are subject to tariffs, just as U.S. goods shipped to the Virgin Islands, Guam, Samoa, and the Northern Marianas are foreign goods for customs purposes. Furthermore, Samoa is exempt from the Nicholson Act, which prohibits foreign vessels from landing fish in U.S. ports.

Puerto Rico and Guam lie *within* U.S. coastwise shipping rules, however — as affirmed in *Huus v. New York* (1901) for Puerto Rico — whereas the rules do not apply to the other three territories. The citizens of Puerto Rico, moreover, do not pay federal income tax but have their own income (and sales) taxes, determined by the local Puerto Rican legislature. The Virgin Islands, Guam, and American Samoa, for their part, have "mirror income taxes": residents pay taxes to their local government in lieu of the federal income taxes they otherwise would pay to the U.S. Treasury.

In sum, there is a considerable diversity of rights and rules operating in the present-day U.S. territories. Some of these constitutional exceptions are not so much instances of political or judicial discrimination, however, as they are designed to preserve indigenous customs and lifestyles among special populations, not unlike those granted to American Indians that were designed to protect indigenous peoples and special populations within the United States, or the special tax breaks granted Puerto Rico's "956" companies (following the number of the legal clause) for the purpose of stimulating economic development, but which are not available to any of the states themselves.

———

Yet the distinctions between residents of the current U.S. territories and American Indians, residents of the nation's capital, and residents of former U.S. territories need to be kept in mind. The territorial inhabitants are U.S. citizens with the nominal exception of American Samoans, but these citizens are not *dual citizens* in the sense of being both U.S. citizens *and* the citizens of one of the several states — and therefore without the same political representation and constitutional protections possessed by citizens of the states. Instead, they are "single citizens" (as I call them). Although "single citizens" are what the political scientist Rogers Smith and others call "second-class citizens" — a term that captures the subordinate status of these persons in the U.S. political system and in constitutional law — the "second-class-citizen" label obscures the fact that most territorial residents do not want to be full citizens (i.e., dual citizens) insofar as that would mean statehood even as they do want fuller political rights, especially the citizens of Guam and Puerto Rico.

American Indians, by the same logic, are thereby "treble citizens," since they are citizens of the United States, citizens of their state of residence, and citizens of their Indian tribe or nation — given that the U.S. Supreme Court has established that Indians living on tribal reservations acquire limited sovereignty on the basis of their Indian identity over the persons and areas of their reservation. Continuing this logic, the residents of Washington, D.C., are somewhere between being "single citizens" and "dual citizens" — "one-and-a-half citizens"? — given their lack of representation in Congress but also their right to vote in presidential elections thanks to the Twenty-third Amendment.

But the Supreme Court in *Rice v. Cayetano* (2000) has cast doubt on parallels that might be drawn between indigenous citizens of the territories (e.g., the Chamorros of Guam and the Northern Marianas,

Samoans) and American Indians or other aboriginal populations living in the states (e.g., Inuit, Eskimos). The Court in *Rice v. Cayetano* refused to accept the denial of special voting privileges to nonnative Hawai'ians and emphatically upheld the Fifteenth Amendment, whereas the Court has upheld distinct forms of political authority in the territories and not applied the Fifteenth Amendment to U.S. citizens of the territories.

In short, the inhabitants of the U.S. territories enjoy — suffer? — a political status between that of citizens of the states and foreign nationals. They occupy not only a murky position in the U.S. Constitution, as the constitutional scholars Gerald Neuman and Alexander Aleinikoff show, but also an uncomfortable and vulnerable position, as we have seen and as many scholars have indicated — among them José Cabranes, Efrén Rivera Ramos, José Trías Monge, E. Robert Statham, and Juan Torruella. But this overseas empire, made possible by the *Insular Cases*, very much remains as part of the United States. Just out of view.

CHAPTER 9

Informal Empire and the End of Territorial Expansion

Take up the White Man's burden —
Ye dare not stoop to less —
Nor call too loud on Freedom
To cloke your weariness;
By all ye cry or whisper,
By all ye leave or do,
The silent, sullen peoples
Shall weigh your gods and you.
RUDYARD KIPLING, "The White Man's Burden," 1899

If the Supreme Court in the *Insular Cases* endorsed the development of a new overseas empire, the territorial expansion legitimated by the decision in *Downes v. Bidwell* and other *Insular Cases* did not continue. In fact, over the course of the two decades of the *Insular Cases*, U.S. grand strategy and foreign policy was already shifting to a more sustainable form of empire as U.S. presidents, federal departments and agencies, and the U.S. military began to move away from land-based sovereignty and toward a more flexible empire, one based on the opening of foreign markets, the presence and exercise of compelling force, and the support of friendly governments and international institutions. The "banana republics" are only the most obvious cases in point — countries effectively controlled by the United Fruit Company and other U.S.-based companies backed by the State Department and, on occasion, the U.S. military. Control over the new, informal empire would be exercised by the White House and through executive agreements, rather than by Congress and through international treaties and legislation. "Since trade ignores national boundaries and the manufacturer insists on having the world as a market, the flag of his nation must follow him," Woodrow Wilson commented in 1907 — before becoming U.S. president — "and the doors of nations which are closed against him must be battered down." The

United States had to have an aggressive economic policy, Wilson added: "Concessions obtained by financiers must be safeguarded by ministers of state, even if the sovereignty of unwilling nations be outraged in the process."

Although the United States of the twentieth century "outraged" the sovereignty of other nations in its push for more open markets, it had virtually ceased from adding additional territory. There were several reasons for this transition to an informal empire. One was the reaction to the war in the Philippines, which was a political liability for the Roosevelt administration, the Republican Party, and other advocates of U.S. expansion, as discussed in chapter 3. At the same time, the negative example of the Philippines contrasted with the United States' successful use of force in Panama in 1903, Santo Domingo (now the Dominican Republic) in 1905, and Cuba (see later discussion).

In the Panamanian case, Roosevelt ordered U.S. forces to intervene to prevent Colombian forces from suppressing the revolution in Panama — thereby allowing Panama to secede from Colombia. The new Panamanian government permitted the United States to build an isthmian canal across the country and lease the Canal Zone — action that Roosevelt said he was prouder of than any other foreign policy action he had made as U.S. president.

In the Santo Domingo case, Roosevelt issued an executive order for U.S. forces to control the customhouses on the island in response to the indebtedness of Santo Domingo to European and U.S. banks and investment houses, the political turmoil on the island, and the pleas by local property owners for a lasting intervention by the United States. So Roosevelt sent in troops after the U.S. Senate had refused to ratify a treaty with Santo Domingo to establish U.S. control over the customhouse. Yet the president declined to annex and directly administer Santo Domingo, despite the opportunity to do so. He had "no more desire to establish a protectorate" in Santo Domingo, Roosevelt told a friend, than "a gorged boa constrictor might have to swallow a porcupine wrong end to."

The early twentieth-century histories of the Philippines, Panama, Santo Domingo, and other Latin American countries suggested that it was easier for the United States to work with supportive regimes than to possess areas outright. It was more convenient for both the White House and the State Department and for U.S. companies trading with or investing in foreign countries, to use diplomatic, economic, and military levers to effect their objectives rather than to annex new areas; presidential administrations and U.S.-based business could thereby deal with the government and political economies of other countries directly, rather than having to involve the U.S. Congress and possibly the courts in international policy.

The historian William Appleman Williams describes the process: "When an advanced industrial nation plays, or tries to play, a controlling and one-sided role in the development of a weaker economy, then the policy of the more powerful country can with accuracy and candor only be described as *imperial*" (emphasis added). "The empire that results may well be *informal* in the sense that the weaker country is not ruled on a day-to-day basis by resident administrators, or increasingly populated by emigrants from the advanced country," Williams further notes, "but it is nevertheless an *empire*" (emphasis added).

Exemplifying the "informality" of the American empire was the absence of a U.S. territorial service. In fact, the Roosevelt administration scrapped plans to establish a civil service program for colonial administration and a consolidated bureau for territorial (or "colonial") administration. The United States did not have the "necessary" bureaucratic "apparatus for the government of dependencies," the Canadian political writer Beckles Willson remarked; in contrast, Great Britain had "an Imperial Service entirely detached from home parties or political influence." Willson and other U.S. policymakers thus asked whether the United States could also "acquire and maintain such a service, free from home politics, without the exaltation of the executive and the exercise of his direct authority."

Secretary Root had approved the establishment of a new Bureau of Insular Affairs in the State Department (the Division of Insular Affairs had previously been located in the War Department). As Root wrote to Secretary of State John Hay on September 4, 1901, he hoped that "the whole business can go where it belongs under civil control in the nearest approach we can make to a Department of Colonial Affairs." But with McKinley's death and the Roosevelt administration's other priorities, there would be no civilian "Imperial Service." A number of departments and agencies assumed authority over the territories, instead — as noted in chapter 8 — until the U.S. Department of the Interior took over the administration of Puerto Rico, Guam, American Samoa, and the U.S. Virgin Islands when the War and Navy Departments relinquished their control; it had overseen the administration of Hawai'i since the Newlands Resolution, and Alaska from 1884 until 1912 (when Alaska had a district government) and then from 1912 to 1959 (when it was an organized territory).

The establishment of an informal empire had several components. One was the establishment of military bases, as suggested by the Navy Department's large role in the administration of the insular territories and as noted in chapters 3 and 8. The informal empire depended on the presence and actions of the U.S. military to complement the promotion of trade and foreign investment. For decades, the U.S. military had the Sangley Point (Manila Bay) and Subic Bay naval bases, Clark Air Base, and several smaller facilities in the Philippines; it had had several military installations in Puerto Rico, the most important of which was the Roosevelt Roads Naval Station, which had been the single largest U.S. naval base and an important training site for U.S. forces as well as NATO and Latin American navies; and Guam continues to house important naval and air bases, as do Saipan (Northern Marianas) and Pago Pago (Samoa). The bases in Hawai'i and facilities in Alaska were also of clear importance, as they are today.

Furthermore, U.S. policymakers first sought to acquire the Virgin Islands because of their potential as naval bases and coaling stations — among the best in the Caribbean. Saint Thomas had an excellent harbor and lay close to the Anegada Passage, the third of the three "navigable breaks in the northern barrier enclosing the Caribbean Sea," according to the military strategist W. V. Judson. (In fact, the Republican platform of 1896 listed the acquisition of the Virgin Islands among its planks.) The United States thus sought to ensure that the islands "would remain the possession of a neutral power" until it eventually bought them in 1917 for $17 million from Denmark, fearing that they might fall into German hands or those of another foreign power.

For much of the twentieth century, the bases in the U.S. territories were the only military installations outside the several states, and throughout the twentieth and into the twenty-first centuries, they continued to be among the most important military installations. Here is where the United States' geographic and informal empires coincided, in fact. The United States had to have territories or colonies to house its bases and refueling stations for the protection and expansion of its commerce. As Woodrow Wilson stated — at the same time that he spoke of the United States' "righteous conquests of free markets" — "Colonies must be obtained or planted, in order that no useful corner of the world may be overlooked or left unused."

But over the last several decades the bases in the "colonies" or territories have come to represent only a small fraction of the United States' military sites — ever since the 1941 lend-lease agreement with Britain in which the United States first acquired bases not on its sovereign soil. Right now, the United States has more than 700 overseas military bases, while still other foreign bases — not included in that count — remain secret or go without formal recognition because of host-nation sensitivity (not to mention the hundreds of military bases within the fifty states). The presence of these foreign bases, in combination with United States' navy, airpower, ground forces, and intelligence and technical capabilities, has allowed the United States to command the open seas throughout the last half of the twentieth century and has given the U.S. military the capability to operate and potentially intervene almost anywhere in the world.

Yet the use of force is typically neither cost-efficient nor popular beyond the short term. Thus the "stick" of the presence, size, and mobility of the U.S. armed forces has been more of a complement to the "carrot" of investment dollars, increased trade, financial assistance, subsidized goods and equipment, and other benefits from U.S. foreign policy and international institutions, as the political scientist Andrew Bacevitch and others point out. During and immediately after World War II, for instance, the United States worked to establish the World Bank, the General Agreement on Trade and Tariffs (later the World Trade Organization), the International Monetary Fund, the Bank for International Settlements, and other international institutions designed to facilitate the operation of the global economy. So even as the United States was fighting Germany and Japan in the early 1940s and even as postwar international relations in the late 1940s were gelling into the cold war, the United States was creating the international institutions necessary for securing the functioning of market economies and the viability of American investment and business internationally. Even at the height of cold war tensions between the United States and the Soviet Union, U.S. presidents and Congresses sought to promote U.S. trade and investment throughout the world.

Another component of the United States' informal empire was the emergence of a new strategic doctrine: the "Roosevelt Corollary" to the 1823 Monroe Doctrine. Whereas the original Monroe Doctrine insisted that European and other foreign powers not interfere in the Western Hemisphere, the Roosevelt Corollary stipulated that the United States itself could intervene in the affairs of Latin American nations. "Chronic wrongdoing or an impotence" that weakened "the ties of civilized society," Roosevelt stated in 1905, during the crisis in Santo Domingo, may "ultimately require" the United States to exert "international police power" in the Western Hemisphere. What constituted the "wrongdoing" or "impotence" that required "police power" was in the eye of the beholder, of course — the United States.

The operation of the Roosevelt Corollary was amply evident in the multiple actions by U.S. forces in the Caribbean and Central America after the turn of the twentieth century. Besides intervening in Hawai'i, Panama, and Santo Domingo, U.S. forces intervened in Nicaragua in 1908 and occupied Nicaragua from 1912 to 1915 and from 1926 to 1933. They occupied Haiti from 1915 to 1934 and occupied the Dominican Republic from 1916 to 1924. U.S. troops were also deployed in Panama in 1918 and in Honduras in 1919 and 1924. And U.S. forces intervened in the Mexican Revolution from 1913 to 1916. But a full treatment of the United States' overt and covert interventions in the Western Hemisphere and elsewhere in the world since the 1920s — for example, the Congo, Chile, Iran, Indonesia — lies beyond the scope of this study.

Supplementing the Roosevelt Corollary was "dollar diplomacy." The Taft administration's policy of the early 1910s was to substitute "dollars for bullets." The idea of dollar diplomacy was that conservative and business elements were to run countries so that they would remain on a sound financial basis and be able to attract and retain foreign capital. Anticipating dollar diplomacy were the "Open Door Notes" written by Secretary of State Hay in 1899 as guidelines for international investment in China. (President McKinley in 1898 had asked that the peace delegation in Paris negotiating with Spain after the war secure "the open door for ourselves.") Elihu Root subsequently affirmed and restated the open-door policy in 1905 and 1906, in the context of U.S. foreign policy vis-à-vis Morocco, where the United States sought to gain access equal to that obtained by Britain, France, and Germany. Root proposed both economic and political reforms for Morocco and initiated public projects for education, transportation, and sanitation systems. In Cuba, Puerto Rico, and the Philippines, meanwhile, the United States was opening up foreign markets, reforming economic and legal systems, and investing in roads, schools, sewer systems, and other infrastructural improvements.

More generally, the open-door policy had four features, as William Appleman Williams sees it: (1) the United States would "win the victories without the wars," since wars manifested policy failure; (2) the United States' superior economic power could direct poorer and less advanced countries in pro-American directions; (3) U.S. foreign economic policy was politically hardheaded and neither legalistic nor moralistic; (4) and U.S. foreign policy would eventually produce increasingly serious "foreign policy crises," ultimately resulting in hostile reaction in the "form of terror."

With the combination of incentives and sanctions available to the United States of the twentieth and twenty-first centuries, few governments have adopted rules unfavorable to American and international business. This is *not* to say that the United States has always been able to install and retain friendly governments. But with the economic incentives available, cooperative foreign governments, capabilities of the U.S. military, and supportive international institutions, the United States has usually been able to influence the policies of other nations without resorting to force. It has, in short, effectively been able to exert a veto power over the kinds of governments established in noncommunist countries around the world.

The present governments of Cuba, North Korea, Iran, and Venezuela stand as conspicuous exceptions. And Libya — a former pariah under President Muammar el-Qaddafi and mentioned in the same breath as Iraq under Saddam Hussein or Panama under Manuel Noriega — is no longer an exception, now that it does business with U.S. oil companies, even though Muammar Qaddafi is still president. Ironically, Cuba for several decades was the prototype of informal empire: area that the United States did not territorially annex but nonetheless effectively controlled. As Beckles Willson in 1903 wrote in reference to Cuba: "Sovereignty is sometimes none the less real because judiciously veiled. Americans . . . still retain a right of veto and of intervention that practically makes Cuba a vassal State. The foreign relations of the republic are absolutely in the hands of the Washington Government. . . . Cuba, in short, while virtually a sovereign State in the management of domestic affairs, is for all other purposes under a very strict American suzerainty."

Cuba — the cause of the Spanish-American War — was once under U.S. occupation, of course, but the United States let it go. The history of Cuba may therefore inform us of a crucial dimension of informal empire: if the United States were to change from being a territorial empire based on geographic sovereignty to one based on informal control, then *the United States had to be able to divest unwanted territory.* Although the Supreme Court had established that states once they had joined the Union could not opt out of the compact (*Texas v. White*, 1868), whether *territories* could secede — or be released — was an open question. It remained an open question until the *Insular Cases.*

———

The argument that the United States did not have to keep all the territories was articulated by academic commentators; by U.S. government attorneys in their briefs for *Neely v. Henkel, Crossman v. United States,* and *Downes v. Bidwell;* and by Justice White in his concurring opinion in *Downes v. Bidwell.* James Bradley Thayer in 1899 hinted at such a possibility in his article in the *Harvard Law Review:* "Never should we admit any extra-continental State into the Union"; it would be "intolerable." Thayer thus wanted a constitutional amendment to ensure that none of the islands — Hawai'i included — "be admitted into the Union." Thayer added, "I take it for granted that we shall not sell them *or abandon them;* that we shall hold them and govern them, or provide governments for them" (emphasis added). By mentioning abandonment, however Thayer implicitly made it an option.

Simeon Baldwin, who took the first, minimal view of the United States, also emphasized that while the United States may acquire possessions "with no possible tie of connection with the American continent" as spoils of war, "a conqueror is not bound" thereby, "and *may not be able to retain* what he receives" (emphasis added). The United States could "get rid of such possessions," Baldwin wrote, given Congress's power "to dispose of the territory of the United States" — even if such power were not expressly contained in the Constitution. Such authority was similar to Congress's ability to maintain temporary territorial governments with "no fixed limit of time," he observed. "We have held Alaska under such conditions already thirty years, and she is hardly more deserving of autonomy now than when she was a Russian province. We have held New Mexico, under different forms of administration, for nearly fifty years," Baldwin added, "and the character and traditions of a Latin race are still so deeply stamped upon her people and her institutions that no demand of party exigency has been strong enough to secure her admission to the privileges of statehood."

The Chicago attorney Frank Mitchell also contemplated the divestment of territory. "Congress may authorize the immediate withdrawal of all American troops and leave the inhabitants to work out their own destiny," Mitchell wrote in 1900. Although Mitchell viewed the option as being "out of the question" — as did Thayer and Baldwin — it was still one of the four alternatives Congress had for the disposal of the Philippines. New York attorney Charles A. Gardiner argued, too, that Congress's powers to "dispose" of Puerto Rico or the Philippines "are unlimited" and as "unreserved" as the power to "dispose of personal property, the prizes, for example, captured in the late war." The Philippines could, therefore, be ceded "to the inhabitants thereof, as a gift," or leased "to tenants, as China is leasing its ports to European powers. We may sell them to any bidder, England, Germany, Japan, as Russia sold Alaska to us." Congress had the power to dissolve a provisional government established in a conquered territory of the United States, Gardiner argued, and could "*put an end to it*" if it so chose (emphasis in original).

James M. Beck, the assistant attorney general — and a future U.S. solicitor general, congressman, and author — argued in his brief for the government in *Neely v. Henkel* that the United States could acquire and then withdraw its claims to territory. Cubans could "decline to form a government, and ask for admission into the United States either as a State or a Territory," Beck observed, or they might "organize a government with which this country will not be satisfied." In any event, there was no "Cuban government at the present time," Beck remarked, "and no certainty that there ever will be one." Cuba's status was undecided. "Until such time" that Cuba's status was decided, moreover, it was "land '*appertaining to the United States*,' an expression used by this court in Jones v. United States [1890] . . . to describe the relation which our Government bears to certain guano islands in the Caribbean Sea" (emphasis added).

The Supreme Court's ruling in *Jones v. United States* was directly on point, Beck observed, since the plaintiff was charged with murder on Navassa, one of the guano islands, which was "under the sole and exclusive jurisdiction of the United States." Although Navassa was "out of the jurisdiction of any particular State or district of the United States," it was "recognized and considered by the United States as appertaining to the United States," and "in the possession of the United States under the laws of the United States then and there in force relating to such islands." The United States could therefore exercise jurisdiction over such territory, the Supreme Court decided, "*for such period as it sees fit over a territory so acquired*" (emphasis added). The United States could either *hold indefinitely* or *release* "appertaining" territory, Beck contended, whether the territory were acquired by discovery (e.g., the guano islands) or by conquest (e.g., Cuba). The sovereignty over such a territory was a political question, for Beck, to be decided by Congress and the executive branch, and not the courts.

U.S. solicitor general Richards reiterated the possibility of territorial secession in his brief for *Crossman v. United States* (1901). For Richards, "The only indissoluble, inseparable parts of the United States" were "the States of the Union, the governing body." While Richards did not think that there was "any power to disintegrate the Union," he did "believe there is power to dispose of territory which simply belongs to the United States." Richards added, "But of course this is a very serious question."

Justice White made a similar argument in his concurring opinion in *Downes*. White speculated that in a situation of war, with the defeated government overthrown and all or part of the area "occupied by the United States," it might be "necessary for the United States to hold the conquered country for an indefinite period, or at least until such time as Congress deemed that it should be *either released* or *retained* because it was apt for incorporation into the United States" (emphasis added). White again brought up the issue of territorial divestment later in his opinion. According to the Court's ruling in *Neely v. Henkel*, White pointed out, "Cuba was not incorporated into the

United States and was a foreign country." The United States could thus possess and hold territory "without incorporating it into the United States." But the United States might also be obliged "*to terminate* [its] *dominion and control*" over a territory (emphasis added). And were a particular territory "unfit" for incorporation, then the U.S. government could for reasons of "political conscience" or "duty under the Constitution" decide to "terminate" its occupation. White's point was that the United States could, upon acquiring territory, either (1) annex it into the Union as an incorporated territory or (2) hold it as an unincorporated territory. If it were unincorporated territory, then the United States could (2a) hold it indefinitely, (2b) eventually incorporate it into the Union, or (2c) release it.

The "divestment corollary" of the Incorporation Doctrine — that is, the idea that the United States could release unincorporated territory — was remarked upon by at least one newspaper. The *New York World* wrote that one of the principles established in *Downes* and one of the doctrines laid down by Chief Justice Marshall was that when the United States acquires territories, "Congress has the power to withdraw the flag and relinquish possession of them." The historian Julius Pratt recognized this very same point in his later analysis of the United States' overseas empire — that one of the purposes of Justice White's Incorporation Doctrine "was to leave Congress free to surrender new possessions like the Philippines if they should prove burdensome and unprofitable."

Political and judicial scholars at the turn of the century agreed. Harry Pratt Judson wrote in 1899 that annexed territory "may be held in trust for the inhabitants, with the expectation of ultimately turning it over to them should they so desire and should they prove themselves capable of orderly government." Alpheus Snow, an expert on territorial rule and international law, wrote in late 1901 that there were "inevitably two classes, and only two classes of dependencies, one manifestly destined, by nature, to be incorporated" into the State "and the other manifestly destined never to be incorporated." It could be that the inhabitants of the "dependencies" will, as is their right, Snow maintained, "insist that they are States naturally free and equal with other States, that they are in a federal union with the American Union, [and] that *Congress is not their Supreme Legislature*." Snow did not actively contemplate or desire complete separation of "dependencies," as he called them, from the Union, however: that would be failure, the "disintegration due to ignorance and incapacity" of the American people and the U.S. government — but it was a possibility.

Philippine governor Taft's remarks to the House Committee on Insular Affairs on March 5, 1902, showed that he, too, accepted the divestment corollary: that the United States might accept the separation of its territories, even if not the entire severance of political ties. For Taft, it was not clear if the Philippine islands were "to have ultimate independence, ultimate statehood, or [an] *ultimate relation like that between Australia and England, or that between Canada and England*" (emphasis added). And Jacob Schurman, who founded the Philippines Independence Commission, the journalist Henry P. Willis, and others repeatedly stated that the "United States should agree *to do for the Philippines what it did for Cuba* and to do it at the earliest possible moment" (emphasis added). In fact, the Democratic Party included the separation of the Philippines from the United States as a plank in its platform of 1904.

Yet what the United States "did for Cuba" was no simple thing; Cuba was the first manifestation of the United States' new informal empire, and its history deserves further attention for what it reveals about the informal empire.

———

The Roosevelt administration publicly treated Cuba as a success. "We have completed our duty to Cuba," navy secretary William Moody told a crowd in Springfield, Massachusetts, in the summer of 1903. "When we went into the war with Spain, . . . we did it with a pledge that we intended to occupy Cuba" only temporarily, until it was pacified, and then "would turn it over to its own people."

Moody spoke of the United States' unprecedented action:

The world was incredulous. If you mentioned the pledge to a foreign diplomat he shrugged his shoulders and said nothing. When the Secretary of War brought into the Cabinet room the papers by which the transfer was made to the constitutional government of Cuba, he said, "*I have not been able to find a single precedent to aid me in my task. There is no example in history which is a parallel.*" Just think! There lies the island of Cuba at the gate-way of the Caribbean, eighty-seven miles from our shores, fair and rich and fertile, the most splendid prize the world contained for us. And she lay absolutely helpless in our hands, absolutely helpless. (emphasis added)

Secretary of War Root, on February 3, 1904, used similar language in his address before the Union Club of New York cheering the United States' release of Cuba and, potentially, the Philippines:

Cuba, poor Cuba! That had struggled so long under intolerable oppression, has its star set in the firmament, and the new Republic governs itself upon the principles of American freedom, — a new Republic that has set its star in the heavens to lead on the republics of all Spanish America. . . . And in the Philippines, where they know not law — for there was no rule of law in the Philippines — where poor, little, brown men had never heard of aught but arbitrary power, they are beginning to learn what liberty means. . . . They are beginning to learn, *and I look forward to the time when the Philippines shall assume towards this country substantially the same relation that Cuba occupies to-day.* This could never have been done but by the exercise of power that rests in the word Sovereignty . . . and through that sovereignty there has already dawned for the people of the Philippines the better day of liberty and law. (emphasis added)

Yet the history of the United States' nonannexation of Cuba tells a different story. If the McKinley administration wanted neither continued Spanish rule nor Cuban independence — as we saw in chapter 2 — it still was not clear how the United States would actually control Cuba. "The Cuban revolution threatened more than the propriety of colonial rule or property relations in the colonial regime," as the historian Louis A. Pérez points out. "It also challenged the U.S. expectation of colonial succession," since "if the United States did not act, [Cuba] would be lost to the United States." The Cuban revolutionaries would take power and set up their own new government, one that would likely be hostile to the interests of Republicans and U.S. businesses. So the U.S. government could not recognize the Cuban Revolution and, instead, had to intervene in Cuba and to find a way to arrange its peaceful transfer to U.S. control.

General Wood wrote to McKinley on August 31, 1900, telling him of "a certain feeling of alarm and apprehension concerning the coming Constitutional Convention and it is undoubtedly true that the radical element will attempt to make some extreme declarations which will not be supported or approved by seventy five per cent of the population." But Wood told the president that "conservative men of all classes, without distinction, are for slow progress in the evacuation of the Island by American forces and Authority. They know, as do all of us here, that a control more or less strong must be maintained for some time, but all are agreed that a Constitutional Government under our supervision is desirable." Wood also let McKinley know that "the Planter's Association and all property owners of the conservative class in Cuba look to the United States as solemnly pledged to establishing a stable government here and they do not want us to withdraw our control or forces" until a stable government was in place.

The McKinley administration shared Wood's view. As Root wrote Wood on January 9, 1901, the administration wanted to promote "opportunities for the introduction of capital and the inauguration of such great private enterprises as have built up this country." But members of Congress worried about the unstable situation in Cuba. Senator Platt, who was chairman of the Senate Committee on Relations with Cuba (Senators Aldrich, Spooner, and Teller were also on the eight-member committee), wrote Root on January 18, 1901— four days after the Supreme Court issued its decision in *Neely v. Henkel*— of his concerns over Congress's restrictions on trade with Cuba:

> I do not see how it is possible to reduce duties on sugar and tobacco, or any other product coming from Cuba, while the Island continues in its present condition. It is a foreign country, but we have treaties with a great number of countries containing favored nation clauses and we are importing sugar and tobacco from these countries. If we were to say that we would [have] received sugar and tobacco from Cuba at a less rate of duty than from the other countries with which we have treaties containing favored nation clauses, demand would immediately be made upon us to reduce the duties from those countries in the same way. If Cuba comes to be independent and is so recognized by our government, then we can make reciprocity treaties with it in which we can reduce duties on products from Cuba in consideration that Cuba reduces duties on products from the United States.

Shortly thereafter, Platt wrote another letter to Root on February 5, 1901, informing him that the Republican members on the committee thought it advisable that he (Root) write up "a resolution authorizing the President to discontinue the military occupation of Cuba whenever certain things shall have been agreed to and incorporated into the constitution of Cuba, making it certain that results which we deem essential are assured." So Root drafted the Platt Amendment — without any input from Cuban politicians.

The Platt Amendment, which passed on March 2, 1901 — attached to an army spending bill — superseded the Teller Amendment and made Cuba a protectorate of the United States. Specifically, Article III gave the United States "*the right to intervene for the preservation of Cuban independence, the maintenance of a government adequate for the protection of life, property and individual liberty*" (emphasis added), and Article VII provided that Cuba was to "lease or sell to the United States lands necessary for coaling or naval stations" (e.g., Guantánamo Bay). Although the Cuban delegation did not like the Platt Amendment and wanted an end to U.S. military occupation, it had no other cards to play. So the Cubans, by a five-vote margin, accepted the amendment as an appendix to their new constitution.

With the U.S. occupation of Cuba and then the passage and adoption of the Platt Amendment, American businesses took control over the sugarcane and tobacco crops. As a result of the indebtedness of Cuban property owners and the collapse of the real estate market, two former U.S. consular agents in 1899 boasted that land could "be bought in unlimited quantities at from one-half to one-twentieth of its value before the insurrection." In fact, more than a quarter of the Cuban sugar mills were U.S. owned by 1902, mills that produced 40 percent of Cuban sugar. Among the prominent investors were the United Fruit Company and the Sugar Trust, both of which often worked through intermediaries. By 1902 the newly organized Tobacco Trust controlled 90 percent of the export trade of Havana cigars, and by 1906 it owned almost a quarter of a million acres of tobacco-growing fields in western Cuba. U.S. investment in Cuba, which had been less than $50 million in 1894, rose to at least $160 million by 1906.

With the establishment of Cuba as a U.S. protectorate and with all the investment by American individuals and companies, many continued to seek Cuba's annexation to the United States and its potential admission as a state. Governor Wood, on October 28, 1901, wrote President Roosevelt about exactly such a possibility: "This is a natural sugar and tobacco country and as we must, in any case, control its destinies, and will probably soon own it, I believe it sound policy to do what we can to develop it and make it prosperous." The Platt Amendment, Wood continued, would give the United States "control which will soon undoubtedly become possession, combined with other sugar producing lands which we now own, we shall soon practically control the sugar trade of the world." Wood thought it likely "that as soon as our home sugar producers realize our policy is to give Cuba a chance they will undoubtedly transfer their industries to Cuba and the Island will, under the impetus of new capital and energy, not only be developed, but gradually become Americanized, and we shall have in time one of the richest and most desirable possessions in the world." Cuba, Wood believed, was "a most desirable acquisition for the United States. She is easily worth any two of the Southern States, probably any three, with the exclusion of Texas."

Although Taft, Root, and other prominent Republicans continued to cautiously favor Cuban annexation, Congress continued to resist. U.S. House Speaker David B. Henderson (R-Iowa), Reed's successor, was "very much opposed to the annexation of Cuba" and "said that the assertions of the beet sugar people would have to be explained away" (as was confidentially reported to Root on December 11, 1901) because sugar beet producers, like many other American producers, did not want to annex Cuba.

Former Louisiana governor H. C. Warmoth, a sugarcane grower, voiced his frustrations over the McKinley and Roosevelt administrations' policies in a hearing before the House Committee on Insular Affairs in January 1902: "The Hawaiian gentlemen who came here told you that they would never be able to produce more than 100,000 tons of sugar, and you recognized their government which they set up there, and you held them in power, and you allowed them to import Japanese and Chinese laborers and fill up the island with those people, and now they produce over 500,000 tons of sugar. You have added Porto Rico to our territory, you have added the Philippines, and we are still working under those circumstances." But now, "We have Hawaii with her 500,000 tons of sugar, we have Porto Rico with

100,000 tons; we have, I know, millions of tons to come from the Philippines. Have we got enough territory? Do you want to go out further and drag in any more of these Spanish populations to compete with American citizens in the production of crops necessary to supply the American people?"

And now there was Cuba, with General Wood urging "the President and Secretary of War to give Cuba [duty-]free sugar, free tobacco, free fruits, free everything else. What are his reasons for this?" Warmoth answered his own question: "That Cuba is poor; Cuba is in danger of anarchy; Cuba is in danger of brigandage; . . . They have said that unless you give them relief that the cane crop this year will not be harvested; that the mills will not grind their cane. Every one of their contentions and statements are found to be false and ridiculous." He then asked: "Does Mr. Akins or Mr. Havemeyer, who own thousands of acres of land in Cuba and who admit they have made money up to date, need help? Does Mr. Hawley and his syndicate, who have bought Chapparra and other estates and thrown millions of dollars into Cuba out of Wall street need aid? Does the Spelman syndicate, who have gobbled up 65,000 acres of the Constantia plantation . . . do they need help?"

Warmoth, other sugarcane growers, sugar beet producers, and others therefore resisted the further integration of the U.S. and Cuban economies. But President Roosevelt and his Republican allies were still able to get reciprocal trade with Cuba, if not Cuban annexation. On December 16, 1903, the Senate passed the highly controversial and twice-defeated reciprocal trade agreement with Cuba, which reduced tariff duties between Cuba and the United States by 20 percent for Cuban products entering the U.S. market, and by 24, 30, and 40 percent — according to the product — for U.S. goods going to Cuba. As a later U.S. Department of Commerce publication summarized, the reciprocity treaty gave the United States "a practical monopoly of the Cuban import market" and provided much of "the stimulus, as well as much of the capital, for the development of the Cuban sugar industry." The passage of the treaty was only possible, though, the historian David Healy reports, because the Sugar Trust had bought a sufficient percentage of the American Beet Company — its chief rival in sugar production — to quell its objections.

With the U.S. investment in the region, with the large American demand for sugar and other goods, and with the Cuban reciprocity agreement in place, sugar production soared in Cuba, as well as in Puerto Rico and the Dominican Republic. Sugar production in the three islands — Cuba being by far the largest producer among them — grew from 429,000 metric tons in 1890 to 1.0 million tons in 1902 and then doubled to 2.3 million tons by 1910. Sugar production then rose to 4.1 million tons by 1918— a tenfold increase in fewer than thirty years. As a consequence, however, all three economies became virtual monocultures, with sugarcane plantations almost entirely replacing coffee plantations and other crops.

Yet the soaring amounts of American investment in and the increased trade with Cuba provided no guarantee that the Cuban government would protect U.S. commercial, financial, and property interests. In fact, the United States repeatedly had to intervene in Cuba under the authority of the Platt Amendment to protect individual Americans, secure endangered U.S. property, and rectify other instances of "chronic wrongdoing or impotence." U.S. forces occupied Cuba from 1906 to 1909, with a rebellion under way, the Cuban economy in shambles, and some $200 million of U.S. investment at stake. And they intervened again in 1912, 1917, and 1922 — not unlike the history of U.S. intervention in other Caribbean and Central American nations. Then, with the overthrow of the Battista regime by Castro in 1959 — recall that Williams's fourth characteristic of the open-door policy is violent resistance — Cuba seized American-owned assets, and the Cuban economy became almost entirely separated from the U.S. economy for the remainder of the twentieth century and into the twenty-first.

In sum, President Roosevelt, his advisers, and other policymakers began to realize soon after the turn of the twentieth century that they could get the benefits of U.S. sovereignty without the costs of military occupation or territorial annexation. So President Roosevelt and later presidential administrations continued to build up the military, the navy especially, and establish naval stations and coaling stations, and then other military facilities, in the territories and, later, other locations around the world. While Cuba now seems to represent a conspicuous failure as an example of informal empire, we might remember that the decades from 1959 to the present had been preceded by quite different U.S. policies between the time of U.S. occupation and the Cuban Revolution of 1959.

———

The Supreme Court's decisions in the *Insular Cases* facilitated the rise of this informal, other sort of empire. The Court allowed for the United States' acquisition of offshore territories that in some instances were only or principally acquired for locating naval and coaling stations, and not for their suitability for statehood. And the divestment corollary — that the United States could divest itself not only of uninhabited, discovered islands (e.g., the guano islands) but also of inhabited, "appurtenant" territories acquired by conquest or treaty cession — enabled the United States to release Cuba and, later, the Philippines. In fact, throughout the early years of the twentieth century, the United States repeatedly chose *not* to annex additional territories, whether Santo Domingo, the whole of Panama — beyond the narrow canal strip — Nicaragua, or other Latin American states, despite the opportunities to do so. At the same time, the United States developed a new doctrine, the Roosevelt Corollary of the Monroe Doctrine, to justify military intervention elsewhere, outside the states and beyond the territories of the United States.

This new doctrine was subsequently endorsed by the Supreme Court, most notably in *United States v. Curtiss-Wright Export Corporation* (1936), a decision that lies at the center of the discretionary power that the Court has accorded the president and Congress in matters of national security. The fact of the Supreme Court's discretion it grants to the executive and legislative branches on matters of foreign and military policy is what the Yale judicial scholar Harold Hongju Koh calls the "national security constitution." For most of the twentieth century and into the early twenty-first century, the Supreme Court has deferred to the military, executive, and U.S. government in matters of national security and grand strategy. There have only been two exceptions: one was the Court's 1971 decision in *United States v. New York Times* (the *Pentagon Papers Case*), in which the Court in a five-to-four split supported the *Times*'s publication of U.S. government documents of the Vietnam War leaked to the press by Daniel Elsberg. The other was recent, when on June 28, 2004, the Supreme Court rejected the Bush administration's claim that the U.S.

government has the absolute power to jail suspected terrorists for reasons of national security, without charging or convicting them of crimes. In *Rasul et al. v. Bush, President of the United States et al.* (2004), *Rumsfeld, Secretary of Defense v. Padilla et al.* (2004), and *Hamdi et al. v. Rumsfeld, Secretary of Defense* (2004) — the first and third were decided six to three, the second, five to four — the Supreme Court ruled that detainees were allowed limited protections under the Fifth Amendment (*Hamdi*) and the right to habeas corpus (*Rasul*). The U.S. government could not hold and subject prisoners to questioning and to physical and psychological stress without a minimum of procedural guarantees. But the Court never cited the *Insular Cases* in the opinions, despite the fact that the decisions in *Rasul* and *Hamdi* concerned the status of detainees at Guantánamo Bay, which the U.S. government has held since 1898. In short, the Supreme Court put (limited) restrictions on how the U.S. government treats suspects in the current war against terrorism, even if it is now apparent that the U.S. military tortures and summarily executes prisoners. Consistent with the decision in *Downes v. Bidwell* and with other of the *Insular Cases*, the Supreme Court has not fundamentally challenged or confronted the United States' empire.

In stark contrast, we *can* imagine Congress and the Court coming to a new understanding with respect to the United States' island territories and the difficult, ambiguous position they (and Washington, D.C.) occupy in the political system and the U.S. Constitution. Harder to imagine is how the constitutionally unique arrangements in the different territories, just like those on American Indian reservations and in the District of Columbia, can be improved upon to the satisfaction of both territorial inhabitants and the interests of members of Congress and the executive branch.

———

But it was the *Insular Cases* that first opened the door to such enduring constitutional permutations. The U.S. Supreme Court had addressed territorial issues before the *Insular Cases*, where, as we have seen in chapter 1, the Supreme Court generally upheld Congress's and the U.S. government's plenary authority over the territories of the United States. Given this territorial history of the United States and given the Supreme Court's record, one could argue, as did Edmund Steele Joy in 1892, that the territories of the United States — and Joy was then writing about the continental territories, to be sure — had no inherent rights to become states, or any other necessary rights beyond a few fundamental ones that virtually all commentators and justices on the Supreme Court agreed inhered to the inhabitants of the U.S. territories.

What the *Insular Cases* did, however, was to force the Supreme Court to forge a single doctrine out of a series of decisions involving the relationship of the U.S. government to its territories. Prior to its decisions in the *Insular Cases* the Court had always *separately* confronted questions of wartime tariffs, military occupations, the status of American Indians, the political rights of Mormons in Utah, the freedoms guaranteed to African Americans in the territories, and other matters. The Court established a mixed set of precedents on these diverse territorial issues, as the legal debates about, briefs filed for, and opinions in the *Insular Cases* clearly show. Perhaps the one exception, the one case of comparable scope to the *Insular Cases*, and to *Downes v. Bidwell* in particular, was the hugely controversial and widely discredited ruling by Chief Justice Taney in *Dred Scott v. Sandford*.

In the *Insular Cases*, then, the Supreme Court had to revisit fundamental issues of national identity and American destiny. The Court had to decide how U.S. sovereignty and the Constitution were to apply to foreign peoples and distant areas, people and areas unfamiliar to Americans but now annexed to the United States, how it was to define the United States for the purposes of the Constitution. And it was because of the Constitution's "absolute silence" on the political status of the territories and the territorial citizens of the United States — as Justice Brown noted in his lead opinion in *Downes* — that the nation's best legal minds and even the justices on the Court could come to such very different understandings of constitutional law and the political system of the United States. No wonder, then, the range and depth of the debates over the constitutional issues at stake in the Court's decision, the richness and length of the briefs prepared for the cases, the historical breadth and scope of the justices' opinions, and the intense and widespread reactions to the decisions by the Supreme Court.

The Supreme Court's decisions did transform what the United States meant for constitutional purposes and for the U.S. political system. The *Insular Cases* took the United States away from the trajectory established by the pattern set by the Northwest Ordinance for territorial development toward statehood. The cases "changed U.S. constitutional history for the sake of empire," the historian Walter LaFeber remarks. The new constitutional doctrine establishing congressional plenary authority over offshore and distant possessions was consistent with the United States' exercise of empire as a great power. While the Court's decisions in the *Insular Cases* may not have fundamentally altered the racism, strategic direction, and economic momentum of the United States at the turn of the twentieth century, they do reveal how the Supreme Court and elite political opinion wrestled with the fact that the United States was most obviously *not* a nation of states and with the question of how the reality of U.S. foreign policy and its new empire(s) could be made consistent with the Constitution. In fact, given the ethnocentrism of the time and the rise of the United States as a great power militarily and economically, we might argue the reverse. We might consider the remarkable closeness of the first several decisions, the length of time it took for the Incorporation Doctrine to become entrenched as judicial policy, and the variation that emerged among the *Insular Cases* with respect to how the Court was to apply separate provisions of the Constitution to the inhabitants and governments of the territories. The decisions in the *Insular Cases* were hardly predestined.

In sum, the *Insular Cases* established that the U.S. Congress and the U.S. Supreme Court had the right to determine the status of areas the United States acquired as a result of the Spanish-American War. Congress and the Supreme Court could determine which territories were incorporated unless treaties explicitly incorporated new areas, and, for those territories that were not incorporated, which particular constitutional provisions applied. The U.S. government could, by virtue of its treaties, legislation, and judicial interpretations, determine what constitutional rights applied to governments, businesses, and individuals of the territories. And the U.S. government could indefinitely defer the granting of political rights to unincorporated territories if it found that such areas were, for whatever reason, unsuitable for inclusion in the Union. In some unincorporated territories this might mean their eventual incorporation into the United States; in others, nonincorporation or even their release.

———

So what was the Supreme Court actually doing when it made its decisions in the *Insular Cases* and stepped onto this new ground?

One response is that the Supreme Court was engaging in *creative pragmatism*, being necessarily flexible in light of the United States' new circumstances. Coudert, the lawyer for the plaintiffs in *Downes v. Bidwell*, *De Lima v. Bidwell*, and many of the other *Insular Cases* thought that Justice White's "ingenious and original doctrine" was not a part of U.S. constitutional law. In fact, Justice Brown's extension doctrine "logically and historically . . . probably had as much to sustain it as the more novel and subtle incorporation doctrine." But Brown's doctrine was inconsistent with Americans' reverence for the Constitution, Coudert observed. And the "more simple, and . . . more logical *ex proprio vigore* doctrine of the original dissenting justices" failed "to satisfy the common sense view that Congress should have a free hand in dealing with peoples of an utterly alien and different civilization." The Incorporation Doctrine, in contrast, "had the advantage of reconciling American reverence for the Constitution . . . with large discretion left to Congress regarding the liberty to be given to the new peoples."

More recent commentators effectively agree. Judge Juan Torruella sees the Incorporation Doctrine as "judicial inventiveness at its ultimate height." Robert Highsaw, a biographer of Justice White, holds a similar view: "The Insular Doctrine permitted the Court to resolve the dilemma that faced it. It was politically impossible for the Supreme Court to rule that the United States could not retain the islands; it was inexpedient to extend to the new peoples immediately all the provisions of the Constitution, differing as much in cultural and political background as the inhabitants of these islands did from the rest of our people." Julius Pratt, too, refers to White's "clever plan for enabling the United States to acquire and govern colonial possessions." And the judicial scholar Loren Beth sees the Incorporation Doctrine as being "realistic," since the new territorial inhabitants were "in no real sense Americans." Rather, because the people of the new territories "had differing cultures, languages, religions, and traditional legal institutions," the Court had to be politically pragmatic. Faced with the sudden reality of the overseas possessions — with all their racial, strategic, and commercial implications — and with the overwhelming reelection of President McKinley in the fall of 1900, the Court reinterpreted the Constitution accordingly, Bruce Ackerman suggests. Although Ackerman does not write about the *Insular Cases*, the turn of the twentieth century, or U.S. territorial expansion, he points out in his account of transformative moments in constitutional history that the Supreme Court may at rare times, under the impetus of popular movements and electoral mandates, reinterpret the Constitution.

A second response to the *Insular Cases* sees the Court's endorsement of the Incorporation Doctrine as conforming to an *unwritten* Constitution. In distinction to the creative pragmatism of the first view, this second view sees the Court as carrying out a more basic logic *internal* to the United States and its Constitution. New Jersey chancellor Eugene Stevenson noted that contrary to the widely held notion that the United States had only a *written* constitution — in contrast to the states of the "old world," which had *unwritten* constitutions — the United States also had an *unwritten* constitution. Foremost among the issues that the Constitution left unaddressed, he commented, was the scope of the geographic area the United States was to control as a sovereign state.

Americans "did not know the elastic nature of their constitution, its adaptability in the hands of clever men to any situation which may conceivably arise," Beckles Willson wrote, elasticity manifest in the decisions in *Downes v. Bidwell* and *De Lima v. Bidwell*, which Willson saw as fundamentally altering the relationship between the U.S. government and the territories of the United States. Although Americans "have for nearly a century agreed to consider themselves ruled by an inflexible Constitution, not to be amended or modified except by the method set forth in the instrument itself," Willson remarked. "This is, of course, a delusion: the *unwritten* and *flexible* American constitution promises in time to be the greater power of the two" (emphasis added).

Alpheus Snow argued, too, that in *Downes v. Bidwell* the Supreme Court was adjudicating and executing the "unwritten Constitution." A majority on the Court "recognize[d] that a written Constitution is only the best evidence of the unwritten Constitution which it evidences." The decision in "the Insular Tariff Cases" has "at last recognized and fulfilled" the framers' purpose, Snow wrote, and "the decision further recognizes that the "American Empire" is a "Federal Empire" — that is, one ruled by the component states and their representatives. The judicial scholar Sarah Cleveland observes that the Court's conclusions in the *Insular Cases* "left the governance of the U.S. overseas territories largely in an *extraconstitutional zone*" (emphasis added). The Supreme Court decided the *Insular Cases* according to the logic of the inherent powers of the United States, she argues. Thus the cases have to be put in the context of the Court's "inherent powers" decisions as also applied to Indians, aliens, and others.

I would suggest a third view, however, one that lies between an interpretation based on creative pragmatism and an emphasis on the flexibility of the Court's interpretation, on the one hand, and one based on the idea that the Court was following an unwritten Constitution of inherent powers and thereby fulfilling a deeper, hidden Constitution that the Supreme Court (rarely) brings to light, on the other hand. This middle view — which encompasses aspects of the first and second views, to be sure — is that of "constitutional construction."

The political scientist Keith Whittington identifies "constitutional construction" as the phenomenon whereby new politics cause new understandings of the political world and of the meaning of the Constitution. This is to say that there come episodes across a wide range of conditions in which political actors forge new meaning out of the shadows and ambiguities of the Constitution. This construction of new constitutional meaning — whether narrow or broad — informs and channels subsequent constitutional interpretation and even the overall direction of the political system. This construction may span different parts of the Constitution's text, Whittington writes; it may bring together substantive areas in a new way; and it may create new constitutional meaning(s) beyond the current and preexisting ones.

As Whittington points out, "The American shift in international posture as marked by the Spanish-American War left the country with permanent noncontiguous, ethnically distinct territories that were not seen as being held in a temporary status until population growth and political organization should allow a transition to statehood," even though he does not include U.S. expansion at the turn of the twentieth century among his case studies. Yet he nonetheless observes that the constitutional construction occurring then "not only affected the size and nature of the territorial jurisdiction of the federal government, but also redefined the nature of citizenship and contributed to shifts in the distribution of powers among branches and levels of government, the nature of the organic structures of government, and the considerations that defined individual rights." The change in the United States' international position "from an expansionist republic" confined to the Americas "to an interventionist global empire *remade* the nature of the United States as a political entity" (emphasis added).

This characterization seems right. It fits the overall changes occurring in the political and constitutional order at the end of the nineteenth century and the beginning of the twentieth. The debates in Congress over going to war with Spain, the Teller Amendment, the annexation of Hawai'i, the Treaty of Paris, the Foraker Act, and trade reciprocity with Cuba are wholly consistent with Whittington's characterization of constitutional constructions as "highly partisan, messy, bitter disputes, in which the losers are driven from the public stage." And Justice Harlan, leading anti-imperialists such as former secretary of the Treasury George Boutwell, and Senators George Hoar and R. F. Pettigrew (R-S.D.) — both of whom opposed the Republican Party leadership — were consequently stranded on the margins of political life. These were highly divisive times.

The notion of constitutional construction — a kind of interpretation, to be sure — allows for a Constitution whose interpretation changes only infrequently, but in ways consistent with the constitutional text itself. Changes in interpretation are open-ended, then, if boundedly so. They can go in different directions and may even conflict in Ackerman's transformative moments. They may also *precede* changes in mass politics, contrary to Ackerman's thesis that the Court follows and endorses popular action. At the same time, constitutional construction does not have to be inconsistent with preceding constitutional meanings or with the founders' designs, but may be assembled in different ways and to different effects — contrary to an emphasis on the openness and flexibility of the Constitution or on the inherent powers of government according to an unwritten constitution.

A study of the *Insular Cases* suggests two amendments to the notion of constitutional construction, however. One is that for understanding the political construction of the constitutional meaning at the beginning of the twentieth century, we need to put the decisions of the

Insular Cases, especially those of 1901, 1903, and 1904, front and center. Whereas Whittington has the Supreme Court acting in the background of legislative and executive action, it may be, as a study of the *Insular Cases* suggests, that the Court's decisions *themselves* may serve as a fulcrum and a forum for the articulation of larger developments in constitutional interpretation. Although we cannot understand the Court's decisions without factoring in race and ethnicity, the strategic concerns of military planners and Republican elites, and the political economy of the tariff along with the increased internationalization of American commerce, the Supreme Court's multiple decisions in the *Insular Cases* served to bring these factors together and enabled the United States to find a way to keep its new island territories for military and business purposes without making them full partners in the American polity. Where the Constitution was silent and constitutional law equivocal, the Supreme Court established new doctrine.

A second amendment would be to note that the constitutional meaning that political actors construct in times of political turmoil may contain its own contradictions and propel its own difficult legacies. We have seen that the decisions in the *Insular Cases* led in two contrary directions — to the emergence of a territorial empire, one politically and constitutionally subordinate to the states and other (incorporated) U.S. territories, and to the emergence of an informal empire based on opening markets, the promulgation of political reforms, the cooperation of friendly governments, the support of international institutions, and the timely use of force. But such constitutional construction may not only be self-contradictory, as we see when we contrast the political development of the island territories (the territorial empire) and the emergence of the United States' increasingly palpable informal empire as a sole superpower throughout the twentieth century and now in the war against terrorism. It may also poorly serve as a resolution for the continuing tensions in the Constitution and in the U.S. political system since the founding between democratic principles and the politics of empire.

Almost every writer on the *Insular Cases* has his or her own particular list of cases, from as few as three to as many as twenty-three. I have chosen an expansive list of the cases, for reasons that I hope the text makes clear. Professor Efrén Rivera Ramos, one of the most prominent students of the Constitution and the territories of the United States, offers a list of twenty-three cases in *The Legal Construction of Identity*, dating from the decisions of May 1901 to *Balzac v. Porto Rico* in 1922. I add twelve cases to Rivera Ramos's list, for a total of thirty-five *Insular Cases*.

The first I add is *Neely v. Henkel* — as do Melvin Urofsky, Loren Beth, Gerald Neuman, Christina Duffy Burnett, and James Kerr in their lists of *Insular Cases* — since *Neely v. Henkel* (actually the first of two cases by the name) addressed the constitutional status of Cuba following the Spanish-American War, and since the decision stands at odds with other decisions by the Supreme Court in cases involving Puerto Rico, the Philippines, Hawai'i, and Alaska. I also add *Binns v. United States*, an Alaskan tax case (David Currie mentions *Binns*, as does Burnett in a recent article), the double jeopardy case of *United States v. Gavieres* (Kerr also discusses *Gavieres*), and two additional tariff cases, *Lincoln v. United States* and *Warner, Barnes v. United States* (which had separate docket numbers but were decided as a single case) and the rehearing of the two cases a year later (John Semonche and Loren Beth each mentions the first *Lincoln; Warner, Barnes* case). I also include a final tariff-related case, *United States v. Heinszen*, in which the Court had to rule on Congress's invalidation of the ability of traders such as Warner, Barnes and Company to sue the U.S. government for the recovery of the tariff duties already collected from them.

In addition, I discuss *Porto Rico v. Rosaly* and *Porto Rico v. Muratti* (the sister case of *Porto Rico v. Tapia*), as does Burnett. Rivera Ramos, Kerr, and Charles Warren include *Porto Rico v. Tapia* among the *Insular Cases* but do not mention *Porto Rico v. Muratti;* Pedro Capo-Rodriguez discusses both cases. Yet *Porto Rico v. Tapia* and *Porto Rico v. Muratti* were important precedents for *Balzac v. Porto Rico.* And *Porto Rico v. Rosaly* addressed the question of the sovereign immunity of Puerto Rico's territorial government.

I also include several other noteworthy cases. In *Ponce v. Roman Catholic Church*, the U.S. Supreme Court recognized the existing Spanish law in Puerto Rico with respect to the Catholic Church, and in *Weems v. United States* (mentioned by Urofsky), the Court adjudicated the applicability of the Eighth Amendment to the Philippines. I include one more case from Puerto Rico, *Ochoa v. Hernandez* (mentioned by Burnett), that addressed the Fifth Amendment's due process provisions with respect to the taking of property. I do not include a number of other Supreme Court cases that involved constitutional issues and the U.S. island territories in the early twentieth century. (For a comprehensive list of Supreme Court cases pertaining to the territories in the years between 1894 and 1921, see Marie Klinkhamer's Appendix B in her biography of Edward D. White.) These (many) other cases were almost all unanimous decisions, with short written opinions that broke no new significant constitutional ground. Many, too, were prize cases. Almost none receive mention in other scholarship on the *Insular Cases*.

CHRONOLOGY

1898

February 15	Sinking of the USS *Maine*
April 19	Teller Amendment on the nonannexation of Cuba
April 21	Congress declares war on Spain
July 7	Hawai'i annexed by joint resolution of Congress
July 26	President McKinley imposes tariffs on goods shipped from Puerto Rico and the Philippines to the states, and vice versa
December 10	Treaty of Paris signed by U.S. and Spanish delegations

1899

February 6	Treaty of Paris ratified by U.S. Senate
February 14	Senate passes resolution not to incorporate Filipinos as U.S. citizens or to annex the Philippines
August 19	United States acquires Eastern Samoa by agreement with Britain and Germany

1900

April 12	Foraker Act, Puerto Rico
April 30	Organic Act, Hawai'i
November 6	William McKinley reelected U.S. president

1901

January 14	*Neely v. Henkel*, 180 U.S. 109
March 2	Platt Amendment, Cuba
	Spooner Amendment, the Philippines
May 27	*De Lima v. Bidwell*, 182 U.S. 1
	Goetze v. United States, 182 U.S. 221
	Crossman v. United States, 182 U.S. 221
	Dooley v. United States, 182 U.S. 222 [*Dooley I*]
	Armstrong v. United States, 182 U.S. 243
	Downes v. Bidwell, 182 U.S. 244
	Huus v. New York and Porto Rico S.S. Co., 182 U.S. 392

September 14	President McKinley is assassinated; Theodore Roosevelt becomes U.S. president
December 2	*Dooley v. United States*, 183 U.S. 151 [*Dooley II*]
	Fourteen Diamond Rings v. United States, 183 U.S. 176

1902

March 8	Tariff on goods from the Philippines set at 85 percent of Dingley Tariff levels
May 20	Establishment of Cuban Republic; end of U.S. occupation
July 1	Act to organize Philippine civilian government
September 15	Horace Gray dies
December 8	Oliver Wendell Holmes takes oath of office

1903

February 23	George Shiras Jr. retires
March 2	William R. Day takes oath of office
June 1	*Hawaii v. Mankichi*, 190 U.S. 197
October 20	Settlement with Canada of Alaska boundary dispute
November 5	Panama independence established
November 17	The Hay-Bunau-Varilla Treaty grants the United States exclusive control of the Panama Canal Zone
December 16	Cuban Reciprocity Treaty passes U.S. Senate

1904

January 4	*Gonzalez v. Williams*, 192 U.S. 1
May 31	*Binns v. United States*, 194 U.S. 486
	Kepner v. United States, 195 U.S. 100
	Mendezona v. United States, 195 U.S. 158
	Dorr v. United States, 195 U.S. 138
November 8	Theodore Roosevelt reelected U.S. president

1905

| April 1 | United States establishes a protectorate in the Dominican Republic |
| April 3 | *Lincoln v. United States; Warner, Barnes & Co. v. United States*, 197 U.S. 419 |

April 10	*Rassmussen v. United States,* 197 U.S. 516
September 2	Roosevelt mediates treaty to end Russo-Japanese War
December 4	*Trono v. United States,* 199 U.S. 521

1906

May 28	*Lincoln v. United States; Warner, Barnes & Co. v. United States,* 202 U.S. 484 (rehearing)
	Henry B. Brown retires
December 17	William H. Moody takes oath of office

1907

May 27	*Grafton v. United States,* 206 U.S. 333
	United States v. Heinszen & Co., 206 U.S. 370
November 16	Oklahoma admitted as forty-sixth state
November 18	*Kent v. Porto Rico,* 207 U.S. 113

1908

| June 1 | *Ponce v. Roman Catholic Church,* 210 U.S. 296 |
| November 3 | William Howard Taft elected U.S. president |

1909

| January 4 | *Kopel v. Bingham,* 211 U.S. 468 |
| October 25 | Rufus W. Peckham dies |

1910

January 3	Horace H. Lurton takes oath of office
March 28	David J. Brewer dies
May 2	*Weems v. United States,* 217 U.S. 349
July 4	Melville W. Fuller dies
October 10	Charles Evans Hughes takes oath of office
November 20	William H. Moody retires
December 18	Edward D. White promoted to chief justice

1911

January 3	Willis Van Devanter takes oath of office
	Joseph R. Lamar takes oath of office
April 3	*Gavieres v. United States,* 220 U.S. 338

| May 15 | *Dowdell v. United States*, 221 U.S. 325 |
| October 14 | John Marshall Harlan dies |

1912

January 6	New Mexico admitted as forty-seventh state
February 14	Arizona admitted as forty-eighth state
March 18	Mahlon Pitney takes oath of office
August 24	Second Organic Act of Alaska
November 5	Woodrow Wilson elected U.S. president

1913

| February 14 | *Porto Rico v. Rosaly*, 227 U.S. 270 |
| June 13 | *Ochoa v. Hernandez*, 230 U.S. 139 |

1914

May 25	*Ocampo v. United States*, 234 U.S. 91
July 12	Horace H. Lurton dies
September 5	James C. McReynolds takes oath of office

1916

January 2	Joseph R. Lamar dies
April 6	United States enters World War I
June 5	Louis D. Brandeis takes oath of office
June 10	Charles Evans Hughes resigns
August 1	John H. Clarke takes oath of office
November 7	Woodrow Wilson reelected U.S. president

1917

| March 2 | Organic Act of Porto Rico (Jones Act) |
| March 31 | Virgin Islands transferred from Denmark to the United States for $25 million |

1918

January 21	*Porto Rico v. Tapia*, 245 U.S. 639
	Porto Rico v. Muratti, 245 U.S. 639
November 11	Armistice Day, end of World War I

{ *Chronology* }

1920

March 1   *Board of Public Utility Commissioners v. Ynchausti & Co.*, 251
               U.S. 401

November 2   Warren G. Harding elected U.S. president

1921

May 16   Edward D. White dies

July 11   William Howard Taft takes oath of office as chief justice

1922

April 10   *Balzac v. Porto Rico,* 258 U.S. 298

BIBLIOGRAPHICAL ESSAY

Note from the series editors: The following bibliographical essay contains the primary and secondary sources the author consulted for this volume. We have asked all authors in the series to omit formal citations in order to make their volumes more readable, inexpensive, and appealing for students and general readers.

The records, briefs, and oral arguments for the decisions in the *Insular Cases* of May and December 1901 may be found in Albert H. Howe, *The Insular Cases: Comprising the Records, Briefs, and Arguments of Counsel in the Insular Cases of the October Term, 1900, in the Supreme Court of the United States, Including Appendixes Thereto*, compiled and published pursuant to H.R. Con. Res. No. 72, Fifty-sixth Cong., 2nd sess. (Washington, D.C.: Government Printing Office, 1901). See the *U.S. Reports* for the appeals, briefs from counsels, and decisions for the set of *Insular Cases*. For the position of the War Department's Division of Insular Affairs, and for a set of briefs arguing for the plenary power of the U.S. government, see Charles E. Magoon, *Reports of the Law of Civil Government in Territory Subject to Military Occupation by the Military Forces of the United States*, submitted to Hon. Elihu Root, Secretary of War (Washington, D.C.: Government Printing Office, 1902).

For correspondence and official memoranda that addressed the politics and judicial histories of the *Insular Cases*, I consulted the papers of Louis D. Brandeis, Henry B. Brown, George B. Cortelyou, William R. Day, Willis Van Devanter, Melville Weston Fuller, John Marshall Harlan, Charles Evans Hughes, William Henry Moody, Theodore Roosevelt, Elihu Root, William Howard Taft, and Edward D. White in the Manuscript Collection at the Library of Congress. I found the most useful documents and correspondence to be the "General Correspondence" file of Secretary of War Root; the "General Correspondence" file, Subject File, "Spanish-American War" of George Cortelyou (President McKinley's personal secretary); the Theodore Roosevelt papers; the William Howard Taft papers; and the William Moody papers (Moody was attorney general and secretary of the navy before becoming an associate justice on the U.S. Supreme Court). Little in the justices' own recorded correspondence bore directly on the *Insular Cases*. Several of the few exceptions to this judicial reticence I cite in the text.

The records of the Senate Committee on Cuba, the Senate Committee on the Philippines and Puerto Rico, the House Committee on Insular Affairs, and the War Department's Bureau of Insular Affairs also contained much relevant background material, although little bore directly on the *Insular Cases*.

Two volumes of collected correspondence were especially helpful. One was Henry Cabot Lodge and Charles F. Redmond, eds., *Selections from the*

Correspondence of Theodore Roosevelt and Henry Cabot Lodge (New York: Da Capo Press, 1971), which contains considerable correspondence between the two men on the topics of U.S. expansion, national politics, legislative strategy, judicial appointments, and the Republican Party. The other volume was *Holmes-Pollock Letters: The Correspondence of Mr. Justice Holmes and Sir Frederick Pollock, 1874–1932*, ed. Mark DeWolfe Howe (Cambridge, Mass.: Belknap Press of Harvard University Press, 1961), which contained some letters that bore directly on the political and constitutional status of the United States' island territories.

Because I wanted to consult a representative sample of newspaper responses to the *Insular Cases*, and because many newspapers of a hundred years ago no longer exist, I consulted N. W. Ayer's and Sons, *American Newspapers Annual* (Philadelphia, 1902), to find the leading newspapers of 1901 from several cities around the United States. I employed a three-part strategy, selecting according to the size of newspaper circulation, the partisanship of the newspaper, and geographic diversity. The largest-selling newspapers around the country were by and far those of New York City, where I looked at the reportage in the *New York Herald, New York World, New York Daily Tribune*, and *New York Times*. I also consulted the *Chicago Record-Herald*, which had the largest circulation in the nation's second-largest city, and two newspapers from the nation's third-largest city, the *Philadelphia Record* and the *Philadelphia Inquirer*. In addition, I looked at newspapers from different regions of the United States (*San Francisco Examiner, Buffalo Evening News and Telegraph, Washington Post*, and *St. Louis Post-Dispatch*), from newly admitted states (*Seattle Times* and *Denver Post*), and from a then-existing territory (the *Santa Fe New Mexican* and *Albuquerque Journal Democrat*). And I balanced partisanship by looking at both Republican and Democratic newspapers from New York City and Philadelphia. I consulted fifteen newspapers in all.

Most of the newspapers in the smaller cities, and especially in the new states and the territory of New Mexico, contained little information on the *Insular Cases;* what news they did contain was typically taken from wire service stories or reprints of articles published in the large metropolitan dailies. In the instances where I do not provide newspaper dates, the news articles or editorials I quote or paraphrase date from one to three days after the relevant Court decision(s). I was unable to obtain copies of Cuban or Philippine newspapers from 1901, and the copies of the Puerto Rican newspaper I consulted with the help of a graduate assistant, Rodrigo Nunes — *La Democracia* — had almost nothing on the cases. Providing background on one of the principal Puerto Rican newspapers, *La Democracia*, is Mariano Negrón-Portillo, "A Study of the Newspaper '*La Democracia*,' Puerto Rico, 1895–1914: A Historical Analysis" (Ph.D. diss., State University of New York at Stony Brook, 1980). Negrón-Portillo offers useful information on the politics and persons in Puerto Rico over the years in question; he does not discuss the *Insular Cases.*

To gauge the scholarly reaction to the United States' new territorial acquisitions at the time, I looked at articles in the leading law, academic, and intellectual journals: Carman Randolph, "Constitutional Aspects of Annexation," *Harvard Law Review* 12 (1898): 291–315; Simeon E. Baldwin, "The Constitutional Questions Incident to the Acquisition and Government by the United Sates of Island Territory," *Harvard Law Review* 12 (1898): 393–416; Christopher C. Langdell, "The Status of Our New Territories," *Harvard Law Review* 12 (1899): 366–392; James Bradley Thayer, "Our New Possessions," *Harvard Law Review* 12 (1899): 464–485; Elmer Adams, "The Causes and Result of Our War with Spain from a Legal Standpoint," *Yale Law Journal* 8 (1899): 119–133; Harry Pratt Judson, "Our Federal Constitution and the Government of Tropical Territories," *American Monthly Review of Reviews* 19 (1899): 67–75; John Kimberly Beach, "Constitutional Expansion," *Yale Law Journal* 8 (1899): 225–234; Charles A. Gardiner, "Our Right to Acquire and Hold Foreign Territory," *American Law Review* 33 (1899): 161–187; Abott Lawrence Lowell, "The Status of Our New Possessions — A Third View," *Harvard Law Review* 13 (November 1899): 155–176; George P. Costigan Jr., "The Third View of the Status of Our New Possessions," *Yale Law Journal* 9 (1899): 124–133; and H. Teichmuller, "Expansion and the Constitution," *American Law Review* 33 (1899): 202–214.

I further consulted William Bradford Bosley, "The Constitutional Requirement of Uniformity in Duties, Imposts and Excises," *Yale Law Journal* 9 (1900): 164–169; Paul R. Shipman, "Webster on the Territories," *Yale Law Journal* 9 (1900): 185–206; Edward B. Whitney, "The Porto Rico Tariffs of 1899 and 1900," *Yale Law Journal* 9 (1900): 297–321; Frank J. R. Mitchell, "The Legal Effect of the Acquisition of the Philippine Islands," *American Law Register* 48 (1900): 193–210; Harry Pratt Judson, "The Constitution and the Territories," *American Monthly Review of Reviews* 21 (1900): 451–456; Clifford Walton, "Change of Sovereignty of a People and the United States Constitution," *American Law Register* 48 (1900): 580–585; John K. Richards, "The Constitution and the New Territories," *American Law Review* 34 (1900): 670–688; and Selden Bacon, "Territory and the Constitution," *Yale Law Journal* 10 (1901): 99–117.

Other political and legal writings on the *Insular Cases* followed in the aftermath of the Supreme Court's decisions of May 27, 1901: L. S. Rowe, "The Supreme Court and the Insular Cases," *Annals of the American Academy of Political and Social Science* 5 (July 1901): 226–250; George S. Boutwell, "The Supreme Court and the Dependencies," *North American Review* 173 (August 1901): 1–8; John W. Burgess, "The Decisions of the Supreme Court in the Insular Cases," *Political Science Quarterly* 16 (September 1901): 486–504; Le

Roy Parker, "The Constitution in Porto Rico," *Yale Law Journal* 10 (1901): 136–145; Lebbeus R. Wilfley, "Our Duty to the Philippines," *Yale Law Journal* 10 (1901): 309–314; Charles E. Littlefield, "The Insular Cases," *Harvard Law Review* 15 (1901): 168–190; Charles E. Littlefield, "The Insular Cases. II," *Harvard Law Review* 15 (1901): 281–297; Eugene Stevenson, "The Relation of the Nation to Its Dependencies," *American Law Review* 36 (1902): 366–386; Emlin McLain, "The Hawaiian Case" *Harvard Law Review* 17 (April 1904): 386–399; and David K. Watson, "Acquisition and Development of National Domain," *American Law Review* 41 (1907): 239–254.

Contemporary historians, social scientists, and political writers — including politicians and publicists — also addressed the political history and culture of the United States' new territories. See Max Farrand, "Territory and District," *American Historical Review* 5 (1900): 676–681; Max Farrand, *The Legislation of Congress for the Government of the Organized Territories of the United States, 1789–1895* (Newark, N.J.: William A. Baker, 1896); Abbott Lawrence Lowell, "The Colonial Expansion of the United States," *Atlantic Monthly*, February 1899, 145–154; Titus Munson Coan, "The Natives of Hawaii: A Study of Polynesian Charm," *Annals of the American Academy of Political and Social Science* 5 (July 1901): 10–17; Rev. Charles C. Pierce, "The Race of the Philippines — The Tagals," *Annals of the American Academy of Political and Social Science* 5 (July 1901): 21–39; Orville H. Platt, "Our Relation to the People of Cuba and Porto Rico," *Annals of the American Academy of Political and Social Science* 5 (July 1901): 145–159; Charles M. Pepper, "The Spanish Population of Cuba and Porto Rico," *Annals of the American Academy of Political and Social Science* 5 (July 1901): 163–178; George F. Edmunds, "The Insular Cases," *North American Review*, 537 (August 1901): 145–153; Hannis Taylor, "Conquered Territory and the Constitution," *North American Review*, no. 540 (November 1901): 577–593; Alleyne Ireland, "Is Tropical Colonization Justifiable?" *Annals of the American Academy of Political and Social Science* 19 (May 1902): 331–339; W. V. Judson, "Strategic Value of Her West Indian Possessions to the United States," *Annals of the American Academy of Political and Social Science* 19 (May 1902): 383–391; James T. Young, "Colonial Autonomy," *Annals of the American Academy of Political and Social Science* 19 (May 1902): 392–407; and Henry R. Burch, "Conditions Affecting the Suffrage in Colonies," *Annals of the American Academy of Political and Social Science* 19 (May 1902): 408–431.

Other scholarly reactions in the first decades of the twentieth century further discussed the United States' territories and territorial policy. See Amos S. Hershey, "The Succession of States," *American Journal of International Law* 5 (April 1911): 285–297; Pedro Capo-Rodriguez, "The Relations between the United States and Porto Rico," *American Journal of International Law* 10 (April 1916): 312–327; Quincy Wright, "Treaties and the Constitutional Separation of Powers in the United States," *American Journal of International Law* 12

(January 1918): 64–95; Pedro Capo-Rodriguez, "Part II: The Relations between the United States and Porto Rico," *American Journal of International Law* 13 (July 1919): 483–525; Pedro Capo-Rodriguez, "Some Historical and Political Aspects of the Government of Porto Rico," *Hispanic American Historical Review* 2 4 (November 1919): 543–585; Charles E. Hughes, "The Centenary of the Monroe Doctrine," *Annals of the American Academy of Political and Social Science* 61, Supplement (January 1924): 7–19; Frederic R. Coudert, "The Evolution of the Doctrine of Territorial Incorporation," *Columbia University Law Review* 26 (November 1926): 823–850; and Dudley O. McGovney, "Our Non-citizen Nationals, Who Are They?" *California Law Review* 22 (September 1934): 593–635.

A handful of books and articles specifically address the *Insular Cases*. James Edward Kerr, *The Insular Cases: The Role of the Judiciary in American Expansionism* (Port Washington, N.Y.: Kennikat Press, 1982), is good on the briefs for the cases, the background personnel to the decisions — besides the justices themselves — and much of the nuts and bolts of the decisions. Efrén Rivera Ramos has a lengthy law article and then book on the *Insular Cases* and Puerto Rico: "The Legal Construction of American Colonialism: The Insular Cases, 1901–1922," *Revista Juridia Universidad de Puerto Rico* 65 (1996): 225–328; Efrén Rivera Ramos, *The Legal Construction of Identity: The Judicial and Social Legacy of American Colonialism in Puerto Rico* (Washington, D.C.: American Psychological Association, 2001). Rivera Ramos's account is particularly strong on the legal and cultural legacies of the Supreme Court's decisions, on the different lenses through which we might understand the cases, and on the particular situation in which Puerto Ricans find themselves.

Rivera Ramos and a number of other scholars also contribute to an outstanding collection of essays on the *Insular Cases* that are contained in Christina Duffy Burnett and Burke Marshall, eds., *Foreign in a Domestic Sense* (Durham, N.C.: Duke University Press, 2001). Each essay addresses one or more aspects of the *Insular Cases*. The editors' introductory essay is highly recommended, as are the essays by José Cabranes, Mark Weiner, Brook Thomas, Efrén Rivera Ramos, Sanford Levinson, Juan F. Perea, E. Robert Statham, Gerald L. Neuman, Mark Tushnet, José Trías Monge, Juan R. Torruella, Roberto P. Aponte Toro, José Julián Álaverez González, Ángel Ricardo Oquendo, Richard Thornburgh, Rogers Smith, and Christina Duffy Burnett. And Christina Duffy Burnett's article "*Untied* States: American Expansion and Territorial Deannexation," *University of Chicago Law Review* 72 (2005): 797, uses a close reading of the Court's opinions and of scholarly writing on the *Insular Cases* to argue that the Incorporation Doctrine represents less of a break with the past than most scholars think, and that the basic purposes of Justice White's opinion was to allow for the "deannexation" of U.S. territories. Also see Amy Kaplan, *The Anarchy of Empire in the Making of U.S.*

Culture (Cambridge, Mass.: Harvard University Press, 2002), for an account of the intersection of the foreign and domestic in American expansion, and Gabriel A. Terrasa, "The United States and Puerto Rico and the Territorial Incorporation Doctrine: Reaching a Century of Constitutional Authoritarianism," *John Marshall Law Review* 31 (1997): 55–93.

Much scholarship on the political development of the United States' present-day island territories features the *Insular Cases* as part of the study. These works, as a class, contain useful historical summaries and analyses. They include Arnold H. Leibowitz, "United States Federalism: The States and the Territories," *American University Law Review* 28 (1979): 459–482; Arnold Leibowitz, *Defining Status: A Comprehensive Analysis of United States Territorial Relations* (Dordrecht: Kluwer Academic Publishers, 1989); Walter L. Williams, "United States Indian Policy and the Debate over Philippine Annexation: Implications for the Origin of American Imperialism," *Journal of American History* 66 (1980): 810–831; Winfred Lee Thompson, *The Introduction of American Law in the Philippines and Puerto Rico 1898–1905* (Fayetteville: University of Arkansas Press, 1989); Lanny Thompson, "The Imperial Republic: A Comparison of the Insular Territories under U.S. Dominion after 1898," *Pacific Historical Review* 71 (1999): 535–574; Lanny Thompson, "Representation and Rule in the Imperial Archipelago," *American Studies Asia* 1 (2002): 3–39; Julian Go, "The Chains of Empire: State Building and 'Political Education' in Puerto Rico and the Philippines," in Julian Go and Anne L. Foster, eds., *The American Colonial State in the Philippines: Global Perspectives* (Durham, N.C.: Duke University Press, 2002); and Stanley K. Laughlin Jr., *The Law of United States Territories and Affiliated Jurisdiction* (Danvers, Mass.: Lawyers Cooperative Publishing, 1995).

Also see George Boughton and Paul Leary, eds., "A Time of Change: Relations between the United States and American Samoa, Guam, the Northern Marianas, Puerto Rico and the United States Virgin Islands," Conference Proceedings, February 8–11, 1993 (1994); Joseph E. Fallon, "Federal Policy and U.S. Territories: The Political Restructuring of the United States of America," *Pacific Affairs* 64 (Spring 1991): 23–41, which provides some provocative analysis; and E. Robert Statham Jr., *Colonial Constitutionalism: The Tyranny of United States' Offshore Territorial Policy and Relations* (Lanham, Md.: Lexington Books, 2002), which uses normative political theory to criticize the constitutional status of the U.S. territories.

Individual studies of Puerto Rico, the Philippines, and Cuba also feature or provide useful background to the *Insular Cases*. See Juan R. Torruella, *The Supreme Court and Puerto Rico: The Doctrine of Separate and Unequal* (Puerto Rico: University of Puerto Rico, 1985), José A. Cabranes, *Citizenship and the American Empire: Notes on the Legislative History of the United States Citizenship of Puerto Ricans* (New Haven, Conn.: Yale University Press, 1979), which is particularly good on U.S. congressional policies on Puerto Rico (as the subtitle suggests), Raymond Carr, *Puerto Rico: A Colonial Experiment* (New York: New York University Press, 1984), which provides a helpful background on Puerto Rican history, and José Trías Monge, *Puerto Rico: The Trials of the Oldest Colony in the World* (New Haven, Conn.: Yale University Press, 1997). Also see Lyman Jay Gould, "The Roots of American Colonial Policy" (Ph.D. diss., University of Michigan, 1958), which discusses the evolution and politics of the Foraker Act.

Louis A. Pérez Jr., in *On Becoming Cuban: Identity, Nationality and Culture* (Chapel Hill: University of North Carolina Press, 1999), *The War of 1898: The United States and Cuba: History and Historiography* (Chapel Hill: University of North Carolina Press, 1998), and *Cuba and the United States: Ties of Singular Intimacy* (Athens: University of Georgia Press, 1990), provides a valuable perspective from the Cuban side and a helpful analysis of Cuban politics. Oscar M. Alfonso, *Theodore Roosevelt and the Philippines 1897–1909* (New York: Oriole Editions, 1974); Philip Lyman Snyder, "Mission, Empire, or the Force of Circumstances? A Study of the American Decision to Annex the Philippine Islands" (Ph.D. diss., Stanford University, 1972); and Michael Cullinane, "*Ilustrado* Politics: The Response of the Filipino Educated Elite to American Colonial Rule, 1898–1907" (Ph.D. diss., University of Michigan, 1989), address the politics, the law, and the persons relevant to understanding Filipino politics under U.S. rule. And Anne Paulet, "Racing the Filipinos: The Question of Filipino Identity and U.S. Policy at the Turn of the Twentieth Century" (paper presented at the conference of the Society of the History of American Foreign Relations, Austin, Texas, June 2004), revisits the parallels between American Indian policy and the politics and war in the Philippines. Also, for an absorbing account of the distinct circumstances of Mormons in the U.S. political system, see Sarah Barringer Gordon, *The Mormon Question: Polygamy and Constitutional Conflict in Nineteenth Century America* (Chapel Hill: University of North Carolina Press, 2002).

A number of writers at the end of the nineteenth century and the start of the twentieth addressed the general subject of the United States' new island territories: Charles Morris, *Our Island Empire: A Handbook of Cuba, Porto Rico, Hawaii, and the Philippine Islands* (Philadelphia: Lippincott, 1899); Horace N. Fisher, *Principles of Colonial Government* (Boston: Page, 1899); James C. Fernald, *The Imperial Republic* (New York: Funk and Wagnalls, 1899); Charles A. Conant, *The United States in the Orient: The Nature of the Economic Problem* (Boston: Houghton, Mifflin, 1901); Alfred T. Mahan, *Retrospect and Prospect* (Boston: Little, Brown, 1902); Alpheus H. Snow, *The Administration of Dependencies: A Study of the Evolution of Federal Empire, with Special Reference to American Colonial Problems* (New York: Putnam's, 1902); John R. Dos Passos, *The Anglo-Saxon Century and the Unification of the English-Speaking People* (New York: Putnam's, 1903); Beckles Willson, *The New America: A Study of the Im-*

perial Republic (New York: Dutton, 1903); William Franklin Willoughby, *Territories and Dependencies of the United States* (New York: Century Company, 1905); and Henry Parker Willis, *Our Philippine Problem: A Study of American Colonial Policy* (New York: Holt, 1905).

Several biographies also discussed the *Insular Cases* and/or had important background information. See James W. Ely Jr., *The Chief Justiceship of Melville W. Fuller, 1888–1910* (Columbia: University of South Carolina Press, 1999); Willard L. King, *Melville Weston Fuller: Chief Justice of the United States 1888–1910* (New York: Macmillan, 1950); Robert B. Highsaw, *Edward Douglass White: Defender of the Conservative Faith* (Baton Rouge: Louisiana State University Press, 1981); Marie Carolyn Klinkhamer, "Edward Douglass White, Chief Justice of the United States" (Ph.D. diss., Catholic University of America, 1943); Walter F. Pratt Jr., *The Supreme Court under Edward Douglass White, 1910–1921* (Charleston: University of South Carolina Press, 1999); Loren P. Beth, *John Marshall Harlan: The Last Whig Justice* (Lexington: University Press of Kentucky, 1992); Tinsley Yarbrough, *Judicial Enigma: The First Justice Harlan* (New York: Oxford University Press, 1995); and Linda Przybyszewski, *The Republic According to John Marshall Harlan* (Chapel Hill: University of North Carolina Press, 1999).

Also see Michael J. Brodhead, *David J. Brewer: The Life of a Supreme Court Justice, 1837–1910* (Carbondale: Southern Illinois University Press, 1994); Robert Jerome Glennon Jr., "Justice Henry Billings Brown: Values in Tension," *University of Colorado Law Review* 44 (1973): 553–604; Charles A. Kent, *Memoir of Henry Billings Brown* (New York: Duffield, 1915); Matthew McDevitt, *Joseph McKenna: Associate Justice of the United States* (New York: Da Capo Press, 1974); Sheldon M. Novick, *Honorable Justice: The Life of Oliver Wendell Holmes* (Boston: Little, Brown, 1989); Robert W. Gordon, ed., *The Legacy of Oliver Wendell Holmes, Jr.* (Stanford, Calif.: Stanford University Press, 1992); G. Edward White, *Justice Oliver Wendell Holmes: Law and the Inner Self* (New York: Oxford University Press, 1993); G. Edward White, *The American Legal Tradition: Profiles of Leading American Judges* (New York: Oxford University Press, 1976); John A. Garraty, "Holmes's Appointment to the U.S. Supreme Court," *New England Quarterly* 22 (September 1949): 291–303; and Louis Menand, *The Metaphysical Club* (New York: Farrar, Straus and Giroux, 2001). For the profiles of the justices serving on the bench from 1901 to 1922, I relied on the above books and articles and, especially, Leon Friedman and Fred L. Israel, eds., *The Justices of the United States Supreme Court, 1789–1969*, vols. 2 and 3 (New York: Chelsea House, 1969).

For information on Coudert Brothers, I consulted Virginia Kays Veenswijk, *Coudert Brothers: A Legacy in Law: The History of America's First International Law Firm, 1853–1993* (New York: Dutton, 1994). For material on former U.S. Treasury Secretary John G. Carlisle, I consulted James A. Barnes, *John G. Carlisle: Financial Statesman* (New York: Dodd, Mead, 1921).

Only a few constitutional law casebooks discuss the *Insular Cases*. These exceptions include Sanford Levinson, Paul Brest, Jack Balkin, and Akhil Amar, *Processes of Constitutional Decisionmaking*, 4th ed. (Aspen, Colo.: Aspen Publishers, 2000); Juan F. Perea, Richard Delgado, Angela P. Harris, Stephanie M. Wildman, and Jean Stefancic, *Race and Races* (St. Paul, Minn.: West Group, 2000), who include long passages from *Downes v. Bidwell* and *Balzac v. Porto Rico* in their text and discuss the U.S. insular policies more generally; and John E. Nowak and Ronald D. Rotunda, in *Constitutional Law* (St. Paul, Minn.: West, 2004), who briefly mention the cases. But also see two older accounts: Thomas M. Cooley, *The General Principles of Constitutional Law in the United States*, 3rd ed., ed. Andrew C. McLaughlin (Boston: Little, Brown, 1898), which addresses the territories in general, before the Spanish-American War; and G. Edward White, *Patterns of American Legal Thought* (Indianapolis: Bobbs-Merrill, 1978), which also touches on the *Insular Cases*.

Discussion of the overall politics, diplomacy, economics, and politicians of the era I found useful were Walter LaFeber, *The American Search for Opportunity, 1865–1913*, vol. 2 of *The Cambridge History of American Foreign Relations* (Cambridge: Cambridge University Press, 1993); Walter LaFeber, "The 'Lion in the Path': The U.S. Emergence as a World Power," *Political Science Quarterly* 101 (1986): 705–718; Walter LaFeber, "The Constitution and United States Foreign Policy: An Interpretation," *Journal of American History* 74 (December 1987): 695–717; Philip S. Foner, *The Spanish-Cuban-American War and the Birth of American Imperialism 1895–1902*, vols. 1 and 2 (New York: Monthly Review Press, 1972); David M. Pletcher, *The Diplomacy of Involvement: American Economic Expansion across the Pacific, 1784–1900* (Columbia: University of Missouri Press, 2001); David M. Pletcher, *The Diplomacy of Trade and Investment: American Economic Expansion in the Hemisphere, 1865–1900* (Columbia: University of Missouri Press, 1998); Matthew Frye Jacobson, *Barbarian Virtues: The United States Encounters Foreign Peoples at Home and Abroad, 1876–1917* (New York: Hill and Wang, 2000); Julius W. Pratt, *America's Colonial Experiment: How the United States Gained, Governed, and in Part Gave Away a Colonial Empire* (New York: Prentice-Hall, 1951); Roger Bell, *Last among Equals: Hawaiian Statehood and American Politics* (Honolulu: University of Hawaii Press, 1984); Joseph A. Fry, *Dixie Looks Abroad: The South and U.S. Foreign Relations, 1789–1973* (Baton Rouge: Louisiana State University Press, 2002); and Richard W. Leopold, *The Growth of American Foreign Policy: A History* (New York: Knopf, 1962).

Also see Richard H. Collins, *Theodore Roosevelt's Caribbean: The Panama Canal, the Monroe Doctrine, and the Latin American Context* (Baton Rouge:

Louisiana State University Press, 1990); David Burton, *Theodore Roosevelt: Confident Imperialist* (Philadelphia: University of Pennsylvania Press, 1968); John Morton Blum, *The Republican Roosevelt*, 2nd ed. (Cambridge, Mass.: Harvard University Press, 1977); John A. Garraty, *Henry Cabot Lodge: A Biography* (New York: Knopf, 1953); Nathan Miller, *Theodore Roosevelt* (New York: Morrow, 1992); Edmund Morris, *Theodore Rex* (New York: Knopf, 2001); Philip Jessup, *Elihu Root*, vols. 1 and 2 (New York: Dodd, Mead, 1938); Lewis L. Gould, *The Presidency of Theodore Roosevelt* (Lawrence: University Press of Kansas, 1991); Lewis L. Gould, *The Presidency of William McKinley* (Lawrence: Regents Press of Kansas, 1980); Donald F. Anderson, *William Howard Taft: A Conservative's Conception of the Presidency* (Ithaca, N.Y.: Cornell University Press, 1968); Warren Zimmermann, *First Great Triumph: How Five Americans Made Their Country a Great Power* (New York: Farrar, Straus and Giroux, 2002); Dexter Perkins, *The Monroe Doctrine, 1867–1907* (Baltimore: Johns Hopkins University Press, 1937); Fareed Zakaria, *From Wealth to Power* (Princeton, N.J.: Princeton University Press, 1998); Ralph Eldin Minger, *William Howard Taft and United States Foreign Policy: The Apprenticeship Years 1900–1908* (Urbana: University of Illinois Press, 1975); Henry Aaron Yeomans, *Abbott Lawrence Lowell 1856–1943* (Cambridge, Mass.: Harvard University Press, 1948); David F. Trask, *The War with Spain in 1898* (New York: Macmillan, 1981); and John L. Offner, *An Unwanted War: The Diplomacy of the United States and Spain over Cuba, 1895–1898* (Chapel Hill: University of North Carolina Press, 1992).

Legal scholarship covering the turn of the nineteenth century and early twentieth century is inconsistent. The best overall account, especially for its context and depth of analysis, is Owen M. Fiss, *Troubled Beginnings of the Modern State, 1888–1910*, vol. 8 of *History of the Supreme Court of the United States* (New York: Macmillan, 1993). Also useful for their overviews on the Supreme Court in the early twentieth century were John E. Semonche, *Charting the Future: The Supreme Court Responds to a Changing Society, 1890–1920* (Westport, Conn.: Greenwood Press, 1978); Melvin Urofsky, *A March of Liberty: A Constitutional History of the United States* (New York: Knopf, 1988); David P. Currie, *The Constitution in the Supreme Court: The Second Century, 1888–1986* (Chicago: University of Chicago Press, 1990); William F. Swindler, *Court and Constitution in the Twentieth Century: The Old Legality, 1889–1932* (Indianapolis: Bobbs-Merrill, 1969); George Sutherland, *Constitutional Power and World Affairs* (New York: Columbia University Press, 1919); and Charles Warren, *The Supreme Court in United States History* (Boston: Little, Brown, 1923). Mark A. Graber also briefly discusses *Downes v. Bidwell* in the context of *Transforming Free Speech* (Berkeley: University of California Press, 1991).

Recent legal scholarship has begun to revisit these broader issues. An extensive overview of the U.S. government's "inherent powers" may be found in

Sarah H. Cleveland, "Powers Inherent in Sovereignty: Indians, Aliens, Territories, and the Nineteenth Century Origins of Plenary Power over Foreign Affairs," *Texas Law Review* 81 (2002): 1–284. More specifically, see Christina D. Burnett, "Island in Limbo: The Case for Puerto Rico Decolonization," *Orbis* 45 (2001): 433–454; Christina D. Burnett, "The Constitution and Deconstitution of the United States," in Sanford Levinson and Bartholomew H. Sparrow, eds., *The Louisiana Purchase and American Expansion, 1803–1898* (Boulder, Colo.: Rowman and Littlefield, 2005); Carlos R. Soltero, "The Supreme Court Should Overrule the Territorial Incorporation Doctrine and End One Hundred Years of Judicially Condoned Colonialism," *Chicano-Latino Law Review* 22 (Spring 2001): 1–36; and Christine A. Klein, "Treaties of Conquest: Property Rights, Indian Treaties, and the Treaty of Guadalupe Hidalgo," *New Mexico Law Review* 26 (1996): 201–255.

For general treatments of the Constitution that put the Court's decisions in a larger political context, two works offered helpful, broad interpretations of the Constitution in American history: Keith E. Whittington, *Constitutional Construction: Divided Powers and Constitutional Meaning* (Cambridge, Mass.: Harvard University Press, 1999); and Bruce Ackerman, *We the People*, 2 vols. (Cambridge, Mass.: Belknap Press of Harvard University Press, 1991). Neither account directly addresses the relationship between the Constitution and U.S. expansion or empire. But for work that does address the juxtaposition between the Constitution and U.S. geographic expansion, see Gary Lawson and Guy Seidman, *The Constitution of Empire: Territorial Expansion and American Legal History* (New Haven, Conn.: Yale University Press, 2004). For a valuable discussion of constitutional doctrine in the late nineteenth and early twentieth centuries, see William M. Wiecek, *The Lost World of Classical Legal Thought: Law and Ideology in America, 1886–1937* (New York: Oxford University Press, 1998).

On economics, trade, and tariffs with respect to the new territories, see Clarence R. Edwards, "Our Trade with Cuba and the Philippines," *Annals of the American Academy of Political and Social Science* 19 (May 1902): 370–376; O. P. Austin, "Our Trade with Hawaii and Porto Rico," *Annals of the American Academy of Political and Social Science* 19 (May 1902): 377–382; César Ayala, "Finance Capital vs. Managerial Control in a Colonial Sphere: United States Agribusiness Corporations in Puerto Rico, 1898–1934," *Research in Political Economy* 14 (1994): 195–219; Ida Tarbell, *The Tariff in Our Times* (New York: Macmillan, 1911 [1906]); Frank William Taussig, *The Tariff History of the United States*, 8th ed. (New York: Putnam's, 1931 [1892]); part 2, especially, of Frank William Taussig, *Some Aspects of the Tariff Question* (Cambridge, Mass.: Harvard University Press, 1915); Jack Simpson Mullins, "The Sugar Trust: Henry O. Havemeyer and the American Sugar Refining Company" (Ph.D. diss., University of South Carolina, 1964); and Peter Trubowitz,

Defining the National Interest: Conflict and Change in American Foreign Policy (Chicago: University of Chicago Press, 1998).

Works that look critically at the history of American empire include R. W. Van Alstyne, *The Rising American Empire* (New York: Oxford University Press, 1960); William J. Pomeroy, *American Neo-colonialism: Its Emergence in the Philippines and Asia* (New York: International Publishers, 1970); Luzviminda Bartolome Francisco and Jonathan Shepard Fast, *Conspiracy for Empire: Big Business, Corruption and the Politics of Imperialism in America, 1876–1907* (Quezon City: Foundation for Nationalist Studies, 1985), which provides evidence of the Havemeyers' manipulation of stock prices for the benefit of individual members of the U.S. House of Representatives and U.S. Senate; David Healy, *U.S. Expansionism: The Imperialist Urge in the 1890s* (Madison: University of Wisconsin Press, 1970), which is particularly thorough; Reginald Horsman, *Race and Manifest Destiny: The Origins of American Racial Anglo-Saxonism* (Cambridge, Mass.: Harvard University Press, 1981), which documents the racism evident in public politics in the United States; Amy Kaplan and Donald E. Pease, eds., *Cultures of United States Imperialism* (Durham, N.C.: Duke University Press, 1993), which contains a handful of chapters that bear indirectly on the *Insular Cases;* and Walter LaFeber, *The New Empire: An Interpretation of American Expansion, 1860–1898* (Ithaca, N.Y.: Cornell University Press, 1967).

Richard J. Watson Jr., in *The Development of National Power: The United States, 1900–1919* (Boston: Houghton Mifflin, 1976), has an approving view of empire, as does Elihu Root, *The Military and Colonial Policy of the United States: Addresses and Reports*, ed. Robert Bacon and James Brown Scott (Cambridge, Mass.: Harvard University Press, 1916).

For accounts of anti-imperialism, see E. Berkeley Tompkins, *Anti-imperialism in the United States: The Great Debate, 1890–1920* (Philadelphia: University of Pennsylvania Press, 1970); Robert L. Beisner, *Twelve against Empire: The Anti-imperialists, 1898–1900* (New York: McGraw-Hill, 1968), which offers short portraits of some of the diverse set of men opposed to imperialism; Daniel B. Schirmer, *Republic or Empire: American Resistance to the Philippine War* (Cambridge, Mass.: Schenkman, 1972), which is provocative but occasionally mistaken; the collection of speeches and essays in R. F. Pettigrew, *The Course of Empire: An Official Record* (New York: Boni and Liveright, 1921), which is particularly good on detailing the economics of the trusts; and the collection of speeches and articles attacking imperialism in *Republic or Empire: The Philippine Question*, ed. William J. Bryan (Chicago: Independence, 1899).

Scholarship that debates the imperialism of free trade includes John Gallagher and Ronald Robinson, "The Imperialism of Free Trade," *Economic History Review* 6 (1953): 1–15; Oliver McDonagh, "The Anti-imperialism of Free Trade," *Economic History Review* 14 (1962): 489–501; D. C. M. Platt, "The

Imperialism of Free Trade: Some Reservations," *Economic History Review* 21 (1968): 296–306; and P. F. Clarke, "Hobson, Free Trade, and Imperialism," *Economic History Review* 34 (1981): 308–312. For work that embeds imperialism and anti-imperialism in discussions of citizenship and identity, see Gerald L. Neuman, *Strangers to the Constitution* (Princeton, N.J.: Princeton University Press, 1996), and "Whose Constitution?" *Yale Law Journal* 100 (1991): 909–991; Rogers M. Smith, *Civic Ideals* (New Haven, Conn.: Yale University Press, 1997); and T. Alexander Aleinikoff, *Semblances of Sovereignty* (Cambridge, Mass.: Harvard University Press, 2002).

For contemporary work on empire, see Chalmers Johnson, *The Sorrows of Empire* (New York: Metropolitan Books, 2004); Andrew J. Bacevitch, *American Empire: The Realities and Consequences of U.S. Diplomacy* (Cambridge, Mass.: Harvard University Press, 2002); Philip Bobbitt, *The Shield of Achilles: War, Peace, and the Course of History* (New York: Knopf, 2002); Niall Ferguson, *Colossus* (New York: Penguin Press, 2004); Neil Smith, *American Empire: Roosevelt's Geographer and the Prelude to Globalization* (Berkeley: University of California Press, 2003), which discusses the "loss of geographic sensibility" coincident with the rise of globalism and the role of geography in the rise of American power; Michael Hardt and Antonio Negri, *Empire* (Cambridge, Mass.: Harvard University Press, 2000); Michael Mann, *Incoherent Empire* (New York: Verso, 2003); and numerous articles in contemporary journals and periodicals. Also see William H. Riker, *Federalism: Origin, Operation, Significance* (Boston: Little, Brown, 1964), which touches on the relationship of federalism to empire.

In order to understand the role of the west in the founders' minds, I consulted Max Farrand, ed., *The Records of the Federal Convention of 1787*, Rev. ed. 4 vols. New Haven: Yale University Press, 1937. For a comprehensive overview of U.S. expansion I relied upon D.W. Meinig's wonderful three volumes: *The Shaping of America: A Geographical Perspective on 500 years of History: Vol. 1, Atlantic America, 1492–1800* (New Haven: Yale University Press 1986); *Vol. 2, Continental America, 1800–1867* (New Haven: Yale University Press, 1993); *Vol. 3, Transcontinental America, 1850–1915* (New Haven: Yale University Press, 1998)."

For accounts of eighteenth- and nineteenth-century American expansion, in particular, see Peter S. Onuf, *Statehood and Union: A History of the Northwest Ordinance* (Bloomington: Indiana University Press, 1987); Peter S. Onuf, *Jefferson's Empire: The Language of American Nationhood* (Charlottesville: University Press of Virginia, 2000); Earl S. Pomeroy, *The Territories and the United States, 1861–1890* (Seattle: University of Washington Press, 1969 [1947]); Jack Erickson Eblen, *The First and Second United States Empires: Governors and Territorial Government, 1784–1912* (Pittsburgh: University of Pittsburgh Press, 1968); Albert K. Weinberg, *Manifest Destiny: A Study of Nationalist Expansion-*

ism in American History (Chicago: Quadrangle Books, 1963 [1935]); Thomas R. Hietala, *Manifest Design: Anxious Aggrandizement in Late Jacksonian America* (Ithaca, N.Y.: Cornell University Press, 1985), which is particularly strong; Alexander DeConde, *This Affair of Louisiana* (New York: Scribner's, 1976), which remains as one of the best discussions of the Louisiana Purchase; and Jon Kukla, *A Wilderness So Immense: The Louisiana Territory and the Destiny of America* (New York: Knopf, 2003). Also see Edmund Steele Joy, *The Right of the Territories to Become States of the Union* (Newark, N.J.: Advertiser Printing House, 1892), which argues for the plenary powers of Congress over the territories and denies that they had any automatic entitlement to statehood. Also see John W. Smurr, "Territorial Constitutions" (Ph.D. diss., University of Indiana, 1960); Arthur Bestor, "Constitutionalism and the Settlement of the West: The Attainment of Consensus, 1754–1784," in John Porter Bloom, ed., *The American Territorial System* (Athens: Ohio University Press, 1973), 13–44; Robert F. Berkhofer Jr., "The Northwest Ordinance and the Principle of Territorial Evolution," in Bloom, *The American Territorial System*; James Bryce, *The American Commonwealth*, 2 vols. (London: Macmillan, 1891); and Grupo de Investigadores Puertorriquenos, *Breakthrough from Colonialism*, 2 vols. (Rio Piedras: Editorial de la Universidad de Puerto Rico, 1986), which contains a very useful overview of the political development of the different nonoriginal states within the United States and their applicability to the situation in Puerto Rico. For a recent account of American empire that puts the *Insular Cases* in the context of preceding U.S. expansion, see James G. Wilson, *The Imperial Republic* (Aldershot, England: Ashgate, 2002).

INDEX

Ackerman, Bruce, 252, 254
Act of July 1, 1902 (Philippines),
133, 152, 153, 160, 186, 191,
193, 194, 195, 201; cruel and
unusual punishment and, 207;
double jeopardy and, 175; Fifth
Amendment and, 167; Foraker
Act and, 150; Philippine Bill of
Rights and, 38; Taft and, 154;
violation of, 190
Adams, Brooks, 31, 65, 181
Adams, Charles Francis, Jr., 180
Adams, Charles Frederick, 112
Adams, Elmer, 48
Adams, Henry, 181
Adams, John, 23, 65, 181, 218
Adams, John Quincy, 65, 181; on
Cuba, 70; on Louisiana
Purchase, 23
Adams-Onis Treaty (1819), 23, 25
Admiralty law, 88, 112
African Americans, freedoms for,
249; Supreme Court and, 224
Aguinaldo, Emilio, 36, 37
Alaska, 106, 200, 202, 237, 257;
administration of, 219, 220,
221, 232; admission of, 216;
boundary dispute of, 260;
incorporation of, 187, 208;
Second Organic Act of, 262;
securing, 2; tariff laws and, 114
Aldrich, Nelson, 73, 242
Aleinikoff, Alexander, 228
Allen, Charles, 100, 105
Allgeyer v. Louisiana (1897), 138, 139,
183, 184
Allison, William, 73
American Academy of Political and
Social Science, 107
American Bar Association, 198
American Beet Company, 245

American Indians, 63, 227;
citizenship and, 42;
land/property and, 21;
Northwest Ordinance and, 20;
regulating trade of, 20;
sovereignty and, 227; status of,
248, 249; and territorial
residents compared, 227
American Insurance Company v. Canter
(1828), 18, 41, 44, 46, 91, 186
American Law Review, 144
American Samoa, 7, 12, 165;
administration of, 221, 231;
annexation of, 38, 216, 259;
citizenship in, 225, 227;
customs and, 226; immigration
law and, 225; income tax and,
226; matai system of, 226;
military bases in, 232; Olympics
and, 213; paradoxes of, 214;
representation in, 226;
sovereignty over, 215; subsidies
for, 220
American Sugar Refining Company,
32, 72; *De Lima* and, 105;
influence of, 73, 74, 76;
prosecution of, 74; Sugar Trust
and, 75
Ames, Fisher: on Louisiana/self-
government, 21
Arizona, 101, 106; admission of, 3,
26, 27, 216, 262
Armstrong, Carlos, 118, 123, 183
Armstrong v. United States (1901), 56,
140, 143, 207, 259; government
argument in, 84; lead opinion
in, 117–18; precedent of, 122,
159, 183; tariffs and, 111–12,
120–21, 139; uniformity clause
and, 207
Arthur, Chester, 93

135, 186; *Dooley I* and, 119, 135; *Dooley II* and, 127, 128; *Dorr* and, 177, 180; *Downes* and, 11, 96, 99, 105–6, 107, 186, 188, 249; extension theory and, 5, 185, 186, 251; Foraker Act and, 92; *Fourteen Diamond Rings* and, 126; on *Goetze,* 117; Harlan and, 97; *Huus* and, 121; incorporation and, 185; *Insular Cases* and, 110, 112; *Kepner* and, 176; latter class of rights and, 89; *Mankichi* and, 170, 171, 172, 182, 185–86, 188; *Mendezona* and, 176; on military, 120; on *National Bank,* 114; on Puerto Rico, 115, 120; territories and, 88, 89, 91, 92, 93, 114, 189; *Trono* and, 185, 190

Brown v. Board of Education of Topeka, Kansas (1954), 57

Bryan, William Jennings, 29; *Downes* and, 101; expansion and, 2; on imperialism, 109; silver and, 108

Buchanan, James, 25, 70

Buffalo Evening News and Telegraph, 100, 179

Burch, Henry R.: on Puerto Ricans, 61

Bureau of Insular Affairs (State Department), 231

Burger Court, *Torres* and, 222

Burgess, John W., 59–60, 107

Burnett, Christina Duffy, 148, 217, 257

Butler, Charles Henry: on White, 189–90

Butt, Archie, 157

Cabranes, José, 8, 228

Calhoun, John C., 83, 179

California: admission of, 3, 26, 38; cession of, 49; representatives from, 27; tariff laws and, 114

Callan v. Wilson, 135, 200

Capo-Rodriguez, Pedro, 257

Cardozo, Benjamin, 198

Carlisle, John G., 118, 119, 122, 129, 141; *Dooley II* and, 128; on imperialism, 143; *Stountenburgh* and, 183

Carlyle, Thomas, 59

Carnegie, Andrew, 29

Carr, Raymond, 220

Castine, Maine, 113–14, 151

Castro, Fidel, 246

Catholic Church of Porto Rico, 162–63

Chamorros, 212, 219, 225, 227

Chaney, John C., 118

Cherokee Nation v. Georgia (1831), 224

Cherokee Tobacco Case (1870), 224

Chicago, Burlington & Quincy Railroad v. Chicago (1897), 211

Chicago Record-Herald, 132; on Brown, 86; on *Downes,* 100–101; on empire, 219; on Harlan, 97

Chinese Exclusion Case (*Chae Chan Ping v. United States*) (1889), 223–24

Choate, Joseph H., 158

Citizenship, 1, 35, 62, 63, 106, 141, 160–61, 213; acquiring, 45; American Indians and, 42; democracy and, 61; First Amendment and, 221–22; meaning/criteria of, 9; nature of, 254; second–class, 225, 227; single/dual/triple, 227; territories and, 214, 224; women's, 224

Civil courts, 134, 194

Civil liberties, 10, 19, 197

Civil rights, 40, 210, 224

Civil Rights Cases (1883), 224

Civil War, 26, 43, 88, 90, 94

Clark Air Field, 214, 232

Clarke, John H., 197, 198, 262

Clay, Henry, 26, 96, 218
Cleveland, Grover, 29, 74, 118;
    expansion and, 59; Fuller and,
    94; Peckham and, 138; Pullman
    strike and, 138, 184; tariffs and,
    71; White and, 90, 91
Cleveland, Sarah, 253
Cold war, territories and, 216, 234
Colonialism, 69, 78, 220, 231, 241
Commerce, 143, 207; interstate, 138,
    184; regulating, 128, 129, 182;
    territories and, 129
Commerce clause, 41, 48, 128
Compromise of 1850, 26
Compromise of 1877, 96
Comstock, Albert, 117
Comstock and Brown, 117
Conant, Charles C., 64
Constitution, written/unwritten,
    252, 253, 254
Constitutional Convention,
    Northwest Ordinance and, 16
Constitutional law, 9, 10, 218, 249,
    254
Contract, freedom of, 19, 46, 138,
    139, 184
Cooley, Thomas, 41, 181
Coudert, Frederic, 55, 82, 84, 138;
    De Lima and, 112; Downes &
    Co. and, 80; on Downes, 99; on
    ex proprio vigore, 251; González
    and, 161; on Incorporation
    Doctrine, 98–99; Mankichi and,
    169, 174; Shively and, 81;
    uniformity clause and, 81
Coudert Brothers (law firm), 55, 58,
    77, 140, 153, 154, 169–70;
    clients of, 76; De Lima and, 112;
    Downes & Co. and, 80; Jones
    and, 162; suit by, 151
Court of the First Instance
    (Philippines), 191
Courts martial, 134, 192, 194, 221
Criminal defendants, due process for,
    168, 169, 205

Crossman, George W., 117
Crossman v. United States (1901), 56,
    86, 111, 116, 189, 208, 236, 259;
    government argument in, 238;
    lead opinion in, 117; precedent
    of, 159, 183; tariffs and, 139;
    uniformity clause and, 207
Cross v. Harrison (1853), 48–49, 114,
    116, 120
Cruel and unusual punishment, 193,
    207, 209, 210, 211
Crumpacker, Edgar D., 154
Cuba, 4, 143, 206; administration of,
    235; annexation of, 32, 33, 64,
    69, 70, 75, 78, 101, 217, 244,
    245; blockade on, 34; economy
    of, 246; independence of, 70,
    135, 216, 241, 243; informal
    empire and, 240, 246–47;
    Insular Cases and, 12, 14;
    intervention in, 230, 236;
    nonannexation of, 259;
    occupation of, 34, 61, 124, 134,
    217, 236, 238—39, 243;
    population of, 29–30, 31; as
    protectorate, 243–44; Spanish-
    American War and, 31, 70, 276;
    trade with, 76, 245, 246
Cuba Libre, 32, 33
Cuban independence movement,
    31–32, 33, 34, 36
Cuban Reciprocity Treaty (1903),
    260
Cuban Revolution (1959), 241, 247
Curie, Charles, 117
Currie, David, 257
Curtis, Edmond W., 121
Curtis, F. Kingsbury, 121
Curtis, Justice: Dred Scott and, 50,
    182
Curtis Mallet (law firm), 58, 118,
    121, 143

Daily Graphic, on Downes, 104
Daniel, John W., 63

Davis, Justice, 96

Day, William R., 147, 152, 260; appointment of, 158; *Dorr* and, 176, 177, 179, 180–86, 189; *Dowdell* and, 195; *Gavieres* and, 193–94; Incorporation Doctrine and, 189; jury trial and, 178; *Kepner* and, 175; *Mankichi* and, 170, 171, 172, 173, 185–86; *Mendezona* and, 176; on territorial government, 186; *Trono* and, 185, 190

Death penalty, 213

Debs, Eugene V., 138, 184

Declaration of Independence (1776), 12, 43, 54, 174

De Lima, Elias, 55, 99

De Lima & Co., 55, 76, 77, 113, 115; attorneys for, 112

De Lima v. Bidwell (1901), 55, 86, 105, 110, 111; defendant arguments in, 84–85, 112–13; lead opinion in, 113–15, 139; precedent of, 118, 122–26, 140, 159, 177, 183, 186, 189, 208, 209; public response to, 105, 151–52; uniformity clause and, 207

De Lôme, Enrique Dupuy, 32

Democracy: citizenship and, 61; empire and, 255

Democratic Party, 218; Philippines and, 240; tariffs and, 70

Denver Post, on *Downes*, 100, 103

Department of Colonial Affairs, 231

Dependencies, classes of, 239–40

Depression of 1893, 65, 75, 109

Deseret, 26

Detainees, protections for, 248

Dewey, George, 34, 36, 67

Dewey, John, 144

Dingley Tariff (1897), 35, 71, 80, 111, 113, 117, 125, 149, 150–51, 260

District of Columbia, 15, 42, 46–47, 101, 106, 178, 188, 200, 202;

constitutionally unique arrangements for, 248; death penalty and, 213; Electoral College and, 224; territorial government for, 224

Division of Insular Affairs (War Department), 220, 231; Report of, 82, 83

Divorce law, 223

Dole, Edward P., 39

Dollar diplomacy, 234

Dominican Republic: intervention in, 230, 234; as protectorate, 260

Dooley, Martin, 75, 108, 110

Dooley, Smith, & Co., 118, 120, 122, 126, 127, 183; reimbursement for, 117

Dooley v. United States I (1901), 56, 127, 135, 139, 140, 149, 152, 189, 208, 259; government argument in, 84, 117–18; lead opinion in, 119; precedent of, 111, 120, 122, 126, 136, 151, 153, 159; public response to, 143; uniformity clause and, 207

Dooley v. United States II (1901), 56, 123, 130, 136, 149, 183, 207, 210, 260; government argument in, 84; lead opinion in, 126–28; precedent of, 142, 147, 155; public response to, 131, 132, 143; territories/trade and, 140; uniformity clause and, 140, 205

Dorr, Fred L., 196; jury trial and, 176–77, 186

Dorr v. United States (1904), 12, 175, 188, 209, 221, 260; commerce/criminal justice and, 181; jury trial and, 176–78, 179; lead opinion in, 185, 186; precedent of, 160, 187, 195, 196, 200–201, 202, 205, 222; property rights and, 183; public response to, 179, 180; ruling in, 149

Double jeopardy, 12, 175, 180, 185, 186, 190–94, 211; protection from, 169, 206, 207, 209; unincorporated territories and, 176
Douglas, Stephen, 26
Dowdell, Louis, 194–95
Dowdell v. United States (1911), 197, 199, 200, 206, 262; precedent of, 160, 196, 205; Sixth Amendment and, 194–95
Downes & Co., 55, 76, 77, 90, 92, 99
Downes v. Bidwell (1901), 7, 55, 57, 98, 126, 135, 136, 142–43, 183, 195, 259; controversy of, 11; Foraker Act and, 78, 207; government argument in, 82, 83, 84, 118; importance of, 80, 103, 110, 111, 115, 116, 215, 229, 248, 249; incorporated/ unincorporated territories and, 5; precedent of, 177, 178, 184, 186, 187, 188, 189–90, 200, 202, 222; public response to, 99–102, 103, 104, 106–8, 121, 125, 141, 143, 219, 239; ruling in, 86, 87, 120, 137, 139–41, 170, 252; uniformity clause and, 205
Dred Scott v. Sandford (1857), 5, 47, 50, 84, 88, 102, 107, 108, 110, 179, 182, 186, 200, 249
Due process, 19, 89, 147, 169, 182, 183–84, 196, 203, 211, 222, 257; criminal, 194; denial of, 159, 195; protection of, 209; substantive, 139
Dunne, Finley Peter, 57, 79, 108

Economic liberty, 58, 129, 183
Edmunds Act (1882), 28
Edmunds-Tucker Act (1887), 28
Eighth Amendment, 134, 193, 257; cruel and unusual punishment and, 192, 207, 210, 211

Eighth Circuit Court of Appeals, 137, 157
Electoral College, 1, 224
Eleventh Amendment, 165, 166; sovereign immunity and, 167
Emancipation Proclamation (1863), 96
Empire, 1, 69, 89, 90, 168, 250, 254; administration of, 220; American, 23, 253; democracy and, 255; Federal, 253; federalism and, 3; informal, 218, 231, 232, 234, 236, 240, 246–48; *Insular Cases* and, 8–9, 215, 217, 219, 220, 228, 229; judicial decision making and, 224–25
Endleman v. United States (1898), 40
Equal protection clause, 89, 222
Establishment clause, 207–8
Ethnocentrism, 9, 76, 250
Everett, Edward, 218
Excessive bail, 192, 211
Expansion, 1–2, 7, 16, 19, 29, 40, 69, 110, 143, 205, 218, 230, 252, 253, 254; constitutional questions and, 3; end of, 216; geographic, 10, 25; history of, 114; imperialism and, 101; *Insular Cases* and, 8
Ex Parte Morgan (1883), 164–65
Export clause, 48, 127, 128, 140, 205
Ex proprio vigore, 181, 197, 210, 251
Extension theory, 186, 251

Farrand, Max, 15, 43
Federal Bankruptcy Act, 201
Federal Death Penalty Act (1994), 212, 213
Federal Employer's Liability Act, 201
Federalism, empire and, 3
Federalists, 21, 22
Federal Safety Appliance Act, 201
Fernald, James: on territories, 53–54

Fuller, Melville Weston, *continued*
and, 11, 110, 223; economic
liberty and, 129, 184; *Ex Parte
Morgan* and, 164; *Fourteen
Diamond Rings* and, 112, 125,
136; *Gonzalez* and, 161; Harlan
and, 124, 180; Holmes and,
145, 180; Incorporation
Doctrine and, 6; *In re Lane* and,
164–65; *Kepner* and, 175;
Lincoln and, 152; *Lottery Case*
and, 129; *Mankichi* and, 171;
Mendezona and, 176; *Neely* and,
136; on Newlands Resolution,
171; *Ponce* and, 162; "separate
but equal" doctrine and, 57;
Shively and, 81; *Sugar Trust Case*
and, 74; on taxation, 128; *Trono*
and, 191; uniformity clause and,
81, 95; *Warner, Barnes* and, 152
Fuller, Paul, 8, 169
Fuller Court, 6, 58, 210

Gadsden Purchase (1853), 18, 19
Gardiner, Charles A., 41, 43, 45,
237; on expansion, 44; on
sovereign power, 42; on tariffs,
44; on treaty-making, 46
Gavieres, Vincent, 193, 196
Gavieres v. United States (1911), 195,
207, 257, 261; lead opinion in,
193–94
General Agreement on Trade and
Tariffs, 233
Gerry, Elbridge, 17
Gideon v. Wainwright (1963), 211
Goetze v. United States (1901), 56, 111,
122, 133, 139, 189, 208, 259;
amicus brief in, 81, 83; Foraker
Act and, 76; government
argument in, 142; import duties
and, 117; lead opinion in, 86,
116; precedent of, 159, 183;
uniformity clause and, 207
Gómez, Máximo, 33

González, Isabel, 161
Gonzalez v. Williams (1904), 165,
181, 260; citizenship and,
160–61; Foraker Act and, 161;
public response to, 161
Grafton, Homer, 191, 195–96, 206;
double jeopardy and, 192, 194
Grafton v. United States (1907), 194,
195–96, 261; anomaly of, 206;
double jeopardy and, 191–92,
207, 209; ruling in, 208
Grand jury, 200; indictment by, 169,
172, 173, 176, 186, 205, 222
Grant, Ulysses S., 96
Granville-Smith v. Granville-Smith
(1955), 223
Gray, Horace, 11, 87, 122, 125, 152,
260; career of, 93–94; *De Lima*
and, 115, 116; *Dooley I* and, 119;
Dooley II and, 127; *Dorr* and,
180; *Downes* and, 11, 148, 187;
Fourteen Diamond Rings and,
126; Holmes and, 144, 145;
Shively and, 81
Griggs, John, 62, 86, 101, 117, 123,
142, 143; on *Downes*, 102;
Goetze and, 83–84; *Insular Cases*
and, 110
Grosvenor, Charles, 86, 130
Guam, 4, 7, 64, 165, 213–14, 219,
223; administration of, 221,
231; annexation of, 69;
citizenship in, 225, 227;
customs and, 226; immigration
law and, 225; income tax and,
226; *Insular Cases* and, 12;
military bases in, 232; seizing,
67, 68; sovereignty over, 215;
subsidies for, 220
Guantánamo Bay, 67, 154, 243, 248

Habeas corpus, 19, 46, 163, 184, 248
Haiti, intervention in, 234
*Hamdi et al. v. Rumsfeld, Secretary of
Defense* (2004), 248

Hanna, Mark, 72
Harding, Warren G., 197, 205, 258
Harlan, John Marshall, 87, 94, 106,
116, 122, 148, 149, 152, 156,
186, 189, 194, 209, 254; Black
and, 211; Brown and, 97; career
of, 96–97; death of, 5, 155, 262;
De Lima and, 115; doctrine of,
142; *Dooley I* and, 119; *Dooley II*
and, 125, 128, 183; *Dorr* and,
178, 179, 180, 185; *Dowdell* and,
195; *Downes* and, 11, 80, 95–
96, 107–8, 110, 135; First
Amendment and, 210; *Fourteen
Diamond Rings* and, 125;
Fourteenth Amendment and,
210; Fuller and, 124, 180;
Grafton and, 192; *Heinszen*
and, 155; on Holmes, 173;
imperial power and, 97–98;
Incorporation Doctrine and,
6; *Insular Cases* and, 79, 136;
Kepner and, 175; *Mankichi* and,
171–72; *Maxwell* and, 210;
Mendezona and, 176; *Neely* and,
112, 135–36; *O'Neil* and,
209–10; *Rassmussen* and, 188;
strict constructionism of, 136;
Taft and, 78; on territorial
claims, 98; *Trono* and, 185
Harrison, Benjamin, 29, 65, 74, 108;
Blaine and, 67; Brewer and,
137; Brown and, 88; expansion
and, 59; McKenna and, 115;
Shiras and, 137
Hart, Alphonso, 118
Havemeyer, Henry O., 32, 76, 245;
on *De Lima*, 105. *See also*
American Sugar Refining
Company; Sugar Trust
Hawai'i, 66, 67, 133, 143, 165, 166;
administration of, 221, 232;
admission of, 3, 216; annexation
of, 4, 10, 38, 39, 52, 68, 90, 117,
169–70, 174, 175, 254, 259;

intervention in, 234; sugar and,
72, 91; treaty with, 39
Hawaiian Constitution, 39
Hawaiian Supreme Court, 169, 170
Hawaii v. Mankichi (1903), 12, 186,
195, 197, 199, 206, 208, 222,
260; criminal due process and,
169; double jeopardy and, 176;
extension theory and, 189;
importance of, 204–5;
precedent of, 160, 178, 184,
187, 188, 196, 200, 201; public
response to, 172, 173—75;
ruling in, 170, 182, 209, 221
Hay, John, 67, 143, 231, 234
Hay-Bunau-Varilla Treaty (1903),
260
Hayes, Rutherford B., 96
Healy, David, 245
Hearst, William Randolph, 156–57
Henderson, David B., 244
Henkel, William, 133
Highsaw, Robert, 157–58, 251
Hill, David, 138
Hoar, George F., 29, 93, 108, 254
Hobson, John A., 65
Holden v. Hardy (1898), 139
Hollander, John, 100
Holmes, Oliver Wendell, 144, 260
Holmes, Oliver Wendell, Jr., 145,
151, 152, 206; *Balzac* and, 204;
Dorr and, 177, 180; double
jeopardy and, 180; Fuller and,
180; Harlan on, 173;
Incorporation Doctrine and,
189; independence of, 144, 173;
Kepner and, 175; *Mankichi* and,
170, 172, 173; *Mendezona* and,
176; territories and, 147; *Trono*
and, 190; *Weems* and, 193
Honduras, intervention in, 234
Hornblower, William, 91, 138
Horsman, Reginald, 58, 59, 218
House Committee on Insular Affairs,
149, 154, 240, 244

Mahan, Alfred Thayer, 1, 4, 66; on
     Cuba, 67; expansionists and, 69;
     on imperialism, 219; U.S. Navy
     and, 65
Malloy v. Hogan (1964), 211
Manifest Destiny, 23
Manila Charter, 196
Manila Freedom, 176
Mapp v. Ohio (1961), 211
Marianas Islands, 67, 68, 143; *See also*
     Northern Marianas
Marshall, John, 84, 103, 112;
     American empire and, 89;
     American Insurance and, 18, 91,
     44; *Loughborough* and, 19, 46,
     49, 94, 148; *Martin* and, 97;
     McCulloch and, 97; territories
     and, 81, 239
Marshall Islands, 216
Martí, José, 31
Martin v. Hunter's Lessee (1816), 97
Mason, George, 17, 18
Mason, William E., 86
Maxwell v. Dow (1900), 210
McCloskey, Robert, 9
McCulloch v. Maryland (1819), 97
McKenna, Joseph, 87, 90, 122, 125,
     153, 156, 186, 191, 197; Brown
     and, 185; career of, 115; *De
     Lima* and, 86, 115–16; *Dooley I*
     and, 119; *Dooley II* and, 127;
     Dorr and, 177, 180; on empire,
     116; *Fourteen Diamond Rings*
     and, 126; *Insular Cases* and, 110;
     Kepner and, 175; *Mankichi* and,
     170, 173; *Mendezona* and, 176;
     Neely and, 11; on occupation/
     cession, 116; on tariff law, 116;
     Trono and, 185; *Weems* and,
     192–93
McKinley, William, 4, 10, 29, 55,
     60–61, 64, 101, 119, 126, 139,
     142, 147, 234; assassination of,
     74, 260; Cuba and, 32, 33, 34,
     134, 135, 217, 241–42; *Downes*

and, 103, 104; expansion and,
     25, 69, 143; on Filipinos, 62–63;
     Foraker Act and, 35–36, 109;
     Guam and, 68; Harlan and, 97;
     Havemeyers and, 73; Holmes
     and, 145; imperialism and, 78;
     Insular Cases and, 6; McKenna
     and, 115; Panama Canal and,
     66, 67; reelection of, 252, 259;
     Spanish-American War and, 68;
     Sugar Trust and, 74–75; tariffs
     and, 71, 72, 75, 259; Wood and,
     242
McKinley Act (1890), 39
McKinley Tariff, 31, 71, 73, 91
McLain, Emlin: on *Mankichi*, 174
McLean, Justice: *Dred Scott* and, 50
McReynolds, James C., 197, 198,
     262
Mendezona, Secondino, 176
*Mendezona y Mendezona v. United
     States* (1904), 179, 181, 186,
     189, 260; double jeopardy and,
     176, 185, 206, 207, 209; ruling
     in, 194, 208
Mexican Cession (1848), 2, 19, 20,
     24, 40
Mexican Revolution (1913–1916), 234
Mexicans, political incorporation of,
     25
Mexican War (1846), 18, 20, 24, 43,
     114
Military bases, establishment of, 232,
     233
Miller, Samuel, 88, 127, 128
Miller, William, 74
Minimum wage laws, 213, 225
Missouri Compromise, 26, 110
Mitchell, Frank, 237
Monge, José Trías, 8
Monroe, James, 70
Monroe Doctrine (1823), Roosevelt
     Corollary of, 234, 247
Moody, William H., 153, 156; career
     of, 154; on Cuba, 240–41;

Northern Marianas, 1, 7, 219, 227;
    annexation of, 216; citizenship
    in, 225; clothing manufacturers
    in, 212; as commonwealth, 216;
    constitutional protections in,
    226; customs and, 226;
    immigration law and, 225;
    Insular Cases and, 12; migrant
    workers in, 226; military bases
    in, 232; minimum wage laws
    and, 213, 225; Olympics and,
    213; paradoxes of, 214;
    representation in, 226;
    sovereignty over, 215; troop
    deaths for, 213
Northwest Ordinance (1787), 14–15,
    16, 22, 25, 26, 27; affirmation
    of, 18; civil liberties and, 19;
    impact of, 19, 20; *Insular Cases*
    and, 250; precedent of, 10, 15;
    text of, 18
Northwest Territory, 17, 27, 43;
    expansion of, 10; government
    of, 14–15; importance of, 16;
    inhabitants and settlers of, 19;
    states of, 16; trans-Appalachian
    West and, 16

O'Brien, Edwin F., 177
Ocampo, Martin, 196
Ocampo v. United States (1914), 206,
    262; precedent of, 160, 200,
    205, 222; probable cause and,
    196–97
Ochoa v. Hernandez (1913), 257, 262;
    property taking and, 159, 167,
    209; ruling in, 208
Oklahoma: admission of, 27, 216,
    261; representatives from, 27; as
    territory, 164
Olney, Richard, 32, 74
Olympics, territories and, 213
O'Neil v. Vermont (1892), 209–10
"Open Door Notes" (Hay), 234
Open-door policy, 235, 246

Oregon, 24; admission of, 3;
    annexation of, 18
Oregon Treaty (1846), 24
Organic Act of Hawai'i (1900), 259
Organic Act of Porto Rico (1917),
    166, 262
Organic acts, 165, 166, 201, 259, 262
Orleans, territory of, 22, 163
Ostend Manifesto (1854), 70
O'Sullivan, John, 23

Palma, Estrada, 33
Panama: independence of, 138, 181,
    260; intervention in, 230, 234
Panama Canal, 247; access to, 220;
    plans for, 66–67
Panama Canal Zone, 216, 260;
    administration of, 220; lease for,
    230
Patterson v. Colorado (1907), 210
Payne-Aldrich Tariff (1909), 150
Peabody & Co., 151, 154
Pearl Harbor, 39, 68
Peckham, Rufus Wheeler, 86, 87, 91,
    94, 122, 149, 152, 181, 186,
    189; *Allgeyer* and, 139, 183–84;
    annexation and, 210; career of,
    138–39; death of, 5, 155, 261;
    De Lima and, 115; *Dooley I* and,
    119; *Dooley II* and, 128, 183;
    Dorr and, 178, 180, 183, 184,
    185; *Downes* and, 95, 110;
    economic liberty and, 183, 184;
    Fourteen Diamond Rings and,
    125; *Heinszen* and, 155, 185;
    Incorporation Doctrine and, 6;
    Insular Cases and, 136; *Kepner*
    and, 175, 190, 191; *Mankichi*
    and, 171, 178; *Mendezona* and,
    176; *Neely* and, 11, 136;
    substantive due process and,
    139; *Trono* and, 185, 190
Peirce, Charles Sanders, 144
Pentagon Papers Case (1971), 247
Pepke, Emil J., 125

Brandeis and, 198; Bureau of Insular Affairs and, 231; on Constitution/flag, 101; Cuba and, 241, 242, 243; economic/political reforms and, 235; expansion and, 143; free trade and, 75; Havemeyers and, 73; *Insular Cases* and, 6; open-door policy and, 234–35; Philippines and, 124, 152; Platt Amendment and, 243; Puerto Rico and, 61–62, 82–83; Whiskey Trust and, 74

Rowe, L. S., 107

Rumsfeld, Secretary of Defense v. Padilla et al. (2004), 248

Russo-Japanese War, treaty for, 261

St. Louis Post-Dispatch, on *Downes*, 100, 141

Samoa, 66, 228. *See also* American Samoa

Sandwich Islands, 39, 106. *See also* Hawai'i

San Francisco Examiner: on *Downes*, 100; on *Fourteen Diamond Rings*, 130, 131, 132; on free trade, 131; Grosvenor in, 130

Santa Fe New Mexican, 121; on *Downes*, 100; on New Mexico/Philippines, 63

Santo Domingo, 22, 247; intervention in, 230, 234

Schilb v. Kuebel (1971), 211

Schurman, Jacob, 37, 240

Schurman Commission, 37

Schurz, Carl, 59, 111

Scott, Sir Walter, 58, 59

Searles, John E., 32

Seattle Daily Times, 100, 103, 141

Second Amendment, 222–23

Self-government, 21–22, 43, 53, 54, 60, 61, 62, 220

Self-incrimination, 205, 210, 211

Semonche, John, 257

Senate Committee on Relations with Cuba, 242

Senate Judiciary Committee, 157

"Separate but equal" doctrine, 57

Sere v. Pitot (1810), 186

Seventh Amendment, 134, 222

Seward, William, 2, 64

Sherman, Roger, 16–17

Sherman, Secretary, 147

Sherman Act, 58, 74

Shipman, Paul, 41, 47, 48

Shiras, George J., Jr., 87, 122, 125, 152; career of, 137; *De Lima* and, 115; *Dooley I* and, 119; *Dooley II* and, 127; *Fourteen Diamond Rings* and, 126; *Insular Cases* and, 136; *Neely* and, 11; resignation of, 11, 145, 260

Shively v. Bowlby (1894), 81

Sixth Amendment, 134, 147, 169, 187, 189, 194–97, 200, 203, 210; due process and, 214; Philippine Bill of Rights and, 195; right to counsel and, 211; territories and, 170

Sixth Circuit Court of Appeals, 147, 156

Slaughterhouse Cases (1873), 139, 210

Slavery, 93, 110

Slave states, admission of, 26

Smith, Rogers, 225, 227

Smith, W. Wickham, 117

Snow, Alpheus, 142; on dependencies, 239–40; on *Downes*, 252; on empire, 253

Southwest Territory, 16

Sovereignty, 1, 8, 14, 33, 95, 166, 215, 219, 220, 229, 233, 236, 241, 249; American Indians and, 227; benefits of, 246; concessions and, 230; extension of, 214; uniformity clause and, 80

Spanish-American War (1898), 4, 9,
14, 67, 147, 203, 214, 225, 250,
253, 257, 259; aftermath of,
133; constitutional controversy
and, 34; Cuba and, 31, 70, 236;
McKinley and, 68; occupation
following, 34, 38, 61, 236;
Puerto Rico and, 64; territories
after, 216; U.S. Navy and, 68
Speech, freedom of, 19, 46, 89, 210,
211
Spelman syndicate, 245
Spooner, John, 73, 242
Spooner Amendment (1901), 123,
130, 152, 153, 259
Spreckels, Claus, 76
Standard (London), on *Downes*,
104
State Department, 68; Bureau of
Insular Affairs and, 231
Statehood, 50, 51, 141, 216, 237,
240, 247; admission to, 178;
development toward, 18, 26, 53,
250, 253
Statham, E. Robert, 228
Stevenson, Eugene, 105–6, 252
Stone, Harlan Fiske: appointment of,
158
Story, Joseph, 114
Stoutenburgh v. Hennick (1889), 118,
183
Subic Bay, 154, 214, 232
Sugar, 67, 101, 105, 242, 243, 245;
production, 244, 246; tariff
rates on, 90–91
Sugar industry, 75, 150, 244, 245,
246; tariffs and, 71–72, 76
Sugar Trust, 32, 74, 76, 77, 105, 140,
245; American Sugar Refining
Company and, 75; Cuba and,
243; Havemeyers and, 73; tariffs
and, 72
Sugar Trust Case (*United States v. E.
C. Knight*) (1895), 6, 58, 74,
129, 138, 183, 184

Supreme Court of Porto Rico, 36,
161, 162, 204; *Balzac* and, 197,
201; *Muratti* and, 200; original
jurisdiction of, 163; U.S.
Supreme Court and, 200

Taft, William Howard, 123, 144,
149, 152, 153, 166, 195, 258; on
Act of July 1, 1902, 154;
appointments by, 155–56, 205;
Balzac and, 199, 200, 204, 208,
221; Brandeis and, 198; as chief
justice, 197; Cuban annexation
and, 244; Day and, 147, 158;
divestment corollary and, 240;
dollar diplomacy and, 234; *Dorr*
and, 203; *Downes* and, 80;
election of, 261; on Filipinos,
62; foreign investors and, 150;
Harlan and, 78; Hughes and,
157, 158; Incorporation
Doctrine and, 5, 202, 205;
Insular Cases and, 6, 79; on
Jones Act, 202; Lamar and, 157;
Lincoln and, 152; McReynolds
and, 198; Philippines and, 38,
146, 152, 240; Pitney and, 159;
Rassmussen and, 187; Roosevelt
and, 145, 146, 150; *Warner,
Barnes* and, 152; White and,
158, 201
Taft Commission, 37, 38, 62, 175
Takings clause, 167
Tammany Hall, 138
Taney, Roger Brooke, 45, 48, 84,
112–13, 114, 249; *Dred Scott*
and, 47, 88, 103, 110, 179
Tapia, Carlos, 199
Tarbell, Ida, 71
Tariff laws, 4, 79, 112, 115, 131;
applicability of, 114; *Insular
Cases* and, 11; rewriting, 155
Tariffs, 45, 48, 58, 67, 82, 88, 111,
113, 118, 120, 136, 222, 226,
245, 257, 259, 260; adverse

effects of, 71; debate over, 70; imposition of, 44, 114, 116; ratification of, 122; sugar industry and, 76; wartime, 152, 153, 249

Taxation, 52, 148, 182, 183; uniform, 53, 81

Teller, Henry M., 33, 242

Teller Amendment (1898), 33, 70, 134, 136, 254, 259; Cuba and, 135, 243

Tenth Amendment, 8, 223

Territorial citizens, 8; and American Indians compared, 227; civil liberties and, 10; political status of, 249; rights of, 12, 222

Territorial government, 27, 181, 186; checks and balances and, 8; creation of, 3, 20

Territories: constitutional questions with, 48, 248; control over, 50–51; defining, 164–65; democratic government and, 60; incorporated, 4, 5, 10, 187, 189, 190, 203, 239, 250; island, 4, 5, 219; nation-states and, 214; nonincorporated, 190, 251; occupation of, 238–39; organized, 165, 166; paradoxes for, 214; political status of, 249; rights of, 44, 225–27; self-government for, 220; separation of, 240; treatment of, 225; unincorporated, 4, 5, 6, 7, 10, 167, 176, 187, 204, 215, 216, 219, 239, 250–51

Territory clause, 43, 46, 92, 140, 148

Terrorism, 248, 255

Texas, 244; admission of, 3, 27; American expansion and, 25; sovereignty of, 218; tariff laws and, 114

Texas v. White (1868), 236

Thayer, James Bradley, 41, 43, 236, 237; on territories, 42

Third Amendment, 222, 223

Thirteenth Amendment, 96, 210

Tillman, Benjamin, 217

Time magazine, 69, 217

Tobacco, 101, 105, 242

Tobacco Trust, 243

Torres v. Puerto Rico (1979), 222

Torruella, Juan, 8, 228, 251

Trade, 65, 66–67, 68, 76, 143, 245

Trans-Appalachian West, 2, 15, 16

Transcontinental Treaty (1819), 23

Transylvania (1780–1784), 18

Treaty clause, 92

Treaty-making powers, 46, 52, 92, 106, 126

Treaty of Guadalupe Hidalgo (1848), 18, 24, 25, 49, 166, 208

Treaty of Paris (1783), 2, 15

Treaty of Paris (1803), 25

Treaty of Paris (1899), 40, 80, 95, 101, 111, 112, 113, 123, 130, 153, 166, 191, 209, 219, 254; annexation and, 6; cessions by, 161; civil rights/political status and, 187; Cuba and, 134, 135; incorporation and, 115; *Neely* and, 133; Philippines and, 36, 177; Puerto Rico and, 84, 162, 207; ratification of, 34, 36, 51, 109, 121, 259; territories and, 126; trade and, 76

Treaty of Washington (1846), 24

Trials: jury, 12, 19, 53, 149, 169, 170, 172, 173, 176–78, 180, 182, 186, 188, 197, 200, 202, 204, 205, 221, 222; speedy/public, 211

Trías Monge, José, 228

Trono, Valentin, 190

Trono v. United States (1905), 207, 261; double jeopardy and, 190, 196; and *Kepner* compared, 190; lead opinion in, 185; ruling in, 194

Trusts, regulation of, 70

Whitney, Paul, 41
Whittington, Keith, 253–55
Wilfley, Lebbeus, 55
Williams, William Appleman, 231,
    235, 246
Williamson, Hugh, 17
Williams v. Mississippi (1898), 224
Willis, Henry P., 240
Willson, Beckles, 235–36, 252;
    Brown and, 106; on Imperial
    Service, 231
Willson, Gus, 106
Wilson, Woodrow, 158, 262;
    appointments by, 205; Brandeis
    and, 198; Clarke and, 198; on
    colonies, 233; on
    concessions/sovereignty, 230;
    on empire, 69; McReynolds
    and, 198; territories and, 229

Wilson-Gorman Tariff (1895), 31,
    71, 91
Wood, Leonard: Cuba and, 34,
    60–61, 241–42; on Platt
    Amendment, 244
Woodruff v. Parham (1869), 127,
    128
Worcester, Dean C., 196
World Bank, 233
World Trade Organization, 233
World War I, 262; territories and,
    216, 217
World War II, territories and,
    216

Yager, Arthur, 197
Yarbrough, Tinsley, 209
Young, Brigham, 28
Young, James, 55, 143

{ *Index* }